EX AUDITU

An International Journal for the Theological Interpretation of Scripture

VOLUME 29   **2013**

Ex Auditu is published annually by Pickwick Publications, an imprint of
Wipf and Stock Publishers, 199 West 8th Avenue, Suite 3, Eugene, Oregon 97401, USA

SUBSCRIPTIONS

Individuals:
U.S.A. and all other countries (in U.S. funds): $20.00
Students: $12.00

Institutions:
U.S.A. and all other countries (in U.S. funds): $30.00

This periodical is indexed in the ATLA Religion Database, published by the American Theological Library Association, 300 S. Wacker Dr., Suite 2100, Chicago, IL 60606, Email: atla@atla.com, www: http://www.atla.com/; *Internationale Zeitschriftenshau für Bibelwissenschaft; Religious and Theological Abstracts; and Old Testament Abstracts.*

Please address all subscription correspondence
and change of address information to Wipf and Stock Publishers.

©2014 by Wipf and Stock Publishers
ISSN: 0883-0053
ISBN: 978-1-62564-792-4

EX AUDITU

An International Journal for the Theological Interpretation of Scripture

Klyne R. Snodgrass, Editor
Stephen J. Chester, Associate Editor
D. Christopher Spinks, Associate Editor

North Park Theological Seminary
3225 West Foster Avenue
Chicago, Illinois 60625-4987
USA

Tel: (773) 244-6243
Fax: (773) 244-6244
email: ksnodgrass@northpark.edu
Web site: http://wipfandstock.com/journals/ex_auditu

EDITORIAL BOARD

Terence E. Fretheim, Luther Seminary, St. Paul, MN
Richard B. Hays, The Divinity School, Duke University, Durham, NC
Jon R. Stock, Wipf & Stock Publishers, Eugene, OR
Miroslav Volf, Yale Divinity School, New Haven, CT
John Wipf, Wipf & Stock Publishers, Eugene, OR

THE EDITORIAL BOARD MEMBERS AND CONSULTANTS represent various disciplines and denominations. Theological interpretation of Scripture is a task to be taken seriously by scholars who are committed to the Christian faith and tradition. However, as one editorial consultant stated: "Let people gradually get used to the idea that a sane hermeneutics is both oriented in advance toward agreement/consent and is simultaneously exigent, discriminating, critical."

EDITORIAL CONSULTANTS

Richard Bauckham
University of St. Andrews, Emeritus
St. Andrews, Scotland

M. Daniel Carroll R.
Denver Seminary
Denver, Colorado

Jan Du Rand
Emeritus, University of Johannesburg
and Extraordinary Professor, North West University

Willie Jennings
The Divinity School
Duke University
Durham, N. Carolina

Robert Johnston
Fuller Theological Seminary
Pasadena, California

R. Walter L. Moberly
University of Durham
Durham, England

Kathleen M. O'Connor
Columbia Theological Seminary
Decatur, Georgia

Iain Provan
Regent College
Vancouver, B.C.

Anthony Thiselton
University of Nottingham
Nottingham, England

Augustine Thompson
University of Virginia
Charlottesville, Virginia

Marianne Meye Thompson
Fuller Theological Seminary
Pasadena, California

Kevin J. Vanhoozer
Trinity Evangelical Divinity School
Deerfield, Illinois

Geoffrey Wainwright
The Divinity School
Duke University
Durham, N. Carolina

Sondra Wheeler
Wesley Theological Seminary
Washington, D.C.

William H. Willimon
The Divinity School
Duke University
Durham, N. Carolina

N. T. Wright
St Mary's College,
University of St Andrews, Scotland

CONTENTS

Announcement of the 2014 Symposium v

Abbreviations vi

Introduction viii
Klyne Snodgrass

Visions of Horror, Visions of Hope: An Orientation for Urban Ministry from the Book of Amos 1
M. Daniel Carroll R.

Response to Carroll 20
Nathan Bills

Early Christian Communities in the Greco-Roman City: Perspectives on Urban Ministry from the New Testament 25
Paul Trebilco

Response to Trebilco 49
Stephen Chester

The Necessity of Lament for Ministry in the Urban Context 54
Soong-Chan Rah

Response to Rah 70
Jessica Rivera

Good Citizenship: A Study of Philippians 1:27 and Its Implications for Contemporary Urban Ministry 74
Dennis R. Edwards

Response to Edwards 94
Kurt N. Fredrickson

Love Yourself: Urban Ministry and the Challenge of Self-Love 98
Chanequa Walker-Barnes

Contents

Prophet, Pagan, Prayer: Urban Theology of Reversal in the Story of Jonah 112
David Leong

Response to Leong 131
Daniel White Hodge

The Ministerial Significance of Early Syriac Theology 137
Vince L. Bantu

Response to Bantu 156
Armida Belmonte Stephens

"No Shortcut to the Promised Land": The Fosdick Brothers and Muscular Christianity 161
Amy Laura Hall

Response to Hall 178
Reggie Williams

The Lord of the Rings 182
Isaias Mercado

Annotated Bibliography on Urban Ministry 187

Presenters and Respondents 201

Ex Auditu—Volumes Available

ANNOUNCEMENT OF THE 2014 SYMPOSIUM

North Park Theological Seminary in Chicago, Illinois, is pleased to announce that the thirtieth Symposium on the Theological Interpretation of Scripture will take place September 25–27, 2014. The symposium will start at 7:00 p.m. on September 25 in Nyvall Hall and will extend through a Saturday afternoon worship service on September 27. The theme in 2014 will be Encounter with God: The Human Response to the Divine Initiative. The following persons have agreed to make presentations:

> Brian Bantum, Seattle Pacific University, Theology
> Beverly Gaventa, Baylor University, New Testament
> Jodie Boyer Hatlem, North Park Theological Seminary, Ethics
> Cheryl Bridges Johns, Discipleship and Christian Formation, Pentecostal Theological Seminary
> Rob Johnston, Fuller Theological Seminary, Theology
> Paul Chang-Ha Lim, The Divinity School, Vanderbilt University, History
> Tremper Longman, Westmont College, Old Testament
> Jonathan Tran, Baylor University, Ethics
> Paul Wilson, University of Toronto, Preaching.

Persons interested in attending the sessions should write before September 1 to:

> Ms. Guylla Brown
> North Park Theological Seminary
> 3225 W. Foster Avenue
> Chicago, Illinois 60625

Meals may be taken at North Park and assistance can be provided in finding nearby lodging.

ABBREVIATIONS

All abbreviations are as specified in Patrick H. Alexander et al., eds., *The SBL Handbook of Style* (Peabody, MA: Hendrickson, 1999). Bibliographical details and any abbreviations not listed here can be found there.

AB	Anchor Bible
ABD	*Anchor Bible Dictionary*
AJEC	Ancient Judaism and Early Christianity
ASMMS	*American Society of Missiology Monograph Series*
BBRSup	Bulletin of Biblical Research Supplement
BTB	*Biblical Theology Bulletin*
CBQ	*Catholic Biblical Quarterly*
EDNT	*Exegetical Dictionary of the New Testament*
HBD	*Harper's Bible Dictionary*
ICC	International Critical Commentary
ISBE	*International Standard Bible Encyclopedia*
IvEph	*Die Inschriften von Ephesos*
JBL	*Journal of Biblical Literature*
JRS	*Journal of Roman Studies*
JSNT	*Journal for the Study of the New Testament*
JSNTSup	Journal for the Study of the New Testament: Supplement Series
JSOT	*Journal for the Study of the Old Testament*
JSOTSup	Journal for the Study of the Old Testament: Supplement Series
JTS	*Journal of Theological Studies*
LHB/OTS	Library of Hebrew Bible/Old Testament Series
MT	Masoretic Text
NICNT	New International Commentary on the New Testament
NICOT	New International Commentary on the Old Testament
NIDOTTE	New International Dictionary of Old Testament Theology and Exegesis
NIGTC	New International Greek Testament Commentary
NIV	New International Version
NRSV	New Revised Standard Version

Abbreviations

NTS	*New Testament Studies*
OBT	Overtures to Biblical Theology
OTL	Old Testament Library
SIG	*Sylloge inscriptionum graecarum*
TOTC	Tyndale Old Testament Commentaries
VT	*Vetus Testamentum*
VTSup	Vetus Testamentum Supplements
WUNT	Wissenschaftliche Untersuchungen zum Neuen Testament

INTRODUCTION

North Park Theological Seminary is an urban seminary in one of the most diverse urban communities anywhere. When I arrived on this campus forty years ago, discussions about urban ministry were intense, and the issues then are still the same issues today. Discussions of urban ministry are nothing new, and I confess that I am not sure we have made a lot of progress. For several decades scholars and pastors have struggled to find solutions to persistent and destructive problems. Good efforts, both secular and ecclesial, sometimes yielded significant results, but urban problems have never been in retreat—problems of poverty, racism, systemic roadblocks, crime, and irresponsibility on all sides. The articles in this volume invite reconsideration of the issues involved. Given that most people in the world by a large margin live in urban centers and given that the issues are at the center of the gospel mandate and have an enormous impact on the lives of people, such reconsideration is not optional.

The symposium focus on urban ministry coincides with the inauguration of a joint Doctor of Ministry in Urban Ministry offered by North Park Theological Seminary and Fuller Theological Seminary. This program will be directed by Soong-Chan Rah, Associate Professor of Church Growth and Evangelism at North Park. Soong-Chan helped plan this symposium, and thanks is expressed to him for his involvement. Thanks are expressed as well to Jessica Rivera who stepped in to respond to Soong-Chan's paper when a death in his family prevented Isaias Mercado from doing so. Jessica and Isaias serve the same church community.

At the symposium twice as much time is given to discussion of the papers as to their delivery, and the journal cannot reproduce the character of those discussions, which are always stimulating and enriching. People in attendance at the symposium include an interesting mix of faculty types, pastors, church leaders, students, and lay people. We are grateful to all who participated. Appreciation is especially expressed once again to all the presenters and respondents who made a significant investment in the life of North Park. The friendship of these people is a gift we value deeply. The authors of papers were given a chance to edit their contributions after the symposium, but the responses are essentially as they were presented. As is obvious, the views expressed are those of the authors and not necessarily those of the journal or of North Park. Special gratitude is expressed to Anne Jorgensen and Elena Canler, students at North Park, for their work on the bibliography and especially to Guylla Brown from North Park's staff, without whom the symposium would be impossible. Anyone who has been to the symposium knows that is true.

The Editor

VISIONS OF HORROR, VISIONS OF HOPE: AN ORIENTATION FOR URBAN MINISTRY FROM THE BOOK OF AMOS

M. Daniel Carroll R.

The invitation to present this paper is a privilege but at the same time a challenge. I was raised in the suburbs, away from the inner-city and far from what are considered to be areas for urban ministry. As an adult, my entry into that world has come in stages.

My exposure to realities associated with urban ministry began in Guatemala, where I spent time as a boy and then later spent thirteen years teaching at a seminary in the capital city. Latin American cities are more of a jumble (and jungle!) than what we find in the United States.[1] The massive movement from rural areas to the peripheries of urban centers by people looking for work, education, and a better life dwarfs any previous internal migration patterns. Poverty bumps up against wealth, and marginalized zones and communities living off of city dumps reflect levels of deprivation not seen in the United States. Beggars, street drunks, addicts (including glue sniffers), and panhandlers are ubiquitous. Drug trafficking and money laundering have drastically changed the urban landscape. They have generated massive new construction projects and more conspicuous consumption, along with waves of violence that are different from the dark days of the dictatorships and civil wars. Like a cancer, the drug trade has penetrated entire barrios, the business world, the police and military, and the halls of government. This and other national and international factors have led to an increase in social, economic, and political disparities in this part of the world that boasts some of its largest metropolises—Mexico City, over twenty-two million; São Paolo, over twenty million; Buenos Aires, more than fourteen million; and Río de Janeiro, over twelve million. More than eighty percent of Latin America and the Caribbean live in cities of more than 750,000. As of 2009 there were almost seventy cities with populations of over one million![2]

---

1. For some of the issues, see, e.g., Tom Angotti, "Urban Latin America: Violence, Enclaves, and Struggles for Land," *Latin American Perspectives* 40, no. 2 (2013) 5–20.

2. http://en.wikipedia.org/wiki/List_of_Latin_American_cities_by_population.

These realities raise theological issues for urban life that traditional Christian theologies did not consider. For example, one of the helpful legacies of Latin American liberation theology was its reflections on systemic sin, that is, the structural evil manifest in social, economic, and political institutions, which is sanctioned by legislation, cultural mores, and sometimes religion.[3] At their most stark, the various spheres of systemic sin maintain their hegemony in violent ways through corrupt law enforcement, extrajudicial, and military personnel. Although liberation theology focused, of course, on the socioeconomic inequalities and the strong-armed tactics of the status quo of the mid to late twentieth century and this from a Marxist framework,[4] its awareness of the "principalities and powers" that weave their spell throughout society is applicable to the urban ministry discussion.

Another stage in my learning curve occurred while my family and I were in Britain for doctoral studies. The Urban Theology Unit in Sheffield was up and running under John Vincent and fancied itself as a beacon of a British liberation theology. It continues to do work on urban matters.[5] In 1985 the Archbishop of Canterbury's Commission on Urban Priority Areas published *Faith in the City: A Call to Action by Church and Nation*. This report caused a stir, as it was in part an indictment of Margaret Thatcher's policies and capitalist agenda. Unemployment was rising, public spending had been reduced, and social polarization and inequalities were more pronounced. The Church of England was wrestling with how to define its presence in cities in decline and its relationship with the working class; it was trying to discern a constructive role in regenerating urban areas in decay.[6] My recent involvement with Christian Community Development Association continues my education in these matters.

I make these observations of contextual realities from various countries, as ideally a theology for urban ministry in today's world needs to think locally, nationally,

---

3. See, e.g., José Ignacio González Faust, "Sin," in *Mysterium liberationis: Fundamental Concepts of Liberation Theology*, ed. I. Ellacuría and J. Sobrino (Maryknoll, NY: Orbis, 1993) 532–41.

4. The use of Marxism was sophisticated, with authors appealing to different branches of Marxist thought. The most penetrating studies were by Juan Luis Segundo (e.g., *Jesus of Nazareth Yesterday and Today*, vol. 1: *Faith and Ideologies*, trans. J. Drury [Maryknoll, NY: Orbis, 1984]) and especially Enrique Dussel. The latter has been prolific on this topic, but much of his work has not been translated from Spanish into English. See his "Liberation Theology and Marxism," in *Mysterium liberationis*, ed. Ellacuría and Sobrino, 85–102; and *Ethics of Liberation: In the Age of Globalization and Exclusion*, trans. E. Mendieta et al. (Durham, NC: Duke University Press, 2013).

5. http://www.utusheffield.org.uk/.

6. *Faith in the City: A Call to Action by Church and Nation* (London: Church House, 1985). A follow-up report, *Faithful Cities: A Call for Celebration, Vision and Justice*, was published in 2006 by the Church of England's Commission on Urban Life and Faith.

and globally. There will be areas of overlap and of dissimilarity. What must be dealt with in this country will not be totally like what is needed in Latin America and the United Kingdom. Diverse histories and cultures create different environments. More drastic circumstances, such as urban ministry matters in Muslim contexts, whether in more peaceful regions or in the war zones of Baghdad, Damascus, Beirut, or Cairo, would call for yet another set of questions. This essay, therefore, is more general in nature. Its goal is to contribute in some small way to a wide-ranging biblical theological optic for urban ministry.

As I have explored some of the urban ministry literature in this country, I have been impressed by the efforts of key authors, such as Robert Linthicum and Mark Gornick, to appropriate insights from both Testaments.[7] They appreciate the tension in the Bible between the dark side of the city in the ancient world and its glorious potential.[8] These theologian-practitioners clearly are aware of systemic sin and the injustices in the use of power that the Scripture denounces. They also underscore the hope of a new, redeemed city in the future, which the text also offers its readers.

My particular area of interest is the prophetic literature. A commonly cited OT text for urban ministry is the letter of Jeremiah to the exiles in Babylon (Jer 29).[9] From that passage several lessons are drawn, such as the importance of a call to engage the city, the mandate for incarnational living, the need to pray for change, the challenges of advocacy for the poor, and proclamation of the gospel—all foundational dimensions for working toward a comprehensive *shalom*.

This essay turns its attention to the book of Amos in its canonical form.[10] After presenting a brief background on the city in the eighth-century BCE, it will attempt

---

7. Robert Linthicum, *City of God, City of Satan: A Biblical Theology of the Urban Church* (Grand Rapids: Zondervan, 1991); Linthicum, *Transforming Power: Biblical Strategies for Making a Difference in Your Community* (Downers Grove, IL: InterVarsity, 2003); Mark R. Gornick, *To Live in Peace: Biblical Faith and the Changing Inner City* (Grand Rapids: Eerdmans, 2002). Also note the creative work by Kris Rocke and Joel Van Dyke, *Geography of Grace: Doing Theology from Below* (n. p.: Street Psalms, 2012).

8. For a concise survey of the biblical material and the tensions in the Bible's presentation of the city, see "City" in *Dictionary of Biblical Literature*, ed. L. Ryken, J. C. Wilhoit, and T. Longman III (Downers Grove, IL: InterVarsity, 1998) 150–54. A classic expression of this tension is expressed in Jacques Ellul, *The Meaning of the City* (Grand Rapids: Eerdmans, 1970). Nathan Bills, in a footnote in his response to this essay, cites his own fine survey, "Urban Imagination in the Old Testament: A Selective Overview," *Missio Dei: A Journal of Missional Theology and Praxis* 3 (2012), http://missiodeijournal.com/article.php?issue=md-3-2&author=md-3-2-bills.

9. Linthicum, *City of God, City of Satan*, 145–62; and his *Transforming Power*, 71–78; Gornick, *To Live in Peace*, 97–126; cf. Eldon Villafañe, *Seek the Peace of the City: Reflections on Urban Ministry* (Grand Rapids: Eerdmans, 1995) 1–39.

10. For the methodological choice for the final form for mission and ethics, see M. Daniel Carroll R., "Ethics and Old Testament Interpretation," in *Hearing the Old Testament: Listening for God's*

to glean something of a prophetic vision of the city for today from that prophetic text. Some of what will be said reinforces what others have taken from other biblical books, but hopefully with new insights as well.

Urban Contexts in Ancient Israel

It is not uncommon for urban ministry studies to state that the OT is an urban book. Evidence of that is said to be the many occurrences of certain terms (especially *ʿîr*, which appears over one thousand times). These studies also state that cities of Judah and Israel (especially their capitals), as well as imperial centers, like Nineveh and Babylon, are of great interest to the biblical authors, and thus to God (and accordingly should be to us).

These observations are true up to a point. What is not asked is how ancient cities may have differed from their modern counterparts. Are they in any way similar? What constituted a "city" in Amos's context, which by all accounts was overwhelmingly rural?

Archaeologist William Dever divides the inhabited sites of Israel and Judah into various "tiers."[11] Three of his categories are pertinent: capital cities, administrative centers, and what he calls "other urban areas" (other tiers are towns, villages, and forts). Each exhibited its own characteristics. The groupings are determined by location (such as being at a trade crossroads, on a prominent elevation for defense purposes, or proximity to an accessible and dependable water supply), size of the site, the presence of monumental and cultic structures, and the remains of luxury items of elite lifestyles.[12]

Address, ed. C. G. Bartholomew and J. H. Beldman (Grand Rapids: Eerdmans, 2012) 204–27; cf. Carroll R., *Contexts for Amos: Prophetic Poetics in Latin American Perspective*, JSOTSup 132 (Sheffield, UK: Sheffield Academic, 1992) 149–75. For a recent, convenient survey of composition theories of the book, see John Barton, *The Theology of the Book of Amos*, Old Testament Theology (Cambridge: Cambridge University Press, 2012). Some scholars propose different ethical perspectives for each hypothetical redactional layer. A recent example is Graham R. Hamborg, *Still Selling the Righteous: A Redaction-Critical Investigation of Reasons for Judgment in Amos 2:6–16*, LHB/OTS 555 (New York: T. & T. Clark, 2012).

11. William G. Dever, *The Lives of Ordinary People in Ancient Israel: Where Archaeology and the Bible Intersect* (Grand Rapids: Eerdmans, 2012) 47–50. This book is not without its critics. See reviews at http://www.bookreviews.org/bookdetail.asp?TitleId=8543&CodePage=8543. His taxonomy, however, is helpful.

12. Dever, *The Lives of Ordinary People in Ancient Israel*, 50–141. For a more technical discussion, see Avraham Faust, *The Archaeology of Israelite Society in Iron Age II* (Winona Lake, IN: Eisenbrauns, 2013) 39–189. Faust also divides sites into various categories. Other helpful studies from different perspectives include Volkmar Fritz, *The City in Ancient Israel*, Biblical Seminar (Sheffield, UK: Sheffield Academic, 1995); John W. Rogerson and John Vincent, *The City in Biblical Perspective*, Biblical

Cities in the kingdoms of Judah and Israel were small in comparison with the prominent metropolises of Syria and Mesopotamia, and they certainly were very much smaller than what we envision for urban centers today (some occupied only a few acres). Size was limited by the amount of available water and the capacity of the surrounding countryside to support an urban population. Cities were walled, which also restricted their size. Many, especially the capitals, would have had an interior enclosure or citadel, inside of which would have been located the palace and/or government buildings, a temple, and the royal quarters. The gate to the city was fortified, as it had a defensive role along with being an important setting for business transactions and legal decisions. Within several cities there apparently also was an open area for a market. In some cases merchants, officials, and a few common folk lived inside the walls, but in other cases this was not so. The rest of the population resided outside the walls and would come into the city for trade, for goods at the market, participation in religious feasts, legal rulings, and for protection in case of attack. Finally, ancient cities would have had to deal with issues that have always occupied cities, such as security, population growth, sewage and human waste, disease, and burial of the dead—all of which would have impacted those urban environments.[13]

This brief description clearly indicates that to consider ancient cities is to enter into a world unlike our own. At the same time, to read the prophetic literature is to encounter accounts of injustice that resonate with modern urban experiences. This carryover is possible because of the vagueness of textual scenes, which do not specify the systems of oppression and seldom identify the perpetrators by name. This literary imprecision allows for a bridge to be drawn between settings separated by millennia.

Social science approaches have attempted to reconstruct in some detail the socioeconomic mechanisms and cultural mores of the eighth century BCE that so enraged the prophets.[14] Because ancient Israel was an agrarian economy, these proposals usually wed thoughts on urban issues with suggestions about the relationship between the cities and the adjacent rural world. They also attempt, among other things, to understand the role of the monarchy and various elites in the injustice,

---

Challenges to the Modern World (London: Equinox, 2009) 3-45; John Goldingay, *Old Testament Theology* (Downers Grove, IL: InterVarsity, 2009) 3:477-507; Douglas A. Knight, *Law, Power, and Justice in Ancient Israel*, Library of Ancient Israel (Louisville: Westminster John Knox, 2011) 157-224.

13. M. Daniel Carroll R., "A Biblical Theology of the City and the Environment: Human Community in the Created Order," in *Keeping God's Earth: The Global Environment in Biblical Perspective*, ed. N. Toly and D. Block (Downers Grove, IL: InterVarsity, 2010) 69-89.

14. For a survey, M. Daniel Carroll R., "Social Science Approaches," in *Dictionary of the Old Testament: The Prophets*, ed. M. Boda and J. G. McConville (Downers Grove, IL: InterVarsity, 2012) 734-47.

ascertain the likelihood of some kind of middle class, and determine the impact of international markets and politics. This research can be illuminating of textual particulars, but it is inevitably speculative. One also would need to sort out what might be the possible input of this work for the task of developing a biblical theology of urban ministry. At the very least, these studies accentuate our need to appeal to the social sciences to comprehend better the realities on this side of the chronological divide.

A way forward is to appreciate that the link to the past is ethical and theological. Though it takes on different shapes today, injustice and systemic abuse continue; the poor and the marginalized still suffer. The prophetic literature serves then as a moral compass for censuring current systems and wrongdoers. It also reveals the heart, the pathos, of God. Yahweh cares deeply about the misery of the down-and-out, the left-behind, and the stepped-on. In other words, in the prophetic books ethical outrage and moral anguish is inseparable from theological convictions about the person of God.[15]

Walter Brueggemann's concept of the prophetic imagination is helpful here.[16] Although his analysis of the prophetic message can suffer from overgeneralization (such as in his consistently negative portrayal of the royal ideology), he correctly recognizes the confrontations of worldviews in the biblical text and explores the various theologies that sanctified a pitiless social construction of reality. A key contribution is his appreciation of the power of poetry in voicing the pain of the oppressed and the divine condemnation of such sin. Imaginative language is key too for the picture of future restoration. These are the elements of a prophetic counter-narrative to the destructive hegemonic story of any society and are the stuff of nonconformist, but obedient, claims on sociopolitical, economic, and religious life. The book of Amos is a wonderful resource for such a perspective in both its denunciation of the present and its vision of renewal beyond the coming judgment.

---

15. A foundational resource in this regard is Abraham Heschel, *The Prophets* (New York: Harper & Row, 1962); cf. Terence Fretheim, *The Suffering of God: An Old Testament Perspective*, OBT (Minneapolis: Fortress, 1984), and from a very different point of view, Jürgen Moltmann, *The Crucified God: The Cross of Christ as the Foundation and Criticism of Christian Theology*, trans. M. Kohl (Minneapolis: Fortress, 1993).

16. This has been a constant theme in his work since the publication of *The Prophetic Imagination*, now in its second edition (Minneapolis: Fortress, 2001); more recently, *The Practice of Prophetic Imagination: Preaching an Emancipating Word* (Minneapolis: Fortress, 2012). Cf. Jamie Gates and Mark H. Mann, eds., *Nurturing the Prophetic Imagination*, Point Loma Press Series (Eugene, OR: Wipf and Stock, 2012).

Urban Reflections from the Book of Amos

The book of Amos is full of Yahweh's judgments: judgments upon the nations surrounding Israel and the imminent judgment upon the people of God. The divine judgment on other peoples is for violence in war and upon Israel for oppression within society. This section explores first the book's treatment of human violence and then the role of religion within a context of societal violence.

Visions of Horror

Violence in the City

The book begins with the Oracles against the Nations (1:3—2:16). The first six decry irrational blood lust in war. Syria/Aram had cruelly threshed the Gilead region of Israel (1:3–5), either literally through torturing its victims or metaphorically in devastating the area (2 Kgs 13:7; Isa 41:15; Mic 4:13; Hab 3:12). The Philistines (1:6-8) and Phoenicia (1:9-10) were involved in buying and selling captives, most likely taken as booty in battle. Edom is censured for unrestrained fury (1:11-12), Ammon for unspeakable brutality against women in war (1:13-15), and Moab for violating the tomb of the dead (2:1–3). These atrocities certainly included attacks on cities and siege warfare, but that is not specifically mentioned (cf. Deut 28:53-57; 2 Kgs 6:24—7:20; 18:27-32; and Lamentations).[17] Conversely, the Oracles predict the destruction of the walls and citadels of the perpetrators' capitals or important cities: Damascus (Syria/Aram), Gaza (Philistia), Tyre (Phoenicia), Teman and Bozra (Edom), Rabbah (Ammon), and Kerioth (Moab).[18] In other words, urban areas come in to play in the Oracles against the Nations.

Our focus, however, is on violence *within* cities, on the plight of the marginalized in urban areas. The book of Amos has a lot to say about what the prophet witnessed in the cities of Israel. His anger expresses the heart of Yahweh, who will not tolerate the violation of the vulnerable. In his characteristically wonderful turn of phrase, Heschel summarizes the target of the prophet's social message in this way:

---

17. For the impact of war and the archaeological evidence, see conveniently Dever, *The Lives of Ordinary People in Ancient Israel*, 320-67. Also note Israel Ephal, *The City Besieged*, Culture and History of the Ancient Near East (Leiden: Brill, 2009).

18. The seventh oracle, which is against Judah, singles out its capital city (Jerusalem). The southern and the northern kingdoms are not condemned for war atrocities.

"When Amos appeared in the North there was pride (6:13–14), plenty, and splendor in the land, elegance in the cities, and might in the palaces."[19]

The term "violence" (*ḥāmās*) does not appear explicitly until 3:10, but the injustices described in 2:6–8 within the Israel oracle (2:6–16) exemplify what today is called social or institutional violence. To degrade, dehumanize, and dislodge the poor is to commit violence against them.[20] It is difficult to identify with certainty the abuses in these three verses, but these sketches must refer to acts of aggression. Each transgression in the passage can be understood in several ways, but all of the interpretive options point to social and economic exploitation of some kind.[21] Amos 2:6 could refer to debt slavery (cf. 8:6) or to bribery in the courts. Either possibility meant potentially catastrophic consequences for the livelihood of the urban poor and rural peasants. Note also the enigmatic, yet compelling, picture of mistreatment in the first part of 2:7 ("They trample upon the heads of the poor as upon the dust of the ground," NIV; cf. 5:11), which is coupled in the next clause with denying justice to the poor (similar wording in 5:12 indicates that this is a legal context). The last line of 2:7 may describe a father and son taking sexual advantage of a poor maiden, who perhaps was working in the household as a debt slave (cf. 2:6). Amos 2:8 depicts the heartlessness of those in positions of power (perhaps local officials or representatives of the government), who take advantage of the needy. Similar callous behavior is portrayed in 4:1, where wives of the well-to-do (maybe from the same group as that of 2:6–8), mockingly caricatured as the "cows of Bashan," seek self-indulgent pleasure gained by exploitation. This insensitivity reappears in 6:3–6, where these social strata enjoy extravagant abundance in a land of want (4:6–9) and do not "grieve over the ruin of Joseph" (v. 6).

The transgressions of 2:6–8 (and of other passages) probably occurred in city precincts, most likely in Samaria.[22] This city is singled out in 3:9 as the pinnacle of

---

19. Heschel, *The Prophets*, 33. Biblically, violence is inherent in human cities since the founding of the first city by Cain (Gen 4:17; cf. 4:23–24; 6:11; 10:8–12). See the sources in n8 above, Rogerson and Vincent, *The City in Biblical Perspective*; and Goldingay, *Israel's Life*, 477–507.

20. Elsa Tamez, *The Bible of the Oppressed*, trans. M. J. O'Connell (Maryknoll, NY: Orbis, 1982) 8–55.

21. Shalom M. Paul provides a detailed summary of interpretive options in *Amos*, Hermeneia (Minneapolis: Fortress, 1991) 77–87 (cf. Carroll R., "Social Science Approaches").

22. The book also mentions Bethel (3:14; 4:4; 5:5–6; 7:10, 13), Gilgal (4:4; 5:5), and Dan (Beersheba, cited in 5:5 and 8:14, was located in Judah). Dan was a city and cultic center in the Northern Kingdom, but it receives only passing mention (8:14). Bethel is categorized as a town by Dever (i.e., 300–1000 population), and like Gilgal was an important cultic center. Bethel is the setting for 7:10–17 and perhaps 9:1. Nathan Bills in his response has reminded me of Walter J. Houston's "Exit the Oppressed Peasant? Rethinking the Background of Social Criticism in the Prophets," which also argues

oppression, whose troubling transgressions would shock even the Philistines and the Egyptians, longtime enemies of Israel. The mention of the capitals and important cities of the surrounding peoples in the other Oracles against the Nations also suggests that Samaria, Israel's capital, is in view in 2:6–8. Within that ancient urban setting the powerless endured legal, economic, social, and sexual violence at the hands of leaders in the various realms of Israelite society.[23] There also is abuse in the religious realm, but we will return to that topic in the next section. Except for the high priest Amaziah (7:10, 12, 14) and King Jeroboam I (7:9–11; cf. 1:1), the evildoers are not identified. Literarily the sins transcend the names of particular individuals.

Descriptions of oppressive violence continue throughout the book. In the well-known chiasm of 5:1–17, the imagery in 5:7 associated with disregarding justice finds its matching pericope in 5:10–13. There that ethical indictment is made concrete, as those in power enjoy the spoils of others' misery.

The vocabulary communicates the unfairness of Israel's world and the utter disdain with which the better-off hold the powerless. They "hate" and "despise" anyone challenging them in legal proceedings at the gate (5:10, 12, 15; NIV, "in court"), and they ensure favorable outcomes for themselves by bribing judges (5:12; cf. 2:6). These rigged rulings perhaps allowed them to accumulate land in unacceptable ways under legal cover and to extract burdensome taxes (probably taken at harvest time) or take other goods with impunity. Intimidation must have been the order of the day. Even those who could challenge these injustices with the truth are silenced (5:13). The sins of those in control of the urban landscape are "many" and "great" (5:12), and they are cruel. The notion of trampling on the poor resurfaces, howbeit with a different Hebrew term (5:11; cf. 2:6; 8:4). The downward socioeconomic spiral of the indigent into the desperate situation of making the agonizing decision to sell family members or oneself into debt slavery also could find its source in the abuses of 5:10–13.

The unscrupulous economic practices of the comfortable are highlighted in 8:4–6. The vocabulary of violence is used again in 8:4. The term for "trample" in 2:6 resurfaces, and that imagery is reinforced by the words "bring the poor to an end." The setting once more must be urban. The mention in 8:3 of the palace (or temple;

---

for the prophetic focus on cities (in *Prophecy and the Prophets in Ancient Israel*, ed. J. Day [New York: T. & T. Clark, 2010] 101–16).

23. See the insightful discussion on the ideals of leadership in the OT in Goldingay, *Israel's Faith*, 708–59.

it is the same word in Hebrew) and of religious rituals in 8:5, along with this market scene, implies that again the location could very well be Samaria.

Merchants manipulate the balances in measuring grain and the prices in the market, fraudulent actions condemned throughout the ancient Near East and in the OT (e.g., Lev 19:35–36; Deut 25:13–16; Prov 11:1; 20:23; Hos 12:7 [MT 12:8]; Mic 6:10). They adulterate the wheat too, mixing the grain with chaff. These dishonest behaviors are connected to the plight of the poor in 8:6, who once again are taken advantage of. They are incapable of changing their plight and are powerless to avoid being bought and sold like commodities (cf. 2:6). The impact on land tenure and the threat to family survival physically and legally would have been significant. Their woeful state of affairs, this violence against their possessions and families, surely was a driving force behind Yahweh's and the prophet's anger.

In sum, the book of Amos is a book of human violence. In the Oracles against the Nations it condemns the armed conflicts between peoples in the present or recent past, and it warns of the coming invasion of an unnamed enemy (3:11; 6:14)[24] and removal into exile (4:3; 5:27; 6:7). Within Israel there also is an internal violence against the powerless. The text presents the sins of the social elite, the government, legal institutions, and the market place and the impact of these actions on the urban (and rural) poor.[25] It portrays these transgressions with emotive language that forcefully communicates the malice in the power differentials within that world. Yahweh's mouthpiece, the prophet Amos, denounces this state of affairs and those behind it. Against these individuals and groups Yahweh has targeted judgments. They are especially deserving of his wrath (3:15—4:3; 5:11; 6:7; 7:9, 11, 17; 9:10).

Violence is rampant in our urban areas, too. The book of Amos does not envision some of the kinds of violence that we experience today, which is connected, for instance, to gang warfare and drug trafficking. It does expose, however, systemic violence in the legal, governmental, and economic spheres. It denounces the mistreatment of the poor and the exploitation of dependent women that permeate urban settings. This reproof has its roots in the person of God, who announces his displeasure and punishment through the prophet. Samaria (and the rest of the country) is not what it is supposed to be. Today cities continue to be violent places. A good share of that violence is subtle, woven into the fabric of the many exchanges of daily life. The book of Amos provides a strong dose of realism about the menacing

---

24. This foe historically would be Assyria, although the empire is not mentioned in the text.

25. Not all of the transgressors would have come from what today we would call the same social class. Government officials, the variety of merchant types, and powerful elders at the gates would not be of uniform economic, political, or social status. All of this complicates the context.

machinations of society. It alerts its readers to be vigilant and serves as an example of moral outrage against wrong.

The means of oppression have changed over the centuries, but not the fact of systemic tentacles that strangle the powerless. The moral (and divine) demand for a prophetic voice to speak against these abuses and to give the exploited their own voice remains. The present is an affront to God and comes at great human cost.[26] Where are the informed prophets to expose these kinds of sins in our communities and cities?

The Role of Religion[27]

Critical commentators often say that the prophet Amos did not censure the worship of other gods but rather concentrated his efforts on condemning injustice and a misdirected Yahwism that condoned such wrongdoing.[28] This is an odd perspective, as they are willing to grant that Amos's contemporary Hosea did denounce the veneration of Baal. Both prophets ministered in the North and dealt with the same society. It would be surprising if Amos did *not* make some reference to aberrant religious practices, even if that was not his primary focus. Allusions to other gods occur at 5:26[29] and possibly at 8:14, although the latter may refer to different appellations of Yahweh at various shrines.[30] The altar and "house of their god(s)" of 2:8 and

---

26. Brueggemann, *The Prophetic Imagination*, 39–57; *The Practice of the Prophetic Imagination*, 21–44.

27. I have written extensively on this topic elsewhere. See Carroll R., *Contexts for Amos*, 49–122, 273–77, 289–306; "'For so you love to do': Probing Popular Religion in the Book of Amos," in *Rethinking Contexts, Rereading Texts: Contributions from the Social Sciences to Biblical Interpretation*, ed. M. Daniel Carroll R., JSOTSup 299 (Sheffield, UK: Sheffield Academic, 2000) 168–89; "Can the Prophets Shed Light on Our Worship Wars? How Amos Evaluates Religious Ritual," *Stone-Campbell Journal* 8, no. 2 (2005) 215–27; "Imagining the Unthinkable: Exposing The Idolatry of National Security in Amos," *Ex Auditu* 24 (2008) 37–54. Cf. Gerald Klingbeil, *Bridging the Gap: Ritual and Ritual Texts in the Bible*, BBRSup 1 (Winona Lake, IN: Eisenbrauns, 2007).

28. A recent statement of this view is found in Barton, *The Theology of the Book of Amos*, 117–20.

29. In support of the worship of astral deities at this point in Israel's history, see, e.g., Hans M. Barstad, *The Religious Polemics of Amos: Studies in the Preaching of Am. 2, 7B–8; 4, 1–13; 5, 1–27; 6, 4–7; 8, 14*, VTSup 34 (Leiden: Brill, 1984) 118–26; Francis I. Andersen and David Noel Freedman, *Amos*, AB 24A (New York: Doubleday, 1989) 529–44; Paul, *Amos*, 194–98. Others claim that astral worship came into the north later (cf. 2 Kgs 17:16–40). Evidence regarding Judah in the seventh and sixth centuries includes 2 Kgs 21:3–5; 23:4–12; Zeph 1:4–6, Jer 7:18; 8:1–2; 19:13; and Ezek 8:16.

30. For these options, see, e.g., Barstad, *The Religious Polemics of Amos*, 143–201; Saul M. Olyan, "The Oaths of Amos 8.14," in *Priesthood and Cult in Ancient Israel*, ed. G. A. Anderson and S. M. Olyan, JSOTSup 125 (Sheffield, UK: Sheffield Academic, 1991) 121–49; Andersen and Freedman, *Amos*, 826–32; Paul, *Amos*, 268–72. This would be akin to Latin America's many variations on the Virgin Mary that have generated pilgrim sites, processions, and religious societies connected to each one.

the high places and sanctuaries of 7:9 are ambiguous references, dedicated either to Yahweh or to other gods. A religiously charged *marzēaḥ* feast is in Amos's sights as well (6:3–7).[31]

The goal at this point is not to try to sort out which deities might be alluded to in these passages; it is to underscore that from the prophet's perspective the theological landscape and religious practices were distorted and that this religious landscape, however we might understand it, was making this unacceptable society possible and communicating that it was normal and sanctified by God. The presence of other gods certainly would have impacted the people's understanding of Yahweh, whose work in their view had to be supplemented in some way by these deities.

The Yahweh of the nation, irrespective of one's social standing, was one of blessing and victory. Amos 4:4–5 lists rituals of celebration. There is no sacrifice for sin, just commemoration for Yahweh's grace toward the people. How striking the juxtaposition with 4:6–11! Surely, there was nothing to praise him for. The general population had suffered hunger, drought, ruined crops, and war. Although Israel crowded the sanctuaries to lift up their hands in worship to their God, they had not truly "returned" to him (repeated five times). Now they must gird themselves for an actual devastating encounter with the God of Hosts (4:12–13).

Ironically, this religious people had silenced the prophets that Yahweh raised up and had compromised the Nazarenes, two groups most deeply committed to Yahweh (2:10–11). What Israel really wanted was to fulfill their religious impulses without worrying about socioethical demands or questioning their nationalism. Pious festivity is what they "loved to do" (4:5). Not surprisingly, they anticipated that the Day of Yahweh would be light—that is, victory over Israel's enemies (perhaps those condemned in the Oracles against the Nations). Instead, that time would be utter darkness and bring inescapable defeat (5:18–20). The book repeatedly forecasts destruction at the hands of an invader, a devastation that would hit the powerful, as well as the entire nation (e.g., 2:14–16; 3:11–12; 5:1–3, 16–17, 27; 6:8–11; 7:1–6, 17; 8:10; 9:1–4, 8–10).

Israel's self-deluding and self-serving nationalistic religion, which was so much sin before Yahweh (4:5), was propagated especially at the principal temple at Bethel. Amaziah reacts against Amos's condemnation of Israel's religious and political structures and makes it clear that the two spheres are fundamentally connected

---

31. In addition to the commentaries, see, e.g., Barstad, *The Religious Polemics of Amos*, 127–42; John L. McLaughlin, *The Marzeah in the Prophetic Literature: References and Allusions in Light of the Extra-Biblical Evidence*, VTSup 86 (Leiden: Brill, 2001) 80–128; J. S. Greer, "A *Marzeah* and a *Misraq*: A Prophet's Mêlée with Religious Diversity in Amos 6:4–7," *JSOT* 32, no. 2 (2007) 243–62.

and mutually supportive (7:9–13). Political decisions and socioeconomic behaviors found divine sanction at this sanctuary; Israel's present arrangement is how things should be. But, the Oracles against the Nations belie the belief that the nation is strong and ever victorious. The book mocks Israel's army's lone trumpeted triumph at Lo-Debar ("no-thing," 6:13). With a clearer appreciation of the country's actual position, the prophet pleads for mercy; he recognizes that "Jacob is so small" (7:2, 5). Soon humiliating defeat (2:14–16), terrible destruction, and a border-to-border invasion (6:14) would engulf Israel. Defeat and exile loomed on the horizon. Those leaders of society and government who had created and sustained this harsh socio-religious construction of reality would lead the march to a foreign land (4:3; 6:7; cf. 5:27).

This amalgam of popular and official beliefs and their rituals is condemned for its fallacies and its distorted understanding of the nature of things and God. The nation is plunging to its doom, mistakenly confident in the always loyal, strong, protective arm of God, but there is another insidious dimension to Israel's religion. *Everyone* goes to the sanctuaries and worships this glorious Yahweh. Sadly, as the marginalized join in these celebrations, they at the same time acclaim this national deity who legitimates the very system that oppresses and exploits them. In Marxist terms, they partake of the opiate of the national god. They wonder at Yahweh's might, but seemingly do not question why he authorizes their misery and unjust existence, why he endorses the unfair rulings at the city gate, and why he does not rescue them as they trudge into debt slavery.[32]

Because of these misrepresentations, the judgment of God would begin at the sanctuaries. Yahweh will not accept such a perversion of his person and of his de-

---

32. In his response and in private communication Nathan Bills has raised the important question concerning the extent of the guilt in the book's condemnation of religion. Are the oppressed also culpable of religious sin? The fact is that the book says that the entire nation of Israel was involved (e.g., 3:14; 4:5; 5:4–6, 25–27; 8:3, 11–14; 9:1), even as it singles out the well-placed as especially deserving of judgment for their religious distortions (e.g., 6:3–7; 7:9–17; 8:4–6; cf. 9:10). The exegetical and theological challenge is to sort out possible degrees of liability and investment in the religious construction of reality and to distinguish that dimension of corporate guilt from the specific condemnation of certain groups within the nation for their injustice. Can the vulnerable be both guilty religiously and innocent socioeconomically, deserving judgment as well as the defense of the prophet in the public square? Is their suffering in the coming earthquake and invasion to some degree merited, or should it rather be understood only as inescapable in the messiness of these judgments (as collateral damage, as it were)? Walter J. Houston calls this tension between the championing of the poor and the totality of judgment the "paradox" of the book of Amos (*Contending for Justice: Ideologies and Theologies of Social Justice in the Old Testament*, rev. ed. [London: T. & T. Clark, 2008] 71–73). Some scholars claim that the reference to Israel in terms of guilt and punishment is restricted to the powerful, but that option does not do justice to the textual data. Of course, this discussion is part of a larger one on the nature and purpose of divine judgments.

mands on a people that claim him as their own. So, Bethel would be destroyed (3:14; 5:5; 9:1), and the other sanctuaries dismantled (7:9; Gilgal, 5:5). True and acceptable religion in the sight of Yahweh was to foster and enact social justice (5:21–24). To seek him (5:4, 6) was to seek the good and justice (5:14–15). This kind of faith, along with commensurate religious practices that would nurture such a community life, would create an Israel of fair treatment for all.

Once again, Latin American liberation theology was perceptive of the continent's religious realities. It saw that the historic Christianity of the region often was complicit, directly or indirectly, in the dictatorships and that through its ceremonies and teaching had perpetuated that culture's fatalism. Liberation theology sought to redefine ecclesial life and reformulate religious ceremonies to promote and sustain substantive social change.[33] Others have pointed out that some strands of Latin American Pentecostalism and neo-Pentecostalism, some of which adhere to a health and wealth gospel and name-it and claim-it theology, blind the poor to the need for social transformation, even as they grow across the continent. The relationship between these newer expressions of Christian faith and the sociopolitical and economic context has been the focus of ongoing research.[34]

The biblical text's critique of religion offers several lessons for urban ministry today in this country. Most importantly, the prophetic message should force us to ask hard and very direct questions about the nature and role of Christian faith and of Christian churches in our cities. Is the theology and are congregations (and the hierarchies in their church associations) in touch with the harsh things of life (4:6–10), or are they disconnected and concentrate on the celebratory in the midst of so much pain and misery (4:4–5)? Does our urban theology accept and pledge allegiance to a national system that exploits its people as part of the natural order of things (5:18–20; 7:10–13)? Have urban churches bought in to the deceptive lies and promises of the broader culture, or do they embrace the centrality of justice for the life of faith (5:24)? How might the faith practices of church services (such as the Lord's Table, confession, the reading of the creeds, the choice of biblical texts, and

---

33. See the sources cited in n4 and the essays in *Mysterium liberationis*, ed. Ellacuría and Sobrino, Part II.4, 543–676. In *Marx and the Failure of Liberation Theology* (London: SCM, 1990) Alistair Kee argues that liberation theology was selective in its appropriation of the Marxist critique of religion, ignoring that Marxism asserts that religion is inherently ideological, the reversal and denial of reality.

34. Sample studies include Benjamin F. Gutiérrez and Dennis A. Smith, eds., *In the Power of the Spirit: The Pentecostal Challenge to Historic Churches in Latin America*, trans. P. Kemmerle (Mexico, D. F.: AIPRAL, 1996); Edward L. Cleary and Hannah W. Stewart-Gambino, eds., *Power, Politics, and Pentecostals in Latin America* (Boulder, CO: Westview, 1997); Paul Freston, ed., *Evangelical Christianity and Democracy in Latin America*, Evangelical Christianity and Democracy in the Global South (Oxford: Oxford University Press, 2008); Robert Brenneman, *Homies and Hermanos: God and Gangs in Central America* (Oxford: Oxford University Press, 2012).

the music) and other activities intentionally cultivate a passion for and a deep commitment to justice? In their messages, various activities, and administration have urban churches and ministries appropriated, intentionally or unawares, the values of secular success promoted in the media? What is the religious opiate that our cities imbibe?

The book of Amos teaches that Yahweh takes worship very, very seriously. His person is at stake in religious rituals and within religious structures. God is willing to destroy sanctuaries and punish religious leadership for theological distortions and for the religious suppression of his clarion call for justice at the gate and in the market place.

Visions of Hope

The book of Amos closes with 9:11–15, a short passage that depicts a future restoration of Israel's cities and countryside. This urban-rural connection mirrors the codependency of urban areas and the surrounding villages and farms in the ancient world.

This passage offers a rather vague hope that lacks the amount of detail in the restoration passages in Isaiah, Jeremiah, and Ezekiel. That is, 9:11–15 anticipates in seed form those fuller visions of the major prophets that include the reestablishment of the monarchy, the rebirth of a united people of God, the creation of a new heart within them, the announcement of a new covenant, the renewed bounty of the land, the incorporation of other nations into the worship of Yahweh, and the rebuilding of the cities (particularly Zion/Jerusalem).[35] These last lines in the book of Amos are a glimmer of hope that may have encouraged Israel, or at least some within it, to seek Yahweh (5:4–5) and endure the imminent disasters that the prophet had predicted. Even if only some individuals or communities were to survive the coming wrath, they could pray that Yahweh would have mercy upon them (5:15) and trust in his promise of this new reality (9:11–15).

Literarily these lines unmistakably connect back to the rest of the book. The scene described here is a clear reversal of all that Israel had experienced and would soon suffer in greater measure. Instead of defeat the nation would occupy a position of privilege among the nations, who now would join in Israel's faith (9:12). Instead of hunger and thirst the people would enjoy miraculous provision of food and drink (9:13). Instead of the destruction of war they would rebuild their cities and replant

---

35. For a good survey of the features of the OT hope, see Goldingay, *Old Testament Theology* (Downers Grove, IL: InterVarsity, 2003) 1:350–516.

their crops (9:14). Instead of removal from their land Israel would dig deep roots for a secure future (9:15).

Significantly, Israel's political future did not include the reconstitution of Jeroboam's line (cf. 7:9–11), which had ruled over this unjust society and had benefited from the status quo. Israel's armies had protected that social world, and the state-sponsored sanctuaries had celebrated the God who supposedly legitimated it. Amos 9:11–15 declares that Israel's hope lay elsewhere, toward the south, in Judah with the Davidic dynasty. Yahweh had roared from Jerusalem and Zion, not Samaria or Bethel (1:2). Israel's government and religious structure, in other words, were illegitimate in the sight of God. Not surprisingly, the high priest orders Amos to leave the country, accusing him before the king of conspiracy as he emphasizes the link between the crown and the temple at Bethel (7:9–13). The future pictured here is about plenty and peace; it also is about a different kind of government. In sum, it is the negation of all that was wrong with Israel.

In addition, these words find their source in the theological traditions that the people knew and had rehearsed (even if in unacceptable ways) in their feasts and readings of the Torah. That is, this was a future connected both to their present experience and to the faith streams of their past (cf. Lev 26:3–13; Deut 28:1–14; 30:1–10).[36]

Several writers have explored the impact of the future on the present. Eschatology was an important theme for Latin American liberation theology. It called Christians to work toward socioeconomic and political anticipations of the future, when justice will rule; their vision was influenced by the socialism of the second half of the twentieth century.[37]

This emphasis on the power of the future is most associated with Jürgen Moltmann. Beginning with the publication of his *Theology of Hope* in the 1960s, he has continued to develop a comprehensive Christian worldview grounded in what he calls a "transformative eschatology."[38] The promise of a concrete future for every

---

36. See, e.g., the discussion in Paul, *Amos*, 288–95; David Allan Hubbard, *Joel and Amos*, TOTC (Downers Grove, IL: InterVarsity, 1989) 236–45.

37. Note, e.g., Gustavo Gutiérrez, *A Theology of Liberation: History, Politics and Salvation*, trans. Sister C. Inda and J. Eagleson (Maryknoll, NY: Orbis, 1973) 213–50; Ignacio Ellacuría, "Utopia and Prophecy in Latin America," in *Mysterium liberationis*, ed. Ellacuría and Sobrino, 289–327. To trigger these changes some, not all, liberationists opted for revolutionary violence.

38. Note his recent *Ethics of Hope*, trans. M. Kohl (Minneapolis: Fortress, 2012). There was a famous public exchange between Moltmann and some liberation theologians about the realism of his vision of the future, about whether the future pulls us forward or whether the misery of the present drives us toward it. Moltmann's view of the debate appears in his *A Broad Place: An Autobiography*, trans. M. Kohl (Minneapolis: Fortress, 2009) 222–32.

dimension of human existence made sure in the resurrection of Jesus, he argues, should drive Christians to work for change in the here and now in order to make visible in some measure the fullness of the kingdom of God. He says:

> Realism teaches us a sense of reality—for what is. Hope awakens our sense for potentiality—for what could be. In concrete action we always relate the potentiality to what exists, the present to the future. If our actions were directed only to the future, we should fall victim to utopias; if they were related only to the present, we should miss our chances.[39]

We are to both wait for and hasten the coming of the Lord (2 Pet 3:12). By this Moltmann means, in words that echo the concerns of this essay: "With every doing of the right, we prepare the way for the 'new earth' on which righteousness will 'dwell.' If we achieve some justice for those who are suffering violence, then God's future shines into their world."[40] This perspective cultivates involvement and encourages endurance in the struggles to change our cities toward the prophetic vision.

In OT circles, of course, the key figure is Brueggemann. In words reminiscent of Moltmann, he titles a chapter on the future "The Burst of Newness and Waiting."[41] Brueggemann's work is very textual. He cites the theological traditions (such as creation) to which the prophets turn to fund their view of the "impossible" future promised by God. By their poetic imagery the prophets tried to engender the practice of courageous hope, an agenda that still demonstrates its power today: "the prophet does not offer plans and blueprints of specificity. Rather the hope that is voiced is lyrical and open, but with enough concreteness that it gives ground for the future"[42]—both theirs and ours. Their message was that the future is not closed and predetermined by those in control of society. God is announcing a fresh start, a different society, a new world. And "we should not miss that the poetry of promise carries with it an implicit summons as well."[43]

An evaluation of how each of these authors conceives of the future and how it impacts the present lies beyond our purview. The point is that the future matters. In urban ministry there is the challenge of articulating a realistic, yet relevant, vision of the future for the city and for life within the city that reverses all the negative features of present existence. In the prophets, howbeit just briefly in the book of

---

39. Moltmann, *Ethics of Hope*, 3.
40. Ibid., 8.
41. Brueggemann, *The Practice of Prophetic Imagination*, 101–49; cf. *The Prophetic Imagination*, 59–79.
42. Brueggemann, *The Practice of Prophetic Imagination*, 114.
43. Ibid., 124.

Amos, this future meant a time of provision and peace, security of hearth and home, and the worship of Yahweh shared by all peoples. The prophetic books juxtapose the realism of violence with this hope of a new reality, a reality that proves that the present is terribly destructive and a delusional lie. As they did, we need to craft a vision of the future that coheres with the present and also appeals to the traditions of our churches and the insights of others who have been faithful in urban work. It is not merely enough to be practical or successful (whatever that might mean in urban ministry circles) as the deepest motivaters of what is to be done. Urban ministry more fundamentally should be theologically sophisticated and steeped in hope.

Conclusion

This essay suggests two emphases from the book of Amos that could help orient urban ministry theologically. The first is the awareness of systemic violence and the complicity of religious life and institutions with the status quo; the second is the power of a vision of a future different from the harsh realities of the present. Both require a sound understanding of the person of Yahweh, something that is inseparable from an ecclesiology that is relevant and a liturgy designed to nurture justice and hope. The city, as Nathan Bills says in his response to this essay, is fundamentally a missiological context.

To read Amos *from* and *for* the city means "reading with the damned"[44]—that is, with the victims of injustice and with the prophetic voices of our time. This kind of active, dialectical engagement between the biblical text and urban life can be a training ground for the moral imagination and ethical sensibilities. In another time and place the novels of Charles Dickens touched the heart of his readers and helped sow the seeds of social reform in mid to late nineteenth-century England.[45] Contemporary secular authors and literary critics, like Robert Coles, increasingly are championing the power of literature to transmit values and shape the mind.[46] How much more should be the impact of the literature of the Bible![47]

Urban ministry needs responsible readers, those who seriously embrace the text and are profoundly committed to our cities. Urban ministry needs readers of

---

44. The title of Bob Ekblad's *Reading with the Damned* (Louisville: Westminster John Knox, 2005).

45. In addition to his novels, look at a collection of Dickens' writing on poverty in other publications of his day such as his *On Poverty* (London: Hesperus, 2013).

46. Robert Coles, *Handing One Another Along: Literature and Social Reflection* (New York: Random House, 2010).

47. Carroll R., *Contexts for Amos*, 140–49.

the Bible who exhibit the virtues of love, hope, and charity, as well as those of courage, justice, and longsuffering.[48] Such readers will have a sound orientation to our violence and will demand that the church be faithful to God and his revelation, and they will long for our future hope in meaningful ways. The book of Amos can serve us toward those ends.

---

48. Richard S. Briggs, *The Virtuous Reader: Old Testament Narrative and Interpretive Virtue*, Studies in Theological Interpretation (Grand Rapids: Baker, 2010).

RESPONSE TO CARROLL

Nathan Bills

I grew up in rural Tennessee on a cattle farm. I am country bred and raised. If I may quote renowned sociologist/country music artist Blake Shelton, who celebrates the bucolic community, "Back woods legit, don't take no lip, chew tobacco, chew tobacco, chew tobacco, spit."

Yet, like billions the world over, I have been pushed and pulled into the urban orbit. Since graduating from college, I have migrated to three metropolitan centers in the South. This road has been educational, and one that has fostered a call to serve with the urban poor. My various experiences with "urban ministry" persuade me that the city is an underappreciated frontier for both the church and academy. In trademark missionary-speak, the city is the "10/40 window" of the twenty-first century.[1]

So, I am very pleased and thankful to be in attendance at this conference that brings church and academy together on this timely theme. I am also extremely grateful to be responding to Professor Carroll's essay. Professor Carroll has made a number of outstanding contributions to OT scholarship, particularly on the book of Amos. What I value most about his work, however, is his commitment to bring his reservoir of learning to bear on issues confronting churches. The church needs more like him.

First, I want to raise a question about the descriptor "urban" ministry that others here have mentioned. The way I have heard the term frequently used—the way I in fact was taught to think about the term—"urban" was coded language for ministry in lower-income neighborhoods, usually of color, in the city. But is this a fair use of the word? We do ourselves a disservice if we restrict "urban ministry" to pocket neighborhoods in the city or a subset of narrowly defined issues such as the church's response to poverty, diversity, justice, etc.[2] I would rather use "urban ministry" to

---

1 Greg Lillestrand, quoted in Eric Swanson, "Nine Game-Changers for Global Missions: Trends that Shape the Future," 4, http://www.leadnet.org/docs/Nine_Game_Changers.pdf (accessed July 14, 2012).

2. On the problematic use of "urban" in discussions of "urban ministry," see Ronald E. Peters, *Urban Ministry: An Introduction* (Nashville: Abingdon, 2007) 25–28; Clifford J. Green, ed., *Churches, Cities, and Human Community: Urban Ministry in the United States 1945–1985* (Grand Rapids: Eerdmans,

denote how the city *as a missiological context* impinges upon the mission of God and God's church.[3] Moreover, because cities exercise immense influence over their surrounding communities, there is a real sense in which churches located outside the city's boundaries will be forced to wrestle with "urban" issues.[4] Thus, I want to resist the label of "urban" ministry if it permits some churches to consign to a select few the challenges made acute by urbanization. Amos would attack the kind of language that insidiously evades responsibilities among neighbors.

One way the church must respond to the urban challenge is to learn to read Scripture for the contextual realities an urbanizing world poses. I want to reiterate Carroll's plea: "Urban ministry needs responsible readers, those who seriously embrace the text and are profoundly committed to our cities." Thankfully, there is plenty of scriptural grist for this task.[5] The Bible, after all, is full of cities. A prominent example, Lady Zion, the female personification of Jerusalem, is one of the most ubiquitous characters in the Bible (no doubt the leading lady of the biblical narrative).[6] Yet, to interpret Scripture as a resource for an urban context will require Spirit-inspired imagination, not least because of the profound differences between biblical cities and their modern day counterparts.[7]

1996) 291–98; and Harvie M. Conn and Manuel Ortiz, *Urban Ministry: The Kingdom, the City, and the People of God* (Downers Grove: InterVarsity, 2001) 160–73. In my "Christian Higher Education and Mission in an Urbanizing World," *Restoration Quarterly* 55 (2013) 77, I further spell out reasons for my hesitation: "Because it linguistically constructs detrimental patterns of relationship, this kind of usage is highly problematic for several reasons. It can exacerbate racial, social, and cultural division, encourage stereotyping, and feed an 'us versus them' mentality. Second, it can unfairly color whole communities with negative realities that apply only to discrete parts—and implicitly deny wider interrelationships, even culpability, among communities—urban, suburban, exurban, and rural. In addition, labeling a particular type of ministry among marginalized communities as 'urban' can denigrate the gifts of faithful Christians living in those communities. Finally, such language represents a failure to imagine all urbanized communities in terms of the promise and potential of the city."

3. See further David Leong, *Street Signs: Toward a Missional Theology of Urban Cultural Engagement*, ASMMS 12 (Eugene, OR: Pickwick, 2012).

4. To mention only one recent example from North America, Elizabeth Kneebone and Alan Berube (*Confronting Suburban Poverty in America* [Washington, D.C.: Brookings Institute, 2013]) have documented the troubling rise of suburban poverty. See also the accompanying website, http://confrontingsuburbanpoverty.org/. "Urban" issues are only going to become more acute for the church's identity and mission in the coming decades, whatever their geography, as the world continues to migrate to the city.

5. Unfortunately, biblical publications attuned to the theme of the city are not as ample as one might hope, but the situation is improving. For a survey and recent bibliography of material relating to the city in the OT, see Nathan Bills, "Urban Imagination in the Old Testament: A Selective Overview," *Missio Dei* 3 (2012), http://missiodeijournal.com/article.php?issue=md-3-2&author=md-3-2-bills. Consult also the multivolume *Constructions of Space* (New York: T. & T. Clark, 2008–).

6. J. Andrew Dearman, "City," *New Interpreters Dictionary of the Bible*, 1:671–677, 676.

7. The Bible offers a complex, at times ambivalent, theological account of the city (see Bills, "Urban

Professor Carroll takes up the message of Amos toward these ends. As he judiciously documents, Amos frequently inveighs against cities.[8] Amos recognizes that cities exercise a powerful influence over the social, economic, and religious realities of their denizens and the adjoining hinterlands, a systemic influence that exceeds the sum of its parts. I agree with Carroll that thinking with Amos will attune our ears and eyes to recognize sinful systems. Amos confronts his readers with a caustic social analysis of institutional evil. In some church cultures whose language of sin is largely dominated by individualistic and personal categories, Amos jolts to a wider, more horrific vision of sin's sweeping, societal effects.[9]

Amos's audience is, to be sure, religious folk. The book is peppered with references describing the people's rapacious appetite for religious rites (e.g., 4:4–5; 5:18–23). YHWH even taunts them about their penchant for uplifting worship "services" (4:4–5). The problem is not the lack of religion, but rather religion's collusion with evil. For Amos it is abundantly clear that Israel's worship is vain and in vain because it is not matched by a corresponding YHWH-shaped ethic.

Thus, Amos delivers his message, in an accent I imagine sounded like Inigo Montoya of *Princess Bride* fame: "Hello, my name is Amos of Tekoa, you disobeyed my father, prepare to die" (5:12). To which the peoples respond, "Inconceivable!" It is "Inconceivable!" largely because of an insidious lacuna in their liturgy: there was no room for lament or judgment talk (e.g., 6:6; 7:13; 8:3), despite the obvious creational signs (4:6–11). Their religious participation helps them neither to name

Imagination"). To illustrate the need for "responsible readers," I want to advocate for a more circumspect reading of one popular text for urban ministry alluded to by Carroll. Jeremiah's letter to the Babylonian exiles (Jer 29) functions as an anthem for urban ministers. "Seek the shalom of the city," Jeremiah instructs the small, exilic population. As Carroll rightly indicates, this passage contains a number of themes that resonate with a Christian urban ethic. However much one appeals to Jeremiah's seemingly "city-blessing" program, the fact that his book ends with a fervent, vindictive oracle against Babylon should cause us to give more "responsible" reflection to the trajectory of Jer 29 as a piece of Jeremiah's whole message into our own day. I do not mean to steal this text away from urban Christians, only to suggest that urban theology, or better, theologies, should reflect the rich, variegated biblical witness concerning the city. On this text, see Ellen Davis, "A Future of Hope: Jeremiah 29," *Missio Dei* 3 (2012), http://missiodeijournal.com/article.php?issue=md-3-2&author=md-3-2-davis.

8. On the urban character of Amos's message, see Houston, "Exit the Oppressed Peasant? Rethinking the Background of Social Criticism in the Prophets," in *Prophecy and the Prophets in Ancient Israel: Proceedings of the Oxford Old Testament Seminar*, LHB/OTS 531, ed. J. Day (London & New York: T. & T. Clark, 2010) 101–16.

9. On the two occasions I have taught graduate urban ministry courses, I have found that the discussion of systemic sin was one of the most appreciated theological aspects of the class. As an entry into sin as a social phenomenon, I had students read Mark E. Biddle, *Missing the Mark: Sin and Its Consequences in Biblical Theology* (Nashville: Abingdon, 2005), chap. 6, "Guilt as a Condition and Consequence: Sin and Systems."

nor to weep over the pervasive evil. Systems collude to cloak the evil. Instead, their anemic worship satiates them with celebration. They may mimic David's melodies (6:5), but their repertoire is quite selective.

What is a prophet to do? First, Amos names the evil, relentlessly. He does not skirt issues but goes for the congregational jugular. Carroll adroitly limns the prophet's grievances, and we might discuss how this role of the prophet—calling out sin—plays out in urban ministry. However, I would like to focus on another aspect of Amos's ministry, already highlighted in this conference. Amos expands the worship repertoire by lamenting for the people, or better, over them. He matches their musical improvisation with a daring composition of his own, a funeral dirge: "Fallen is Virgin Israel, never to rise again, deserted in her own land, with no one to lift her up" (5:2; NIV). It is Israel's failure to lament that will lead to the people's destruction, and ironically, their eventual lament (e.g., 5:16–17; 8:7–14). Urban ministry, Carroll contends, must not turn a blind eye to the pain of the marginalized. Israel did, and for that she would die. Israel was not indispensable, and neither are we.

Carroll's last section delves into the prophetic vision of restoration. Amos concedes glimmers of hope (5:4–6, 14–15; 9:11–15). But when considered within the purview of Amos's entire message, these hopeful prophecies reverberate more like visions of resurrection than resuscitation.[10] Of course, we want hope—we need hope—especially in many urban congregations. Genuine hope resides as a threatened minority in many urban neighborhoods. In Amos, though, hope is a marginal character. What is not marginal in Amos, and what is quite common in urban boroughs the world over, is a more popular, cheaper, false hope. This hope trolls the streets, selling its commodities indiscriminately. For this reason, I contend that God's people should give Amos a fair hearing without assuaging his harsh words of judgment by turning too quickly to visions of shalom. Walter Brueggemann has eloquently identified the danger: unless we first hear the prophet criticize and dismantle the dominant consciousness, God's people will not be prepared to embrace the radical alternative.[11] The church that finds itself colluding with the dominant consciousness[12] might need to reckon a bit more with Amos's words of judgment

---

10. On the metaphor of resurrection, see Donald Gowan, *Theology of the Prophetic Books: The Death and Resurrection of Israel* (Louisville: Westminster John Knox, 1998).

11. Walter Brueggemann, *The Prophetic Imagination*, 2nd ed. (Minneapolis: Fortress, 2001), esp. chap. 3. He states, "I believe the proper idiom for the prophet in cutting through the royal numbness and denial is the *language of grief*, the rhetoric that engages the community in mourning for a funeral they do not want to admit. It is indeed their own funeral" (51).

12. Here I find Carroll's interpretation of Amos's audience a bit perplexing. He argues that an "insidious dimension to Israel's religion" is the fact that all of Israel is implicated in the religious apostasy.

and his stipulation of lament. If not, such a church risks fumbling biblical hope by grasping for a seductive parody. If Amos teaches the church the importance of taking our worship seriously, then his theology asks if the church offers in worship settings meaningful venues to vocalize, and listen to the voice of, the world's pain. Moreover, Amos confronts lopsided celebratory tones by exposing the church's part in perpetrating the violence, and calling it to repentance. "Perhaps," Amos somberly suggests, "YHWH God Almighty will show mercy" (5:15). Might the church consider the "perhaps"?

Only when God's people reckon with the pain, suffering, and sin can they begin to mobilize for genuine hope. This kind of hope may demand some among us to linger a bit longer over the criticism, to acknowledge the violence and ruins of our own making, however disconcerting.[13] Lament, and yes, at times judgment, must have their say and their day. Amos helps the church come to grips with Friday, to find its place among the grieved on Saturday, so that God's folk will know how to recognize, welcome, and faithfully celebrate Sunday. Other prophets in the canon tutor Israel more so in the new beginnings of Sunday. Amos does it ever so slightly. To read Amos is to learn to weep in the darkness, our darkness, with the damned.

In and through the darkness we will find that YHWH God Almighty will be with us, just as we say that he is (5:14).

The oppressor and oppressed alike are guilty of cultic perversion, and therefore, are fitting targets of the prophesied punishment. Yet, he does not cite any texts as evidence. I have two difficulties with this interpretation. First, when Amos does describe whom he is addressing, the less ambiguous characterizations seem not to correspond to the poor and oppressed (e.g., 2:6–8; 3:15; 4:1; 5:10–11; 6:1, 4–6; 8:4–6, 13–14). Carroll might respond that Hosea is much clearer on this topic. Is it fair, though, to read Amos's message through the sociological lens of Hosea? Second, it seems that Amos 9:8–10 does suppose a discriminate judgment between the righteous and the sinners. Cf. Walter Houston, *Contending for Justice: Ideologies and Theologies of Social Justice in the Old Testament* (New York: T. & T. Clark, 2008) 55, 71–73.

13. A robust re-engagement of the genre of biblical lament is an initial, if not fundamental, step in Christian efforts in urban contexts of over-whelming challenges. See Soong-Chan Rah's contribution in this volume.

EARLY CHRISTIAN COMMUNITIES IN THE GRECO-ROMAN CITY: PERSPECTIVES ON URBAN MINISTRY FROM THE NEW TESTAMENT

Paul Trebilco

Wayne Meeks, in his now classic study *The First Urban Christians*, wrote that within a decade of Jesus' death

> the Greco-Roman city became the dominant environment of the Christian movement. So it remained, from the dispersion of the "Hellenists" from Jerusalem until well after the time of Constantine. The movement had crossed the most fundamental division in the society of the Roman Empire, that between rural people and city dwellers, and the results were to prove momentous.[1]

What then did it mean to be a Christian in the context of a city in the Greco-Roman world? What was it like to be a group of Christians in Rome, Ephesus, Corinth, or Antioch in the first century CE? What does "urban ministry" look like in these contexts?

In this paper I will focus first of all on the likelihood that, when they gathered, the early Christians generally did so in houses, in tenements, and at times out of doors. How did these gathering places contribute to different features of their life together? I will then go on to discuss key facets of Christian communities in an urban environment that are related to this—their sense of community, the practice of hospitality, their perception of being a family and their sense of "doing good to all." Finally, I will turn to the evidence for contextualizing their proclamation in each urban context.

The House and Tenement Church and Socio-Economic Levels

When we think of Christian communities in the first century, we must of course avoid thinking of church buildings. It was not until near the end of the second century at the earliest that Christians owned buildings in which they could meet for

---

1. W. A. Meeks, *The First Urban Christians: The Social World of the Apostle Paul* (New Haven: Yale University Press, 1983) 11. Subsequent work has shown that Galilee itself had strong elements of urban life and should not be seen as solely "rural"; see J. W. Rogerson and J. Vincent, *The City in Biblical Perspective* (London: Equinox, 2009) 52.

worship;[2] prior to that time we need to think of Christians generally gathering in "house churches" for teaching, for worship, and for all facets of their life together. Such gatherings are spoken of in several places. In 1 Cor 16:19 we read: "The churches of Asia send greetings, Aquila and Prisca, *together with the church in their house*, greet you warmly in the Lord." Note also Col 4:15: "Give my greetings to the brothers and sisters in Laodicea, and to Nympha and *the church in her house*."[3] A range of other verses indicate that Christians often met in houses.[4] What insights do recent studies of the house church give us into our theme of urban ministry?[5]

The nucleus of the house church would often have been a particular household, with new converts from other households and from non-Christian families joining the group.[6] They would have met regularly, probably at least weekly (1 Cor 16:2). John Reumann asks what happened in house churches and answers in this way: "Just about everything that one can list as purpose or activity in early Christianity."[7] He adds, "prayer, preaching, teaching, and study took place [there]; baptism, *agape*, and Lord's Supper; prophecy, speaking in tongues, hymn singing, lessons read aloud from the Septuagint, revelation, and interpretation—1 Cor 14:26, the 'service of the word'; healings and miracles (1 Cor 12:28–30); developing plans and programs to aid mission witness, members in need, prisoners, and of course Paul's collection for the saints in Jerusalem."[8]

When it comes to the number of people in a house church meeting in a private house, this clearly depends on the relative wealth or poverty of members of the group and the size of the house owned by the wealthiest person. The average number of

---

2. See C. Osiek and D. L. Balch, *Families in the New Testament World: Households and House Churches* (Louisville: Westminster John Knox, 1997) 35.

3. See also Phlm 2; Rom 16:5.

4. See Acts 2:46; 5:42; 8:3; 12:12; 16:14–15, 31–35; 18:7; 20:20; Rom 16:23.

5. See the studies by J. H. P. Reumann, "One Lord, One Faith, One God, But Many House Churches" in *Common Life in the Early Church: Essays Honoring Graydon F. Snyder*, ed. Julian V. Hills et al. (Harrisburg, PA: Trinity, 1998) 106–17; R. W. Gehring, *House Church and Mission: The Importance of Household Structures in Early Christianity* (Peabody, MA: Hendrickson, 2004); E. Adams, "First Century Models for Paul's Churches: Selected Scholarly Developments Since Meeks," in *After the First Urban Christians: The Social Scientific Study of Pauline Christianity Twenty Five Years Later*, ed.T. D. Still and D. G. Horrell (London: T. & T. Clark, 2009) 60–78.

6. See P. Oakes, *Reading Romans in Pompeii: Paul's Letter at Ground Level* (Minneapolis: Fortress, 2009) 69–97; see also Reumann, "One Lord," 110.

7. Reumann, "One Lord," 111.

8. Ibid.

people that could be accommodated in a wealthy person's house was probably thirty to forty, and often scholars have assumed that house churches were around this size.[9]

Recent work by Friesen and Longenecker on the socio-economic level of early Christians is important here. They argue that we should think of the vast majority of early Christians as low on the social level. Although they see the situation somewhat differently, they argue that between 82 percent and 90 percent of the population in the ancient world hovered at or just above subsistence, with something like 7 percent to 15 percent having moderate surplus and 3 percent being extremely wealthy.[10] In thinking of house churches we have perhaps been subtly misled by the archaeological discoveries of what are actually the houses of the rich.[11] We envisage meetings in free-standing buildings, generally with a courtyard, and scholarly works give us floor plans of excavated houses.[12] But Jewett reminds us that *oikos* has a broad range of meanings and "can refer to a Roman atrium, a Greek peristyle house, a Hellenistic

9. V. Branick, *The House Church in the Writings of Paul* (Wilmington, DE: Glazier, 1989) 38–42, argues that thirty to forty people could be accommodated at a meeting in a wealthy person's house; J. Murphy-O'Connor, *St Paul's Corinth: Texts and Archaeology*, 3rd rev. ed. (Collegeville, MN: Liturgical, 2002) 182, suggests fifty was the maximum, but that thirty to forty people was more likely; B. Blue, "Acts and the House Church" in *The Books of Acts in its Graeco-Roman Setting*, ed. D. W. J. Gill and C. Gempf (Grand Rapids: Eerdmans, 1994) 142–43 (see also 175), argues for larger numbers: seventy-five in a large reception hall, with more being accommodated in adjoining rooms, but this is in a large mansion. On housing in this period, see Osiek and Balch, *Families in the New Testament World*, 5–32.

10. See the figures in S. Friesen, "Poverty in Pauline Studies: Beyond the So-Called New Consensus," *JSNT* 26 (2004) 347, who sees 90 percent at or just above (and occasionally dropping below) subsistence, 7 percent with moderate surplus, and 3 percent extremely wealthy; and B. W. Longenecker, *Remember the Poor: Paul, Poverty, and the Greco-Roman World* (Grand Rapids: Eerdmans, 2010) 53, who sees 82 percent at or just above subsistence, 15 percent with moderate surplus, and 3 percent extremely wealthy. This is a revision of B. W. Longenecker, "Exposing the Economic Middle: A Revised Economy Scale for the Study of Early Christianity," *JSNT* 31 (2009) 243–78, where he notes (p. 269) "Studies of the early Christian movement cannot be immune to the pressing 'realities of poverty' that affected the majority of the imperial world." Friesen, "Poverty in Pauline Studies," 343, defines "subsistence" as "the resources needed to procure enough calories in food to maintain the human body." See also Oakes, *Reading Romans*, 62–67, who notes of his own work in this area: "I have been rather startled to discover that the figures in our model can be mapped very closely onto his [Friesen's]." See also P. Lampe, *From Paul to Valentinus: Christians at Rome in the First Two Centuries* (Minneapolis: Fortress, 2003) 153–83; D. G. Horrell, "Domestic Space and Christian Meetings at Corinth: Imagining New Contexts and the Buildings East of the Theatre," *NTS* 50 (2004) 357–59; R. Jewett, *Romans: A Commentary*, Hermeneia (Minneapolis: Fortress, 2007) 62–63; S. Friesen and W. Scheidel, "The Size of the Economy and the Distribution of Income in the Roman Empire," *JRS* 99 (2009) 61–91.

11. D. G. Horrell, "Domestic Space," 356, notes the houses Murphy-Connor considers (see next note) are all "upper-class homes belonging to the wealthy."

12. See for example, Murphy-O'Connor, *St Paul's Corinth*, 178–82; the section discussing a Roman villa at Anaploga in the environs of Corinth is entitled "A Typical House" (178). D. Horrell has challenged Murphy-O'Connor's reconstruction; see Horrell, "Domestic Space," 349–69, and Murphy-O'Connor's reply in *Keys to First Corinthians: Revisiting the Major Issues* (Oxford: Oxford University Press, 2009) 190–93.

style courtyard with adjoining rooms, or even an apartment building with shops on the ground floor."[13] A house is not simply a stand-alone villa, and poor Christians were almost certainly not living in such buildings, unless they were the slaves of the owners of such houses. When it comes to visualizing the meeting places of many of the early Christians, we should think of the houses of the poor—tenements with poorer quality housing the higher up the tenement one lived,[14] or small makeshift houses, or living in a back room or mezzanine floor associated with a shop, or in a workshop itself, or in temporary shacks.[15] Or perhaps we should think of at least some of the earliest Christians as slum-dwellers. Jewett in his recent commentary on Romans speaks of the "slum conditions" in which some of the early Christians in Rome lived.[16] Many of them were what we might call "the urban poor."

Ostia provides much evidence for apartment buildings or *insulae*. In a study of housing in Roman Ostia, James Packer estimated that 2.9 percent of the population lived in private mansions, 12.8 percent in better quality apartments and around 69 percent in crowded *insulae*, with 15.3 percent being homeless and seeking shelter in public buildings and other places.[17]

---

13. Jewett, *Romans*, 64.

14. See J. E. Stambaugh, *The Ancient Roman City* (Baltimore: John Hopkins University Press, 1988) 175: "The farther tenants climbed up the increasingly narrow stairs, the more rickety and cramped were their rooms."

15. See Horrell, "Domestic Space," 361. Different cities had somewhat different housing. For example, Horrell notes (361) that there is no evidence in Corinth for five or more storied *insulae*.

16. See for example Jewett, *Romans*, 812, where he writes with regard to Rom 13:10 ("do not steal") of "church members living in close proximity in the city of Rome, where the slum conditions made preservation of property difficult and the widespread poverty made theft appealing as well as damaging."

17. The figures are from J. E. Packer, "Housing and Population in Imperial Ostia and Rome," *JRS* 57 (1967) 85–86; see also J. E. Packer, *The Insulae of Imperial Ostia*, Memoirs of the American Academy in Rome 31 (Rome: American Academy in Rome, 1971) 69–71. The figures presented by Packer are slightly unclear. Ostia was rebuilt during the second century CE, but Packer (*The Insulae of Imperial Ostia*, 43–44) shows that Pompeii and Herculaneum, both destroyed during the first century CE, had numerous similar *insulae*. Note also B. S. Billings, "From House Church to Tenement Church: Domestic Space and the Development of Early Urban Christianity—The Example of Ephesus," *JTS* 62 (2011) 549: "Further problematic is the fact that only a tiny percentage of the population of a large Greco-Roman city were domiciled in what are usually referred to as 'houses,' such as those found at Pompeii and Herculaneum . . . The vast majority were residents of multi-storey apartment blocks (*insulae*)." E. Adams, "First-Century Models for Paul's Churches," 66, thinks that 99 percent of the population lived in "abject poverty." Such persons congregated in "lean-tos, 'shanties,' *insulae*," etc., not the villas of antiquity. For a critique of scholarship envisaging more affluent houses for congregational meetings see Adams, "First-Century Models for Paul's Churches," 66–68. For a recent discussion of housing in Ostia, see J. DeLaine, "Housing Roman Ostia" in *Contested Spaces: Houses and Temples in Roman Antiquity and the New Testament*, ed. D. L. Balch and A. Weissenrieder, WUNT 285 (Tübingen: Mohr/Siebeck, 2012) 327–51.

At Ostia apartment blocks were normally four stories high, with the ground floor often containing shops, the majority of which served their owners as both work and living areas, although some shops had an associated back room or mezzanine floor.[18] In the upper floors families would have lived in either single rooms or two-room apartments.[19] *Insulae* were to be found in many other cities too.[20] In Rome they were mainly built of brick and concrete, although there would have been much wood in the upper storeys, including wooden partitions.[21]

Packer also makes two other important points. First, with regard to the distribution of the population, he notes that "Instead of being spread over a relatively large area . . . people were crowded together in big apartment-houses near the centre of the city. . . . In an age when transportation and communication were slow and laborious, it made sense to concentrate as large a number of people as possible near the heart of the town."[22] Second, he notes that the typical person living in both Ostia and Rome "must have lived almost entirely outside his [or her] apartment, in the streets, shops, arcades, arenas, and baths of the city. The average Roman domicile must have served only as a place to sleep and store possessions."[23]

If we are to think of most (though not all) early Christians as poor, living at or near subsistence level, then we need to generally think of tenement churches rather than churches in free standing villas. Of course, there may have been some of the latter, but I suggest they would be the exception, not the rule.[24] In Acts 20:9, relating to Troas, we are told that during a long Christian meeting Eutychus fell out of a third-story window; we can suggest then that, at least on this occasion, the Christians of Troas gathered in a typical tenement.[25] What difference does it make to think

---

18. See Packer, "Housing and Population," 83–85.

19. Ibid., 85. Factory buildings were very similar, with factories on the ground floor and residential accommodation in mezzanines and upper floors. Packer notes concerning residents in Ostia: "the great majority of these people must have inhabited one-and two-room apartments" (ibid., 87).

20. See A. G. McKay, *Houses, Villas and Palaces in the Roman World* (London: Thames and Hudson, 1975) 217; Osiek and Balch, *Families in the New Testament World*, 20, 31. On Rome, see Lampe, *From Paul to Valentinus*, 63–65. He notes (p. 64) that generally *insulae* "did not rise above five or six stories."

21. L. Thommen, *An Environmental History of Ancient Greece and Rome* (Cambridge: Cambridge University Press, 2012) 104, 124.

22. Packer, "Housing and Population," 86–87.

23. Ibid., 87.

24. Jewett, *Romans*, 63, notes that Lampe's work strongly suggests the bulk of the early Christians lived in slum districts in Rome. He argues that this "requires a revision of the prevailing concept of house churches, because most of the population in these districts lived in crowded *insulae* buildings."

25. See Lampe, *From Paul to Valentinus*, 369.

of many house churches actually being tenement churches in Ephesus or Rome or elsewhere?

First, where would Christians living in a tenement have actually met? Probably they met in workshop areas on the ground floor or in one of the small single-room or two-room apartments higher up the building. Space for the Christian gathering would then have been made available by a particular family from a part of the tenement that they rented.[26] Such an area would have been highly accessible to others in the tenement, as well as to those living nearby. Or perhaps they met in a shop? Or outside? All of these are possible.

First Corinthians 14:23–25 is revealing: "If, therefore, the whole church comes together and all speak in tongues, and outsiders or unbelievers enter, will they not say that you are out of your mind? But if all prophesy, an unbeliever or outsider who enters is reproved by all and called to account by all. After the secrets of the unbeliever's heart are disclosed, that person will bow down before God and worship him, declaring, 'God is really among you.'"

Notice the presupposition that when the whole church comes together, "outsiders or unbelievers" are free to enter as they please. Perhaps the unbeliever who is envisaged as entering a Christian gathering could have been a family member of a believer. In 1 Cor 7:12–15 it is clearly presupposed that whole households did not always convert and that at times one partner in a marriage would become a believer and the other would not. Gordon Fee notes: "Perhaps the *apistoi* ["unbelievers"] referred to in 7:12 [who are married to believers] are the kind Paul could envision being present at a Christian gathering [in 1 Cor 14:23–25], especially if the Christian meal was being eaten at the same time."[27] So perhaps the unbeliever who enters the Christian gathering is a family member.

But the situation of an unbeliever just "turning up" also fits very well with the gathering occurring in a tenement building, where people were living in very close proximity and where a group that met in the tenement would be unable to control that space. As Stambaugh comments, "The layout of the insula made privacy a hard

26. Jewett, *Romans*, 65, suggests as well as workshop areas they may have used "temporarily cleared space used by Christian neighbors in upper floors." However, Gehring, *House Church*, 149–150, is rightly critical of the idea that partitions on upper floors could be moved weekly. They may have been of wood or other material, but this does *not* mean they were portable and could be easily cleared away to create larger spaces; see also Oakes, *Reading Romans*, 91n44.

27. G. D. Fee, *The First Epistle to the Corinthians*, NICNT (Grand Rapids: Eerdmans, 1987) 681n33. He also writes (p. 685 on 14:23): "Paul may very well have in mind an unbelieving spouse accompanying the believer to his or her place of worship." We also note that in 1 Cor 7:12–15 Paul does not recommend that a believer automatically divorce an unbeliever—rather the unbeliever is "made holy" through the believing partner. But if the unbeliever initiates separation, then "let it be so."

thing to find. The apartment itself might well be full of neighbors, since several unrelated individuals or small familiae might share a cenaculum [an apartment], taking turns cooking in the medianum [a long central room] . . . and retiring for privacy or sleep into an individual cubiculum [a sleeping room] . . . Street noises probably penetrated even to the interior cubicula and made sleep difficult (Martial 12.57.3–17). Life had an inevitably communal nature in such surroundings."[28]

So someone who also lived on the same floor—or upstairs or downstairs in the same tenement—could simply become curious, particularly with regard to the noise of singing (1 Cor 14:15; Col 3:16) or speaking in tongues (1 Cor 14:26). But we need to note that an unbeliever "wandering in" would also fit people gathering in a stand-alone house, since such houses were more accessible, more open and less private than our own houses today.[29]

Edward Adams has suggested that some Christian gatherings were in rented space, rather than in domestic space. He notes that in 1 Cor 11:20–21 Paul speaks of the church coming together and that "when the time comes to eat, each of you goes ahead with your own supper, and one goes hungry and another becomes drunk." Paul then adds in v. 22: "What! Do you not have homes (*oikias*) to eat and drink in? Or do you show contempt for the church of God and humiliate those who have nothing?"

Here Paul *contrasts* eating together and eating in their own homes, which suggests that eating together did not occur in a believer's home. Similarly, in 1 Cor 11:33–34 we read "when you come together to eat, wait for one another. If you are hungry, eat at home (*en oikō esthietō*), so that when you come together, it will not be for your condemnation." Here again there is a contrast between eating together and eating at home.[30] This leads Adams to suggest that none of the homes of the

---

28. Stambaugh, *Ancient Roman City*, 178. This applies to Rome, but we have no reason to think that it was dissimilar in other cities. See also Osiek and Balch, *Families in the New Testament World*, 34–35.

29. See Osiek and Balch, *Families in the New Testament World*, 24–25; D. L. Balch, *Roman Domestic Art and Early House Churches*, WUNT 228 (Tübingen: Mohr/Siebeck, 2008) 35–38, E. Adams, "Placing the Corinthian Communal Meal," in *Text, Image, and Christians in the Graeco-Roman World: A Festschrift in Honor of David Lee Balch*, ed. A. C. Niang and C. Osiek, Princeton Theological Monograph Series (Eugene, OR: Pickwick, 2012) 30n48: "Though Roman houses (or at least elite houses) too were, to some extent, open to uninvited guests."

30. See Adams, "Placing the Corinthian Communal Meal," 28–29. He notes (p. 28, emphasis original): "The rhetorical questions of 11:22 and the injunction of 11:34 would have significantly less persuasive force if some of the congregants, i.e., the members of the hosting household, *were* eating in their own house." He also argues that Rom 16:23 means (p. 27) "that Gaius was renowned for extending hospitality to travelling Christians from all over," rather than that all the Christians in Corinth met in Gaius's house.

believers in Corinth served as the physical space of the assembly in which they ate the communal meal. Rather, he thinks they ate outside the home, perhaps in some form of rented dining facility such as a restaurant.[31] In addition, if virtually all the members of the church lived in very small apartments in crowded conditions, then such rented space would provide them with the opportunity to gather in larger numbers than in the living quarters of any member. Meeting in a public or semi-public dining facility would fit with 1 Cor 14:23 with its presupposition that outsiders could easily enter the gathering. Adams also suggests that "In warmer months, though, the believers could have dined outside, either in a large garden or free public space (probably outside city limits)."[32]

I am not suggesting that no early Christian groups met in homes, since the phrase "the church in their house" (1 Cor 16:19; see also Col 4:15; Phlm 2; Rom 16:5) still suggests some groups met in houses or tenements, but this does not mean they all did, or that they always did; the evidence Adams focuses on suggests that they *also* met in other places.

Second, we tend to take the distinction between public and private for granted, but for early Christians living in over-crowded *insulae* the situation would have been quite different. As Billings puts it, they were "living out their lives in an essentially 'face to face' social environment in which the modern disjunction between public and private space, and between the public and private spheres of life, was often blurred, indistinct, or simply not present."[33] We need to be aware of our own instinctive views here; we would tend to think of house churches as much more *private* spaces than public buildings like churches. But clearly they need not be private at all. The dichotomy between public and private is not an obvious part of the world of poor NT Christian living in the city. Perhaps the lack of a distinction between public and private space helps us to understand why there was no distinction between public and private faith, a distinction that so dominates contemporary life. For that distinction, so well-known to us, is not to be found among the early Christians. All of life had public dimensions; all of faith had public dimensions too.

Third, we have noted that Paul anticipates that unbelievers will enter during worship. Note again what Paul says in 1 Cor 14:24–25: "But if all prophesy, an unbeliever or outsider who enters is reproved by all and called to account by all. After the secrets of the unbeliever's heart are disclosed, that person will bow down before God

---

31. Adams, "Placing the Corinthian Communal Meal," 30.

32. Ibid., 35. He adds (n69): "An outdoor setting might help to explain Paul's prohibition of women's speech in 1 Cor 14:35–36 (if these verses are authentic)."

33. Billings, "From House Church to Tenement Church," 568.

and worship him, declaring, 'God is really among you.'" This is at least one dimension of the evangelism strategy of the church in the city, for this demonstrates a real openness to unbelievers, to non-members, entering what must have been moderately public space. Here worship and mission come together.

Fourth, we have noted recent work that emphasizes the poverty of the vast majority of those in the ancient world, including the early Christians. Perhaps we tend to think of urban ministry as ministry to the poor in the inner city. When it comes to NT Christians, we should think of ministry *by the poor* to the poor. We should think of groups *without* a rich patron who owned a large house and who might help everyone materially and financially.[34] Rather, we should think of Christians with very limited resources, sharing what they had with each other in communal meals (including the Lord's Supper) and in many other ways.[35]

Connected to this is the collection Paul organized among Gentile churches for the Jerusalem church, which was experiencing severe hardship.[36] We should take seriously what Paul says in 2 Cor 8:1-2: "We want you to know, brothers and sisters, about the grace of God that has been granted to the churches of Macedonia; for during a severe ordeal of affliction, their abundant joy and their extreme poverty (*bathous ptōcheia*) have overflowed in a wealth of generosity on their part." This act of great generosity was undertaken by Christians who were themselves extremely poor.[37] It was an act of great mercy by the poor for the poor.[38]

Finally, I note what a minimal church structure is involved in the house or tenement church. They had a very simple group structure, with perhaps two leaders

---

34. Jewett, *Romans*, 65, emphasizes the difference between a house church meeting in the home of a patron and a tenement church that existed without the benefits of a patron. He contrasts (p. 67) the "love-patriarchalism" of the house church with a patron and the "agapaic communalism" of the tenement church. He discusses 2 Thess 3:10 in particular with regard to the latter; see also R. Jewett, "Tenement Churches and Communal Meals in the Early Church: The Implications of a Form-Critical Analysis of 2 Thess 3:10," *Biblical Research* 38 (1993) 23-43; "Tenement Churches and Pauline Love Feasts," *Quarterly Review* 14 (1994) 43-58.

35. See Jewett, *Romans*, 67-69.

36. On the collection see Rom 12:6-8; 15:25-29; 1 Cor 16:1-4; and 2 Cor 8-9. See D. J. Downs, *The Offering of the Gentiles: Paul's Collection for Jerusalem in its Chronological, Cultural, and Cultic Contexts*, WUNT 2/248, Tübingen: Mohr/Siebeck, 2008).

37. See M. J. Harris, *The Second Epistle to the Corinthians: A Commentary on the Greek Text*, NIGTC (Grand Rapids: Eerdmans; 2005) 562-63. He notes that Paul's Greek means "poverty at the deepest," "rock-bottom poverty," "extreme/profound poverty." Paul also speaks of "the lavishness and liberality" of their generosity.

38. In his very helpful response to this paper, Stephen Chester rightly points to 2 Cor 8:14 with its reference to the Corinthians' "present abundance." In my view, many Christians were poor, but equally clearly all Christians were not poor at all times.

sharing the leadership of each group.[39] Since the Lord's Supper was at this stage a full meal (see 1 Cor 11:20–22), and since there is no hint in the two places where Paul speaks of it (1 Cor 10:14–22; 11:17–34) that the management of the meal was in the hands of an official of any kind, perhaps responsibility for presiding at the meal rotated among members, or it was the responsibility of whoever did the teaching.[40] But Paul addresses his remarks about the Lord's Supper in 1 Cor 11:17–34 to the *whole* church, which suggests that responsibility for the proper conduct of the meal, and probably the ordering of their life together too, rested finally upon all members.[41] Further, when a group grew, it would simply have split into two house churches. We also know of no city-wide leadership structure prior to the time of Ignatius (around 105–110 CE). Only in Corinth do we hear of all the Christians in one city gathering together, and this probably only happened in the earliest days when the church was small, and even then only on some occasions.[42] So we have a simple group structure. One author notes in the context of a discussion of house churches, "The first-century Church maximized the effectiveness of its functions by minimizing the complexity of its forms."[43]

Community and Hospitality

That "church" means "house church" or "tenement church" in the NT leads us to think of a certain sort of community. It was small, intimate, perhaps even intense. This does not mean community was easy! We get the sense of disagreements and disappointments in community. The Pastorals point to real disagreement between

39. Here I am referring to local leaders as opposed to itinerant leaders, but even itinerant leaders often worked in groups. See further G. D. Fee, "*Laos* and Leadership under the New Covenant," *Crux* 25.4 (1989) 3–13, esp. 7–8 and 9–10. For example, 1 Cor 16:16; 1 Thess 5:12–13; Heb 13:17; and 1 Pet 5:1–4 refer to leaders, but always in the plural. Phil 4:3, where Paul asks a loyal yoke-fellow to mediate between Euodia and Syntyche may be an exception, but here since the two women are probably also leaders, Paul is asking one leader to work with two others. Even the Pastorals presuppose a joint leadership structure; see P. R. Trebilco, *The Early Christians in Ephesus from Paul to Ignatius*, WUNT 166 (Tübingen: Mohr/Siebeck, 2004) 448–73.

40. If they met in a family home or in someone's rented space in a tenement, the hosts may have made the arrangements for the meal and had a presiding role over the Lord's Supper; when they met in a restaurant, or outdoors, leadership may have been undertaken by whoever did the teaching.

41. See R. Banks, *Paul's Idea of Community*, rev. ed. (Peabody, MA: Hendrickson, 1994) 82.

42. See 1 Cor 14:23; Murphy-O'Connor, *St Paul's Corinth*, 183; see further P. Trebilco, "Studying 'Fractionation' in Earliest Christianity in Ephesus and Rome," in *Reflections on the Early Christian History of Religion. Erwägungen zur frühchristlichen Religionsgeschichte*, ed. C. Breytenbach and J. Frey, AJEC 81 (Leiden: Brill, 2013) 293–333.

43. R. Zdero, "The Apostolic Strategy of House Churches for Mission Today," *Evangelical Missions Quarterly* 47 (2011) 346.

different house churches, and 3 John indicates people have been refusing to accept one another, as we will note shortly. In these communities there was no place for anonymous observers. People knew one another.

One small cameo of this is the use of the word *allēlōn* ("one another") in the NT. It is used over fifty-five times in many NT books to exhort the addressees to act in community-enhancing ways. Many of the verses are well known:

> John 15:12: "This is my commandment, that you love *one another* as I have loved you."

> Rom 12:10: "Love *one another* with mutual affection; outdo *one another* in showing honour."

> Rom 12:16: "Live in harmony with *one another*; do not be haughty, but associate with the lowly; do not claim to be wiser than you are."

> Gal 5:13: "For you were called to freedom, brothers and sisters; only do not use your freedom as an opportunity for self-indulgence, but through love become slaves to *one another*."

> Eph 4:32: "Be kind to *one another*, tender-hearted, forgiving *one another*, as God in Christ has forgiven you."

> 1 Pet 1:22: "Now that you have purified your souls by your obedience to the truth so that you have genuine mutual love, love *one another* deeply from the heart."

> 1 John 4:7: "Beloved, let us love *one another*, because love is from God; everyone who loves is born of God and knows God."[44]

Many more passages could be cited. We get a very strong sense of love, intense engagement, and care for one another.[45] We should not romanticize this; they had their disputes, and perhaps the repeated exhortations remind us that they did not love one another as various authors thought they should. But the ideal is held up before readers many times.

Perhaps we can connect this with our thinking about tenement churches. One can imagine people "living in each other's pockets." The density of population perhaps led to a certain sort of highly-engaged community, which only those who have lived in this sort of community can really appreciate.

---

44. See also Mark 9:50; John 13:14, 22, 34, 35; 15:17; 16:17; Rom 1:12; 12:5; 13:8; 14:13, 19; 15:5, 7, 14; 16:16; 1 Cor 11:33; 12:25; 16:20; 2 Cor 13:12; Gal 5:15, 26; 6:2; Eph 4:2, 25; 5:21; Phil 2:3; Col 3:9, 13; 1 Thess 3:12; 4:9, 18; 5:11, 15; 2 Thess 1:3; Heb 10:24; Jas 4:11; 5:9, 16; 1 Pet 4:9; 5:5, 14; 1 John 1:7; 3:11, 23; 4:11, 12; 2 John 5.

45. See further Jewett, *Romans*, 807.

One key feature of loving one another was hospitality. Sometimes it is spoken of directly, as in Rom 12:13–14: "Contribute to the needs of the saints; extend hospitality to strangers. Bless those who persecute you; bless and do not curse them." Or 1 Pet 4:9: "Be hospitable to one another without complaining."

Generally, however, hospitality is somewhat hidden in NT texts. The key words occur a number of times,[46] but often hospitality is simply presupposed, and we must read between the lines to see it. Where did Paul stay throughout his many travels? Where did any of the early Christians stay when they travelled? Usually he stayed with other Christians. We have already noted that a key part of the house church was sharing a meal, the Lord's Supper, together. We only hear about this in 1 Cor 11 because the Corinthians had been getting it all wrong.

Second and Third John show us the vital role played by hospitality in the life of these early Christians. In 2 John 10–11 we read: "Do not receive into the house or welcome anyone who comes to you and does not bring this teaching; for to welcome is to participate in the evil deeds of such a person." Of course, "receiving into the house and welcoming" includes hospitality and food. Here hospitality or the denial of hospitality is being co-opted as part of a strategy to control false teaching.[47] Do not feed or engage in table fellowship with those who deny your understanding of the gospel (see 2 John 7–9) and so are involved in "evil deeds."

Again in 3 John 5–7 we see the vital role of hospitality: "Beloved, you do faithfully whatever you do for the brothers and sisters, even though they are strangers to you; they have testified to your love before the church. You will do well to send them on in a manner worthy of God; for they began their journey for the sake of Christ, accepting no support from non-believers." Here the addressees are commended for their love for the brothers and sisters, even though they are strangers. This involves more than hospitality but certainly not less. Food is right through these verses!

---

46. *Xenia*, "hospitable": Acts 28:23; Phlm 22; *xenizō*, when used with the meaning "to receive as a guest": Acts 10:6, 18, 23, 32; 21:16; 28:7; Heb 13:2; *xenodocheō*, "to show hospitality": 1 Tim 5:10; *xenos* with the meaning "host": Rom 16:23; *philoxenia*, "hospitality": Rom 12:13; Heb 13:2; *philoxenos*, "hospitable": 1 Tim 3:2; Tit 1:8; 1 Pet 4:9. Other texts presuppose it: e.g., Matt 10:11–14; 25:35, 40, 43; Mark 9:37–38; Luke 9:48; Acts 2:46; 9:43; Rom 15:7; 16:2. On hospitality among the early Christians see A. E. Arterbury, *Entertaining Angels: Early Christian Hospitality in its Mediterranean Setting*, NT Monographs 8 (Sheffield, UK: Sheffield Phoenix, 2005).

47. See J. Painter, *1, 2, and 3 John*, Sacra Pagina (Collegeville, MN: Liturgical, 2002) 354. He notes: "Commentators often note the un-Christian nature of such teaching and practice. But this instruction does not concern a response to the poor or needy. It is a policy to refuse aid to a rival mission that, in the view of the Elder, was deceived and deceiving in its work. To aid what the Elder evaluates as 'evil works' was to participate in the deception and its destructive consequences."

In 3 John 10 we see the other side of the coin: "So if I come, I will call attention to what he [Diotrephes] is doing in spreading false charges against us. And not content with those charges, he refuses to welcome the brothers and sisters, and even prevents those who want to do so and expels them from the church." Diotrephes is doing what the elder in 2 John had recommended, denying hospitality to those with whom *he*, Diotrephes, disagrees. This upsets the elder in 3 John because Diotrephes and the elder are on different sides of this dispute.[48]

A key part of the life of the earliest Christian assemblies in Greco-Roman cities then was eating together and staying with one another. To quite some extent urban ministry meant hospitality, sharing food, and accommodating visitors. We can suggest that sharing food was practiced more broadly than just with fellow-believers. When unbelievers entered a house church gathering, as 1 Cor 14:23–25 tells us they did, did they go away hungry? If they were family members of some of the participants, certainly not. For other unbelievers I think this is very unlikely too.

Recall too the significance of table fellowship; this involved entering into a covenant-like relationship with people. Sharing one's home and one's table was to honor people, to enter into a sacred trust with them.

So table fellowship, sharing food, hospitality, and accommodating others was a vital part of the life of the early Christians, and I suggest a vital part of ministry in the city. It is not as if they discussed the matter and decided that an important strategy for urban ministry was hospitality. This was simply part of their life together that impacted all they did and was vital for the ethos of the movement. At its heart we can suggest that it imitated and perpetuated Jesus' own table fellowship, continuing his emphasis on the present-day anticipation of the messianic banquet.

The early Christians as "family"

Implied in much of what I have already covered is that one key way in which the early communities of Christians perceived of themselves was as a family. Perhaps the most obvious way to see this is to note that *adelphos*—"brother" or "sister"— was the most common way of referring to other believers in the NT and is found with a metaphorical (as opposed to biological) meaning 271 times. The word occurs in

---

48. See also *Didache* 11:4–9; 12, where we see the other side of hospitality, the over-burdening demands that could be made by visitors who may exploit hospitality. The response of the *Didache* is not to ban the practice but to regulate it. It was too important to ban. Where else would a visiting apostle-prophet stay other than with a church member? But clearly there were some issues associated with the misuse of hospitality.

every NT book except Titus and Jude.[49] When early Christians wanted to address each other, or write of each other, the first word that came to mind was *adelphoi*—"brothers and sisters."[50] This is because they saw themselves as part of a family, a family that included people of different backgrounds, ethnicities, social and economic status, and so on. Much other evidence shows that they saw themselves as "fictive kinship groups."[51]

What impact does it have on urban ministry that believers saw themselves as a new family? Of course, seeing themselves theologically as a new family helps us to understand some of what I have already said. The sense of loving one another and of feeding and housing each other can be directly related to being a family; that is how you treat family members!

Five other things can be emphasized here. First, the early Christians had a clear sense of *belonging*, of being part of a new community, of such intimacy that it could honestly be described as a family. The family was the most crucial social unit in both a Jewish and Greco-Roman context, and it was here that people found their sense of identity and of belonging. For the early Christians to regard themselves as a new family indicates that it was *in this group* that they found a new sense of belonging, of connectedness, and of love for one another. I do not want to suggest that non-Christians could not find this in other places such as associations, clubs, or their own natural families. Clearly though this was something that the early Christians experienced that was vital to them and that was also characteristic of the movement.

Second, we get the clear sense that part of being in this new family for believers was that old hostilities had been overcome. Ephesians 2 is our clearest witness to this; the wall of ethnic hostility, "the dividing wall, that is, the hostility between us" (Eph 2:14), between Jew and Gentile, had been broken down. Age-old antipathy, hatred, and enmity were now experienced as overcome. Through Christ, God "has

---

49. See further K. O. Sandnes, *A New Family: Conversion and Ecclesiology in the Early Church with Cross-Cultural Comparisons*, Studien zur Interkulturellen Geschichte des Christentums 91 (Bern: Lang, 1994); R. Aasgaard, *"My Beloved Brothers and Sisters!" Christian Siblingship in Paul*, JSNTSup 265 (London: T. & T. Clark, 2004); P. Trebilco, *Self-Designations and Group Identity in the New Testament* (Cambridge: Cambridge University Press, 2012) 16–67.

50. That *adelphoi* was inclusive and clearly included sisters as well as brothers is shown by a number of texts. Note for example, Phil 4:1–2, where Paul speaks of *adelphoi mou* and then immediately urges Euodia and Syntyche to be of the same mind, which shows these two women are clearly included among the *adelphoi*. Or note that Paul uses *adelphoi* of his readers in Rom 1:13; 7:1, 4; 8:12; 10:1; 11:25; 12:1; 14:10, 13, 15, 21; 15:14, 30; and 16:17. Rom 16 shows that women are clearly to be thought of as among the addressees and so are included in each use of *adelphoi*, but *adelphos* can also be used just for a brother as in Mark 3:35, where *adelphē* is added to *adelphos*.

51. See for example T. J. Burke, *Family Matters: A Socio-Historical Study of Kinship Metaphors in 1 Thessalonians*, JSNTSup 247 (London: T. & T. Clark, 2003) 169–75.

shattered all the barriers that divide the human family and has made possible a new community."⁵²

Or note Col 3:11: "In that renewal there is no longer Greek and Jew, circumcised and uncircumcised, barbarian, Scythian, slave and free; but Christ is all and in all!" These are the huge dividing walls of this period, and they were experienced as overcome in this new family who have become "God's chosen ones, holy and beloved" (Col 3:12), who have together been clothed "with the new self, which is being renewed in knowledge according to the image of its creator" (Col 3:10). Again, we should not romanticize. There were clearly ongoing issues and challenges of living out the new creation, but a new unity, a new sense of family across previously unbridged and unbridgeable divides, was experienced as a gift of renewal through their salvation.

Third, thinking of the early Christians as family is a very helpful way to think of status. The Greco-Roman city was highly differentiated in terms of status and honor. Hierarchy pervaded all spheres of life, including patron-client relationships. By contrast, calling each other brothers and sisters is quite a different way of thinking about status and about relationships. It does not mean there were no distinctions. There were older brothers and younger brothers, and as time progressed increasing distinctions were made along gender lines. Thinking of radical egalitarianism is probably going too far, but there is a crucial difference between the status differentiation within a family understood to be made up of brothers and sisters and those in the wider society. Calling each other *adelphoi* involved a sense of mutuality and sharing that was quite different from the clearly delineated hierarchy of the wider world. This was a quite distinctive way of thinking about community.

Fourth, part of being a member of this new family was to experience hostility from one's former family or from outsiders in general. There was a cost to this new experience. First Peter is clearest with its strong language of being "aliens and exiles." This refers to the ongoing social experience of the early Christian assemblies. Having *once* been part of the wider society as families and as individuals, they *now* had joined a quite different group and saw themselves as outsiders. They experienced the wider culture as something in which they did not fit. Hostility and suffering resulted; belonging came at a price.⁵³ This no doubt reinforced the sense of belonging to the family of the early Christians.

---

52. H. M. Conn and M. Ortiz, *Urban Ministry: The Kingdom, the City and the People of God* (Downers Grove, IL: InterVarsity, 2001) 146. The point made in the text stands regardless of the authorship of Ephesians.

53. See 1 Pet 1:1; 2:11, 23; 3:9, 16; 4:14-16; see J. B. Green, "Living as Exiles: The Church in the Diaspora in 1 Peter," in *Holiness and Ecclesiology in the New Testament*, ed. K. E. Brower and A. Johnson (Grand Rapids: Eerdmans, 2007) 311-25. First Thessalonians is another clear example; see 1 Thess

Fifth, from where did this sense of being a family come? In Mark 3:34–35 Jesus addresses a crowd sitting around him and listening to his teaching by saying, "Here are my mother and my brothers! Whoever does the will of God is *my brother and sister* and mother." Jesus establishes a new family and redefines the meaning of *adelphoi*; the term refers to those who do the will of God, as this is expressed by Jesus. So brothers and sisters becomes a designation for followers of Jesus. The widespread metaphorical usage of brothers and sisters in the NT has its roots in Jesus' teaching that his followers were a new family and in Jesus' establishment of a kinship model of community.[54] Following this precedent, it is understandable that the earliest post-Easter followers of Jesus *continued* to use the term for each other.

Note also Rom 8:29: "For those whom he [God] foreknew he also predestined to be conformed to the image of his Son, in order that he might be *the firstborn among many brothers and sisters.*" As Christians are conformed to the image of Jesus Christ, the Son, they become co-heirs with him (Rom 8:17), but they can *also* be called *brothers and sisters (adelphoi)* of Christ, brothers and sisters of the firstborn Son, as well as of one another.[55] It is clear they are brothers and sisters *through* the work of Jesus, for he is the firstborn to whose image the many *adelphoi* are now to be conformed. As they are conformed to *his* image, they become *each other's adelphoi* precisely *through* Christ. It is because of his relationship to each believer that Christians become *adelphoi* of one another. Romans 8:29 is thus a foundational statement for Paul's use of brothers and sisters of Christians.[56] Accordingly, Christians used this language because of strongly theological reasons connected to Jesus' ministry and their understanding of Christology. This new community was not a human creation or an organisation devised by people who naturally got on with each other. Far from it. It was experienced as a gift, a *consequence* of the new creation in Christ (Gal 6:15; 2 Cor 5:17).

So urban ministry is ministry by brothers and sisters, part of a new family who experience a sense of belonging, a family where enmity has been overcome and love has been created, yet a family that then is called to suffer together as aliens in a land where they no longer belong. Part of urban ministry for first-century Christians was

---

1:6; 2:2, 14; 3:3–4. See J. M. G. Barclay, "Thessalonica and Corinth: Social Contrasts in Pauline Christianity," in *Pauline Churches and Diaspora Jews*, WUNT 275 (Tübingen: Mohr/Siebeck, 2011) 182–87.

54. For discussion on this see Trebilco, *Self-Designations*, 39–42.

55. On this, see J. M. Scott, *Adoption as Sons of God: An Exegetical Investigation into the Background of ΥΙΟΘΕΣΙΑ in the Pauline Corpus*, WUNT 2/48 (Tübingen: Mohr/Siebeck, 1992) 248–55.

56. See Johannes Beutler in *EDNT* 1:29. Note that Paul never says that the corollary of God being Father is that Christians are all brothers and sisters of one another.

an invitation to join this new family and become brothers and sisters, and with the invitation came the challenge to truly live as family.

Doing Good to all[57]

But we should not think that the early Christian communities existed for their own benefit alone. It is *not* the case that they kept their activities within the family, or that the only engagement with others was for evangelism. Of course, they did look after one another, and Paul's collection is the clearest example of that. But there is a surprising amount of material in the NT that suggests that these small, often suffering communities, sought to assist those outside their groups in very practical ways.

Note 1 Thess 5:15: "See that none of you repays evil for evil, but always seek to do good to one another (*eis allēlous*) *and to all* (*kai eis pantas*). As A. Malherbe writes, "Paul does not think that passivity is a proper response to being wronged,"[58] and so Paul says that they are to do good to one another, which refers to actions within the community. He then generalizes this by saying "and to all," which is clearly a reference to outsiders.[59] This sense is confirmed by the beginning of 5:15: "See that none of you repays evil for evil." The group has clearly been persecuted recently,[60] and so the "evil" they have encountered is from outsiders; these outsiders are thus in view at both the beginning and the end of v. 15. Accordingly, they are to do good *beyond* the family to all. And here and in other passages discussed in this section, to "do good" is purposely broad. Malherbe suggests the good is "what is beneficial, as opposed to *kakon* in the sense of injury or harm,"[61] and so encompasses a whole range of positive activities.

---

57. On this see V. P. Furnish, "Inside Looking Out: Some Pauline Views of the Unbelieving Public," in *Pauline Conversations in Context: Essays in Honor of Calvin J. Roetzel*, ed. J. C. Anderson, et al. JSNTSup 221 (Sheffield, UK: Sheffield Academic, 2002) 104–24; V. P. Furnish, "Uncommon Love and the Common Good: Christians as Citizens in the Letters of Paul," in *In Search of the Common Good*, ed. D. P. McCann and P. D. Miller (New York: T. & T. Clark, 2005) 58–87.

58. A. J. Malherbe, *The Letters to the Thessalonians. A New Translation with Introduction and Commentary*, AB (New York: Doubleday, 2000) 322. The principle of not repaying evil for evil is also found in Matt 5:44–48; Luke 6:27–36; Rom 12:17; 1 Cor 6:7; and 1 Pet 3:9; see Malherbe, *The Letters to the Thessalonians*, 321.

59. G. D. Fee, *The First and Second Letters to the Thessalonians*, NICNT (Grand Rapids: Eerdmans 2009) 212–13.

60. See 1 Thess 1:6; 2:2, 14; see also J. M. G. Barclay, "Conflict in Thessalonica," *CBQ* 55 (1993) 512–30.

61. Malherbe, *The Letters to the Thessalonians*, 322, quoting J. B. Lightfoot, *Notes on Epistles of St Paul from Unpublished Commentaries* (London: Macmillan, 1895) 81.

Further, in Rom 12:9–21 Paul gives some general exhortations about living the Christian life. In vv. 9–12 he focuses on relationships within the community. Then in 12:13–21 he predominantly turns to relationships with outsiders:

> Contribute to the needs of the saints; extend hospitality to strangers. 14 Bless those who persecute you; bless and do not curse them. 15 Rejoice with those who rejoice, weep with those who weep. 16 Live in harmony with one another; do not be haughty, but associate with the lowly; do not claim to be wiser than you are. 17 Do not repay anyone evil for evil, but take thought for what is noble in the sight of *all people* (*pantōn anthrōpōn*). 18 If it is possible, so far as it depends on you, live peaceably with *all people* (*meta pantōn anthrōpōn*). 19 Beloved, never avenge yourselves, but leave room for the wrath of God; for it is written, "Vengeance is mine, I will repay, says the Lord." 20 No, "if your enemies are hungry, feed them; if they are thirsty, give them something to drink; for by doing this you will heap burning coals on their heads." 21 Do not be overcome by evil, but overcome evil with good.

There is an interesting alternation between insiders and outsiders here. In v. 13 "the saints" who are to be assisted through the addressees making a contribution to their needs are other Christians.[62] The thought of assisting in material needs then leads naturally to an exhortation to offer hospitality.[63] Outsiders are clearly in view in the exhortation to "Bless those who persecute you; bless and do not curse them" (v. 14). This leads to a more general injunction which might have both insiders and outsiders in mind: "Rejoice with those who rejoice, weep with those who weep" (v. 15). Verse 16 then concerns relations with insiders.

In vv. 17–21 the focus clearly turns to outsiders. Particularly in view is that the Roman Christians are not to repay evil for evil, or to avenge themselves, which amounts to the same thing. It is God who will repay; rather, they are to live in ways that all people regard as noble,[64] to live peaceably with all, to give food or drink to their enemies.[65] This is summarized in 12:21 as "Do not be overcome by evil, but overcome evil with good." Here then we clearly get a sense of doing good, giving food and drink, and so on, well beyond the family.

---

62. See Trebilco, *Self-Designations*, 128–133.

63. This probably refers primarily to other Christians, but hospitality to genuine strangers, i.e., outsiders, may also be in view.

64. 12:17 is an allusion to Prov 3:4, which is also alluded to, if not cited, in 2 Cor 8:21.

65. The end of v. 20 ("for by doing this you will heap burning coals on their heads") is greatly debated. Jewett, *Romans*, 777–78, gives the different options and argues that "the congruity with the synoptic tradition of loving the enemy and Paul's argumentative context of 'genuine love' and overcoming evil with good makes it likely that he had the impact of hospitality in mind."

This is not limited to Paul. Note 1 Pet 3:9–11: "Do not repay evil for evil or abuse for abuse; but, on the contrary, *repay with a blessing*. It is for this that you were called—that you might inherit a blessing. 10 For 'Those who desire life and desire to see good days, let them keep their tongues from evil and their lips from speaking deceit; 11 let them turn away from evil and *do good*; let them seek peace and pursue it.'"[66] One is to do good to all, even to those who are doing one evil or from whom one suffers abuse. Instead of repaying in kind, one is to repay with a blessing.

We clearly see here a strong interest in "doing good to all"—we might add "in the city"—which is all the more noteworthy because it is clearly an injunction given to persecuted and suffering communities. A number of other texts continue the emphasis on doing good beyond the family of faith.[67]

This encourages us, rather compels us, in quite different social circumstances, likewise to do good to all. An important dimension of urban ministry in the NT is sharing in tangible and material ways with the wider community in the city. This expansive vision of doing good to all is surprising, even startling, when we consider it comes from marginalized and often persecuted groups. It presents a clear model of positive engagement. In the completely different social contexts in which we live, doing good to all clearly encompasses a call to work for peace with justice for all people. Of course, much else in the NT argues for precisely this too.[68]

Contextualization

Part of urban ministry for the earliest Christians was clearly speaking about the gospel. As 1 Pet 3:15 puts it, they were urged "to make your defence to anyone who demands from you an accounting for the hope that is in you."

I want to suggest that the gospel was put into words in somewhat different language in different cities. The "urban" in "urban ministry" was taken seriously. Cities were different, had different histories and identities, and different ideas resonated in

---

66. Ps 34:13–17 is quoted in 1 Pet 3:10–12. In this regard, see also 1 Pet 2:17: "Honor *everyone*. Love the family of believers. Fear God. Honor the emperor."

67. See 1 Thess 3:12: "And may the Lord make you increase and abound in love for one another and *for all*, just as we abound in love for you"; Gal 6:9–10: "So let us not grow weary in doing what is right, for we will reap at harvest-time, if we do not give up. So then, whenever we have an opportunity, let us work for *the good of all*, and especially for those of the family of faith"; and Acts 24:16: "Therefore I do my best always to have a clear conscience toward God and *all people*."

68. I am very grateful to Stephen Chester for making the very important point in response to this paper that the early Christians were also "prepared to be offensive" to outsiders in various ways with regard to matters such as idolatry, ancestral traditions, and sexual ethics, precisely because such offence "was demanded by the message of the cross." His point is very well made indeed.

different places. I suggest the early Christians took this difference seriously and that through a process that we can call contextualization, the gospel came to *different* expression in somewhat *different* language in Jerusalem, in Ephesus, and in Rome. If you like, the gospel was proclaimed in different accents or even in different dialects.[69]

Several examples of the way in which the local identity of particular cities shaped the expression of the Christian faith could be given. The best-known example is of course in Acts 17, Luke's account of Paul preaching before the Areopagus in Athens. According to Luke, Paul picks up on the proverbial interest in knowledge in Athens; he speaks of the altar to the unknown God, and then points out that "what you worship as something unknown I am going to proclaim to you" (17:23). He makes this God known to them as Creator of all and then returns to the theme of knowledge when he says that the past has been a time of *unknowing* or *ignorance*, but that people must now repent (17:29–30). Here Paul translates his message into concepts that Athenian listeners could understand, and so builds a very Athenian linguistic bridge of communication across which they could travel.[70]

A less well-known but very significant example of the translation of the gospel into local language is found in the Christology of 1 and 2 Timothy, probably written to address readers in Ephesus.[71] *Epiphaneia* ("appearance, manifestation") or the associated verb is used in four places in these books. In 2 Tim 1:10 we read: "this grace . . . has now been revealed through *the appearing* of our Saviour Christ Jesus." In 1 Tim 6:14 we read: "I charge you to keep the commandment without spot or blame until *the appearing* of our Lord Jesus Christ."[72] In Titus, written to Crete, *epiphaneia* and the related verb are found three times.[73]

It is clear that the concept of "epiphany," "appearance" is a vital component of the author's Christology.[74] "Epiphany" is used of the first "appearance" of Jesus and

---

69. In general see D. Flemming, *Contextualization in the New Testament: Patterns for Theology and Mission* (Downers Grove, IL: InterVarsity, 2005).

70. R. C. Tannehill, *The Narrative Unity of Luke-Acts: A Literary Interpretation* (Minneapolis: Fortress, 1990) 2:215, says, "Starting from a cultural value acknowledged by the audience enables Paul to engage them in the discourse." See also B. W. Winter, "Introducing the Athenians to God: Paul's failed apologetic in Acts 17?," *Themelios* 31, no. 1 (2005) 38–59.

71. See Trebilco, *Early Christians in Ephesus*, 206–9.

72. See also 2 Tim 4:1, 8.

73. *Epiphaneia* is found in Titus 2:13 and the associated verb 'to appear' in Titus 2:11; 3:4.

74. I. H. Marshall, "The Christology of the Pastoral Epistles," *Studien zum Neuen Testament und seiner Umwelt* 13 (1988) 169, sees the concept of epiphany as "the controlling factor in the christology of the Pastorals." See also A. Y. Lau, *Manifest in Flesh. The Epiphany Christology of the Pastoral Epistles*, WUNT 2/86 (Tübingen: Mohr/Siebeck, 1996); I. H. Marshall, *A Critical and Exegetical Commentary on The Pastoral Epistles*, ICC (Edinburgh: T. & T. Clark, 1999) 287–96.

also of his second "appearance," which is elsewhere called his *parousia*.[75] God's saving activity in Jesus is bracketed by two epiphanies with a period in between. Using the concept of epiphany, Christ is spoken of as a divine figure who is the manifestation in this world of the unseen and transcendent God.[76]

What can we say about the use of the concept of epiphany? First, *epiphaneia* ("appearance") occurs elsewhere in the NT with this sense only in 2 Thess 2:8, and the verb *epiphainein* has a different sense in its other two occurrences.[77] Secondly, while the verb is found in the Septuagint and the noun in 2 and 3 Maccabees and similar ideas are found in Jewish apocalyptic literature,[78] the concept of "epiphany" is not an important one in Jewish literature.

By contrast, *epiphaneia* is often used in Greco-Roman religions of the self-manifestation in this world of a divine being, with appropriate signs of majesty and power. It can refer to the appearance of a god during processions or to help people in time of need, or as the motivation for the foundation of a temple.[79] It can also be used to refer to the emperor. Accordingly, both the noun and the verb are found in Ephesian inscriptions honouring Julius Caesar as "the manifest (or appearing) god," or honouring Artemis as "the most manifest goddess."[80] This is important since, as we have noted, 1 and 2 Timothy were probably written for Ephesian readers.

It is significant then that the author uses the concept of epiphany. Given the prominence of this concept in Hellenistic religions and its comparative unimportance in Jewish literature, a strong case can be made that here the concept of epiphany, and the associated epiphany scheme, has been adopted from the sphere of Hellenistic religions and used by the author as a vehicle for christological clarifi-

---

75. For the first "appearance" of Jesus, see 2 Tim 1:10, and Titus 2:11; for the second "appearance" of Jesus, see 1 Tim 6:14; 2 Tim 4:1; 4:8; Titus 2:13. For *parousia* see Matt 24:3, 27, 37, 39; 1 Cor 15:23; 1 Thess 2:19; 3:13; 4:15; 5:23; 2 Thess 2:1, 8; Jas 5:7, 8; 2 Pet 3:4, 12; 1 John 2:28.

76. Marshall, "Christology," 170, notes "Christ is seen as reflecting God and is understood in relation to God who thus occupies the central position." See also 1 Tim 6:14–16.

77. See Luke 1:79 and Acts 27:20.

78. See Marshall, "Christology," 169.

79. See Lau, *Manifest in Flesh*, 182–89.

80. In 48 BCE the cities of Asia set up an inscription at Ephesus in which they honoured Julius Caesar as "*the manifest god* descending from Ares and Aphrodite"; see *SIG* 760. An inscription of 104 CE speaks of a person's decision "to adorn and reverence the religious and public realms of your greatest and most notable city, for the honour and reverence of the *most manifest goddess* Artemis"; see *IvEph* 27, lines 384–85; translation from G. M. Rogers, *The Sacred Identity of Ephesos: Foundation Myths of a Roman City* (London: Routledge, 1991) 173. An edict of 162–64 CE speaks of temples being founded and altars dedicated to Artemis among both Greeks and barbarians "because of the visible *manifestations* effected by her"; see *IvEph* 24B, lines 13–14.

cation.⁸¹ Accordingly, it is a clear example of language and thought forms from the local city, in this case from Ephesus, being used as a vehicle for the expression of the gospel. Note too that Howard Marshall argues that the use of the concept of epiphany in a translation process relating to Christology has *not* changed the essential teaching of the older, traditional material about Christ.⁸² It is *faithful* contextualization.

Here then we clearly see the concern to *address* a particular urban context in relevant and meaningful language, in this case concerning Christology. This is a true *local, urban* embodiment of early Christian preaching. The gospel preached by the author of the Pastorals *belonged* in Ephesus. It would have had meaning elsewhere too, but the way the gospel was expressed and the language that was used definitely reflects the local, contextual embedding of Christian faith.

We could go on to a number of other examples, such as the way in which the book of Revelation picks up the local Leto-Apollo myth in Rev 12 or uses local terminology from Greco-Roman magic to proclaim the supremacy of Christ in Western Asia Minor.⁸³ Some features of the message of Titus, addressed to readers on Crete, are particularly fitting for a Cretan context.⁸⁴ Ignatius too uses local language to speak of what it is to be a Christian.⁸⁵ In a number of instances the language of the Christian faith has a strong *local* dimension and was at home in a particular place. Expressions of Christianity that were truly local to particular cities developed.

What we see then is a clear attention to the needs of "outsiders." How are *they* to hear this gospel? If it comes in a completely strange tongue, it will pass the hearers by.⁸⁶ Perhaps this can be seen as an exercise in hospitality, in making the outsider feel at home by speaking in a way that resonates with them and that they can understand.⁸⁷ This does not involve changing the gospel but rather contextualizing the message into the local accent, even the local dialect, so that others can truly hear it.

---

81. See Marshall, "Christology," 168–69.

82. See ibid., 169–75.

83. See Trebilco, *Early Christians in Ephesus*, 395–400.

84. See G. M. Wieland, "Roman Crete and the Letter to Titus," *NTS* 55 (2009) 338–54; he notes (p. 354) the letter's concern "for effective communication of the content of Christian faith in terms that would have resonated with religious beliefs, aspirations, and practices current on Crete in the Roman period."

85. See P. A. Harland, "Christ-Bearers and Fellow-Initiates: Local Cultural Life and Christian Identity in Ignatius' Letters," *Journal of Early Christian Studies* 11 (2003) 481–99.

86. This would be to apply the principle of "other-regard" to the outsider in the same way that Paul applies it to the outsider or unbeliever in 1 Cor 14:23–25.

87. See J. D. Myers, "What is Translation? An Act of Love and Hospitality," *Word & World* 31 (2011) 332–34.

Of course, we also see Christian teachers teaching local Christians in language with which *they* could identify.

The context of the city then is important in urban ministry. The gospel, the same gospel I believe, was preached differently in Rome, Ephesus, and Jerusalem. One size does not fit all. Local language and local situations were important for the earliest Christians. They noticed the differences and took them into account in preaching and teaching. They took the *place* of their hearers into consideration and sought to build bridges of communication so the message could be heard and become real and *belong* in a particular city. We see real engagement with urban culture, urban images, and city mythologies in order to preach the gospel and express beliefs in ways that were understandable. Urban ministry looks different in different places.

The one gospel is expressed in different language in different places, yet it is the one gospel. We can and should translate it into the vernacular in each of our cities, but we must ensure that it is the one gospel we are translating.

Perhaps too this encourages other translation exercises or similar exercises in creativity. Our ways of doing urban ministry, our structures that support ministry, and the ways we fund ministry are all matters about which the NT expresses principles that we could discuss if we had time. These are also issues the NT encourages us to translate into the vernacular so that our forms of ministry, our structures, and so on exhibit flexibility and creativity, all so that the one transforming gospel can be proclaimed, embodied, and incarnated in each locale.

Conclusions

In some ways our contexts are hugely different from that of the first century CE. Our social organization, our political structures, and our communication strategies are vastly different. Our visions of the possibilities of social change would have baffled people in the first century.

Yet in many ways the pluralist, post-Christendom world in which we live has many features in common with the first century and with life in the city in particular. Certainly in my New Zealand context the church is often a small minority, marginalized and made to feel alien. Of course, many of our brothers and sisters in the faith throughout the world know what it is like to suffer and to endure abuse for the name of Christ (1 Pet 5:9). Many have rediscovered the significance of the house church, either out of necessity because that is the only form of church that is possible or in a search for intimacy and care, which often involves a turn away from what they see as irrelevant institutions more concerned with their own perpetuation than with propagating the faith.

So I hope these insights are relevant to urban ministry. Much else could have been covered, but I hope principles and practices from urban ministry in the NT that are relevant today have emerged: the vital role of the house and tenement church and the principles that emerge from its life; the importance of community, hospitality, and seeing the church as family; the importance of doing good to all; and the calling to translate the gospel into the vernacular. These are integral facets of what I think our *earliest* brothers and sisters in the faith would have regarded as their urban ministry.

RESPONSE TO TREBILCO

Stephen Chester

Paul Trebilco provides for us a fascinating overview of early Christian urban congregations. He begins from their social locations, i.e., from the connected issues of their socio-economic level and the physical location of their worship, whether in houses, tenement apartments, or elsewhere. The issue of social location becomes the launch pad from which he discusses key aspects of the communal life of the congregations and their interactions with the broader urban contexts of which they were part.

From the perspective of NT scholarship there is nothing surprising about Trebilco's starting point. The socio-economic level of early Christian urban congregations has been widely discussed among NT scholars. Yet the question of starting point is not one that should be taken for granted, for the other issues discussed in the paper—the early Christians' sense of community, their practice of hospitality, their perception of being a family, their sense of doing good to all—could also legitimately be approached from other perspectives. They could, for example, have been fruitfully approached from the starting-point of Jew/Gentile relationships, the great issue of ethnicity and identity in the early Christianity. They could have been fruitfully approached from the perspective of gender, but here they are approached in connection to socio-economic level. There is something, I suspect, about the title "urban ministry" that serves to put the issue of socio-economic level in our minds and make it a natural part of our discourse. This is a good thing. Socio-economic level may receive extensive attention in critical studies of congregational life more broadly, and of urban ministry in particular, but in the general discourse of our culture and church life it is much less discussed. All kinds of issues are quite rightly viewed through the lenses of ethnicity and gender, but less so through the lens of socio-economic level or class. What is unspoken or unsayable is usually just as powerfully at work in human interactions as that which can be named, and so Professor Trebilco does us a service by putting the issue of socio-economic level front and center in the discussion.

In relation to what he tells us about socio-economic level in early Christianity and the physical locations of early Christian worship, I find myself almost entirely in agreement. In contrast to earlier phases of scholarship in which attempts were made to characterize the socio-economic level of the entire early Christian movement, the discussion of recent decades presents us with a much more variegated picture. Some congregations might meet in the freestanding house of a relatively well-off believer, but we need also to reckon with tenement apartments, makeshift houses, and the back rooms of shops or workshops. Therefore that we should think of NT Christians as exercising "ministry by the poor, to the poor," as Trebilco suggests, is likely to be correct in very many cases. Yet it seems to me entirely credible to think of the diversity of patterns of socio-economic level within early Christianity extending so widely that some congregations contain several believers wealthy enough to own freestanding houses while other congregations contain none at all. As Trebilco notes, Paul urges the Corinthians to contribute generously to the Jerusalem collection by reminding them how the Macedonian believers have been generous despite their extreme poverty (2 Cor 8:2). Yet Paul also tells the Corinthians that their plenty will supply the need of those in Jerusalem who will receive the collection (2 Cor 8:14). While he countenances the possibility that at some future time circumstances might be reversed, it is difficult on the basis of these texts to argue that Paul regarded the Corinthians and the saints in Achaea as poor. We do not know his scale of comparison, but at the time he wrote Paul regarded the Corinthians as better off materially than either the Macedonian churches or the church in Jerusalem.

Trebilco's paper is also stimulating in following the work of Eddie Adams in arguing that we should not always think of early Christian congregations as meeting in homes.[1] The book of Acts is suggestive here, for while the house of Lydia is shown as quickly becoming the hub of the first Christian congregation in Philippi, she is first encountered at a riverside place of prayer (16:13) to which Paul and his co-workers subsequently return (16:16). Similarly, in Ephesus Paul is shown as holding daily discussions of the gospel for two years in the lecture hall of Tyrannus (19:9). In neither instance is there an account of Christian worship in these locations, but it is difficult to imagine a sharp boundary being maintained between such worship and Paul's evangelistic activities at the riverside or in the lecture hall. Trebilco reminds us that in 1 Cor 14:20–25 Paul provides us with a hypothetical discussion of a service of worship becoming an occasion for evangelism, and Paul clearly regards this as desirable. Indeed, the permeable boundaries in ancient Mediterranean societies between what we would conceive of as "private" domestic space and more public locations

---

1. E. Adams, "Placing the Corinthian Communal Meal," in *Text, Image, and Christians in the Graeco-Roman World: A Festschrift in Honor of David Lee Balch*, eds. A. C. Niang and C. Osiek, Princeton Theological Monograph (Eugene, OR: Pickwick, 2012) 22–37.

form another major emphasis of the paper. In its domestic location early Christian worship may have been almost as accessible to those outside the group as it would have been in nondomestic locations. This raises a set of interesting questions for us today in relation to worship and its physical location. Whatever our personal preferences, we may too quickly assume that it is self-evident where services of worship should take place without asking in which location it might be most possible for outsiders to experience Christian worship as it expresses the gospel.

When we turn to the discussion of key facets of the life and witness of the early Christian communities, I again find very little with which to disagree. Everything that is written is amply supported by evidence drawn from the NT texts. However, I did notice that we are twice warned against romanticizing the early churches and their communal life. That Trebilco felt the need to give these warnings made me think about the principle of selection. While it is understood that one paper can never cover everything, why were these particular facets of the life of the early urban congregations selected? Why community, hospitality, the sense of family, and the necessity to do good to all? On any account these are indeed important issues worthy of inclusion, but they also seem to be features of early Christian practice that we can, with the appropriate qualifications and warnings not to romanticize them, embrace as positive in our own contemporary western cultural context without much difficulty. Such a positive embrace might become less easy if we started taking them really seriously in the life of our congregations, but nevertheless, at least in the abstract, these are things about our ancestors in faith that we can admire. But what about the aspects of the life of the early urban congregations that we might find rather grittier and more challenging? What about their emphasis on ethical standards, above all their intense concern with sexual purity? What about not only the openness of their worship to outsiders but also the exclusive priority of their claim upon the loyalty of members?

This aspect of exclusivity does surface in Trebilco's discussion of family, for he notes concerning believers that "Having *once* been part of the wider society as families and individuals, they *now* had joined a quite different group, and saw themselves as outsiders. They experienced the wider culture as something in which they did not fit." We can think here, perhaps, especially of those whose personal relationships with social superiors were disrupted, such as believing slaves with unbelieving masters or believing wives with unbelieving husbands. As Wayne Meeks expresses it, "the Christian groups were exclusive and totalistic in a way that no club nor even any pagan cultic association was . . . to be 'baptized into Christ Jesus' nevertheless signaled for Pauline converts an extraordinarily thoroughgoing resocialization, in which the sect was intended to become virtually the primary group for its members, supplanting all other loyalties."[2] If this is so, then it is not surprising if there were those in the households of the wider society who perceived the new allegiances of the believers as in competition with existing ones and as a betrayal. However, the issue of exclusivity does not only relate to family and group relationships. It also applies to the message of the early Christians. The same texts that urge doing good to all also say things like "the message about the cross is foolishness to those who are perishing, but to us who are being saved it is the power of God" (1Cor 1:18), or "You know that you were ransomed from the futile ways inherited from your ancestors, not with perishable things like silver or gold, but with the precious blood of Christ" (1Pet 1:18–19). How is the outsider to whom the Christians are doing good supposed to respond to such acts of kindness when they are accompanied by the suggestion that, as things stand, this very outsider will shortly perish for all eternity or that the outsider's ancestral traditions are rightly to be characterized as worthless? How is the outsider to react to the wholesale adoption by Gentile believers, who have no ancestral tradition at all on which to base it, of the traditional Jewish critique of Greco-Roman religion as idolatry? Even the easily accessible hypothetical worship service of 1 Cor 14:20–25 is scarcely unthreatening. What Paul imagines is that in prophecy the outsider will be reproved and examined by all, with the result that the secrets of the outsider's heart will be laid bare.

I do not raise these points because I doubt the sincerity or seriousness of the New Testament's injunctions to do good to all. I do not doubt it, nor do I believe that the early Christians were offensive to outsiders because they enjoyed giving offence. They were prepared to be offensive in these ways because they perceived that the message of the cross demanded it. They were prepared to be offensive because they perceived it to be in the long-term best interests of outsiders themselves. The urgency of their message about salvation had to be communicated. Thus the exclusivity of the message and the potential for offense it entailed were theologically and pastorally grounded. The potential offensiveness of the Christian message and of Christian praxis were from the point of view of the believers presumably entirely consistent with, perhaps even expressive of, the desire to do good to all. The question this raises for urban congregations today is, of course, how are we to be appropriately offensive in speaking and embodying the message of the gospel? This is a truly

---

2. Wayne Meeks, *The First Urban Christians: The Social World of the Apostle Paul*, 2nd ed. (New Haven: Yale University Press, 1983) 78.

dangerous question, for there are all kinds of ways in which we might abuse it to serve our own interests. There are also all kinds of ways in which we could make entirely inappropriate and insensitive applications of texts such as the ones I just quoted in order unjustly to denigrate non-Christians, or indeed implicitly to devalue important ministry already taking place in urban contexts. It is, however, not only dangerous but also unavoidable. There are many things in the life of the contemporary Western city that urgently need to be addressed under the rubric of "futile ways," either inherited from our ancestors or of our own, more recent, invention.

Trebilco points us in the right direction toward answering this question in responsible ways when he concludes his paper by raising the issue of contextualization. He draws our attention to ways in which the NT reveals to us early Christian communities translating the gospel into local language. For example, the vocabulary of epiphany is used to express Christ's identity in a way that has particular resonance in the context of Ephesus. This act of translation is in one sense an exercise in hospitality that ensures that the outsider can truly hear the gospel in a tongue that is not completely strange. Yet precisely because it speaks in a local accent, this contextualization serves also to present the challenge of the gospel all the more clearly. The identification and putting into practice of such faithful acts of contextualization are among the principal challenges confronting us in contemporary urban ministry. What does it mean, as an expression of God's love for all, for our congregations faithfully to communicate and embody the scandal of the cross?

THE NECESSITY OF LAMENT
FOR MINISTRY IN THE URBAN CONTEXT

Soong-Chan Rah

The plenary speaker's voice resounded throughout the large church sanctuary. Nearly four thousand participants had convened for one of the largest church planting conferences in the U.S. Current and future church planters gathered to hear from more successful church planters and pastors. In one session the platform speaker repeated the mantra "The sky's the limit; so reach for the stars." A catch phrase replaced any reference to Scripture. Vague abstract platitudes were offered for the church planter in the audience to apply in any way deemed relevant.

Maybe even more disturbing than the theologically vacuous plenary session was the persistent theme of striving for success and moving toward the triumph of the church in the U.S. The U.S. church should reach for the stars and change the world through strategic initiatives. The problem of church decline would be conquered. Multiple urban churches would be planted to reshape the surrounding culture and save the city. The church in the U.S. would employ any practical, applicable, and workable method to insure success and a triumphal outcome.

The triumphal push toward solving the problems of the church in the U.S. finds expression in Christianity's engagement with the urban context. In recent years there has been a surge of interest in urban ministry coupled with a resurgence of interest in justice ministry among evangelicals. In both scenarios the narrative of an affluent and privileged individual fixing the problems of the poor has emerged as a central motif. Cities are problems to be solved. A successful suburban church, therefore, has the obligation to fix the problems of our cities through urban ministry or urban church planting. A triumphalistic narrative shapes urban ministry.

The twenty-first-century American Christian theological imagination is limited by a dominant narrative. The narrative of suffering and lament has been silenced by a narrative of triumph and success. The book of Lamentations offers a counter narrative to the success-driven, triumphalistic narrative of the church in the U.S. Lamentations calls us to embrace a narrative of suffering to understand the fullness of God's ongoing work in the urban context.

The Historical Context of Lamentations and Twenty-First-Century Urban Ministry

The destruction of Jerusalem and the subsequent exile of God's people in 586 BCE serve as the context and impetus for the poetry of Lamentations. The fall of the last stronghold of a formerly great nation inaugurates the exilic period. This disaster of catastrophic proportions gestures toward the culmination of suffering for God's people. When this tragedy occurs, the people of God tumble to the depth of despair.[1] In Jeremiah 29 we are given a glimpse of two possible responses to this national tragedy. Jeremiah sends a letter "from Jerusalem to the surviving elders among the exiles and to the priests, the prophets and all the other people Nebuchadnezzar had carried into exile from Jerusalem to Babylon" (Jer 29:1).

Jeremiah first confronts the temptation of the exiles to withdraw from the world. Jeremiah 29:4–7 reveals YHWH's command for the exiles:

> This is what the Lord Almighty, the God of Israel, says to all those I carried into exile from Jerusalem to Babylon: 5"Build houses and settle down; plant gardens and eat what they produce. 6Marry and have sons and daughters; find wives for your sons and give your daughters in marriage, so that they too may have sons and daughters. Increase in number there; do not decrease. 7Also, seek the peace and prosperity of the city to which I have carried you into exile. Pray to the Lord for it, because if it prospers, you too will prosper.

The traditional and expected formula of "seek the peace and prosperity of Jerusalem" is turned on its head with the command to "seek the peace and prosperity of the city to which I have carried you into exile," i.e., Babylon. YHWH implores his people to continue to live life, even in the midst of shattered dreams and expectations. Life continues even as a community struggles with its place in the world. Withdrawal from the reality of a fallen world is not an option.

American Christianity's relationship to the city yields a complex and shifting narrative. In the early stages of American church history we observe a Christianity

---

1. The despair over the fall of Jerusalem is amplified by the high view of the city held by its residents. Jerusalem was David's city. The Psalms attest "The name of the LORD will be declared in Zion and his praise in Jerusalem" (Ps 102:21); and "Praise be to the LORD from Zion, to him who dwells in Jerusalem" (Ps 135:21). Jerusalem was home to the temple of the LORD and the place of affirmation that Israel had a covenantal relationship with YHWH. "The destruction of Jerusalem, the loss of statehood, the deportation of the leaders, and the cessation of cultic religion were epochal events for they marked the end of one era and the beginning of another . . . The significance of the Book of Lamentations consists in its close connection with the tumultous [sic] events of that era and its vital interpretation of the flux of contemporary history." Norman Gottwald, *Studies in the Book of Lamentations* (London: SCM, 1954) 19.

that held an optimistic view of the future of the American continent and American cities. Historian Winthrop Hudson summarizes the expectation of the colonists for the American continent: "they were executing a flank attack upon the forces of unrighteousness everywhere. Their role, John Winthrop had reminded them, was to be 'a city set on a hill' to demonstrate before 'the eyes of the world' what the result would be when a whole people was brought into open covenant with God . . . this was God's country with a mission to perform."[2] William Clebsch notes "the vision of the new world as locus for a new city . . . The new world prompted Christians from the sixteenth century through the nineteenth to think of America as the last and best of human societies following the westward course of empire."[3] Colonial American Christians anticipated that the cities of the New World would become cities set on a hill, New Jerusalems and Zions.

This optimistic view of the American city shifts over the course of the nineteenth and twentieth centuries. The many decades between the end of the Civil War and the end of the Second World War witnessed drastic changes in the landscape of the city. The migration of African Americans from the southern former slave states coupled with the influx of non-Protestant and non-Western European immigrants into the northern and east coast cities resulted in the notable growth of these cities.

The influx of these "unwanted elements" in the cities, however, meant that whites, who had previously seen the American cities as places of great hope and promise, now saw them as dangerous places. Robert Orsi comments that,

> in the feverish imaginations of antebellum anti-Catholic literary provocateurs, city neighborhoods appeared as caves of rum and Romanism, mysterious and forbidding, a threat to democracy, Protestantism, and virtue alike. Journalism, anti-Catholic and anti-immigrant polemics, temperance pamphlets, and evangelical tracts together created a luridly compelling anti-urban genre that depicted the city as the vicious destroyer of the common good, of family life and individual character, and counter-posed the city to an idealized image of small-town life.[4]

---

2. Winthrop S. Hudson, *Religion in America,* 3rd ed. (New York: Scribner's Sons, 1981) 20–21.

3. William A. Clebsch, *From Sacred to Profane America* (New York: Harper & Row, 1968) 39. Harvie Conn also notes that the colonial Puritan hoped that "New England would one day become the New Jerusalem." Harvie M. Conn, *The American City and the Evangelical Church* (Grand Rapids: Baker, 1994) 28.

4. Robert Orsi, *Gods of the City* (Bloomington: Indiana University Press, 1999) 6. Randall Balmer adds: "Evangelicals suddenly felt their hegemonic hold over American society slipping away . . . The teeming, squalid ghettoes . . . festering with labor unrest, no longer resembled the precincts of Zion that postmillennial evangelicals had envisioned earlier in the century." Randall Balmer, *The Making of Evangelicalism* (Waco, TX: Baylor University Press, 2010) 33.

Meanwhile, the suburban communities offered an attractive alternative for former residents of the city. Amanda Seligman notes that, "in the years after World War II, a modern form of suburb, fostered by new tools, opened up around the country. Innovative financing techniques, subsidized by the federal government, enabled millions of white Americans to purchase property beyond city limits."[5]

The culmination of this shifting perspective is white flight. The twentieth century witnessed the departure of whites and white churches from the city in significant numbers. Isabel Wilkerson in *The Warmth of Other Suns* notes:

> [A]fter World War II, Chicago, Detroit, Cleveland, and other northern and western cities would witness a fitful migration of whites out of their urban strongholds. The far-out precincts and the inner ring suburbs became sanctuaries for battle-weary whites seeking, with government incentives, to replicate the havens they once had in the cities.[6]

The suburbs became the new outposts for white Christians fearful of the changes in the city. Twentieth-century Christians, therefore, adopted a strong sense of distinction and separation between the city and non-city regions. This demarcation led to the perception of the modern city as the center of all that is wrong with the world, while the suburbs could be seen as what is right with the world. The suburbs have become the New Jerusalem with the cities now relegated to being Babylon. White Christians were now tempted to disengage from the evil city in the same manner of temptation facing the exiles of Jer 29.

If the first temptation addressed in Jer 29 reveals the temptation to disengage from the city, the second temptation warns of an overengagement with the city. The people of God are tempted to acquiesce to idolatrous temptations and to listen to false teachers and prophets. Jeremiah 29:8–9 instructs, "Yes, this is what the Lord Almighty, the God of Israel, says: 'Do not let the prophets and diviners among you deceive you. Do not listen to the dreams you encourage them to have. 9They are prophesying lies to you in my name. I have not sent them,' declares the Lord."

Jeremiah refers to false prophets who would tell the exiles what they wanted to hear. The false prophets claimed that the exile would be short-lived and that Jerusalem would be restored soon.[7] The exiles were tempted to embrace the teach-

---

5. Amanda I. Seligman, *Block by Block: Neighborhoods and Public Policy on Chicago's West Side* (Chicago: University of Chicago Press, 2005) 210–11.

6. Isabel Wilkerson, *The Warmth of Other Suns* (New York: Vintage, 2010) 378.

7. J. A. Thompson observes that "the false prophets had told the people that their stay would be short, and Jeremiah needed to assert that this was a *falsehood* . . . [the false prophets] were associates of diviners and dreamers (27:9) . . . It was an attempt to speed up the divine purposes. But Yahweh

ing of false prophets who offered a quick resolution to their suffering. These claims were made using the idolatrous practices of the times, mainly divination and magic.

Jeremiah confronts the work of the "diviners" who would attempt to deduce the future through magical means. Divination practices were "closely associated with various forms of magic and sorcery."[8] Divination reflects a desire to know and control the future by removing uncertainty. For a people in exile the readily available practice of divination would be a real temptation. Divination and idol worship would serve as a persistent temptation as it operated with a degree of material certainty.

Peter Steinke identifies this temptation as magic. "Many are drawn to magic because of its promise of quickness. Before you know it—Presto! Repeat the cant 'Abracadabra.' Magic is not only quick but also direct. All sorcerers go for the end product, without the process. Here it is. No messy stuff. No questions. No confusing dialectic to toss and turn in your brain. It seems as if every magician possesses the master key to the door."[9]

YHWH worship, on the other hand, held no such promises. YHWH does not operate like a vending machine. The worship of God does not follow a simplistic pattern yielding the exact desired outcome. Unlike divination, YHWH worship holds no seductive promises of success based upon magic. Defeated exiles would be tempted to forsake the complexity of YHWH worship for the simplicity of magic and to embrace the lies of the false prophets offering quick solutions.

In U.S. church history the shift of ministry emphasis toward the suburban expressions of the church results in the rise of quick and easy answers to ministry. There exists no shortage of magic formulas in the suburban ministries that proliferate in the latter half of the twentieth century. The latest church growth book and church resource are tantalizingly available. Frustrated pastors weary of waiting for their church to turn around will have no problem accessing resources with the latest and greatest idea to make it happen. Churches in the U.S. are not supposed to struggle, and they are not supposed to decline. American ingenuity and know-how will solve these problems. There is a simple answer if we would only apply ourselves. Jeremiah 29 challenges these presuppositions. There are no easy answers.

Churches in the suburbs exhibited significant numerical growth in the latter half of the twentieth century. Winthrop Hudson notes that while twenty-six million

---

will not be hurried in his plans for his people." J. A. Thompson, *The Book of Jeremiah*, NICOT (Grand Rapids: Eerdmans, 1980) 547.

8. D. E. Aune, "Divination," *ISBE* 2:972.

9. Peter L. Steinke, *A Door Set Open: Grounding Change in Mission and Hope* (Herndon, VA: Alban Institute, Kindle Edition, 2010) Kindle Location 716–19.

dollars was spent on new church buildings in 1945, that number steadily increased to over one billion dollars by 1960.[10] Harvie Conn asserts that these numbers reflect the expansion of churches in the suburbs requiring new buildings.[11] While church attendance increased in the suburbs, Herbert Gans's 1967 research on a quintessential suburban town revealed that families that move from the city to suburbia entailed no change in church or synagogue attendance.[12] The move to the suburbs did not yield a high rate of conversion that led to increased church attendance. Instead, suburban church growth relied on the population shift of the white community from urban centers to suburban outposts. Harvie M. Conn summarizes studies conducted by Dennison Nash and Peter Berger: "the impressive increases in church membership statistics in suburbia were only a reflection of the increased number of families with school-aged children in the country, the postwar 'baby boom' that had helped to produce the suburban migration itself."[13]

The homogenous unit principle (HUP) operated as one of the key magic formulae employed to grow suburban churches. Whether intentional or not, the HUP applied by suburban churches affirmed the wisdom of white flight. The HUP would allow the suburban churches to capture the migration of whites to the suburbs and lead to the numerical growth of the suburban churches. In turn, the growth of the suburban church would justify the proliferation of church growth movement principles that would offer the method of growth applicable to all churches.

Recently gentrification has occasioned the return of the white middle-class to the city, including suburban Christians with a heart for urban ministry. However, many of these relocators may still cling to assumptions about the city rooted in the narrative of white flight. Even as whites relocate to help the city, a dysfunctional messianic narrative rooted in white middle-class identity may emerge. They may see themselves as saviors to the fallen city populated by the sinful people of color. The white middle class that had successfully grown the church in the suburbs could now apply those ministry principles to the spiritually vacuous urban context solving

---

10. Hudson, *Religion in America*, 384n45.

11. Conn, *The American City and the Evangelical Church*, 97.

12. Herbert Gans, *The Levittowners: Ways of Life and Politics in a New Suburban Community* (New York: Columbia University Press, 1967) 264.

13. Conn, *The American City and the Evangelical Church*, 98. See Dennison Nash and Peter Berger, "The Child, the Family, and the 'Religious Revival' in Suburbia," *Journal for the Scientific Study of Religion* 2, no. 1 (1962) 85–93; and Dennison Nash, "And a Little Child Shall Lead Them: A Test of an Hypothesis That Children Were the Source of the American 'Religious Revival,'" *Journal for the Scientific Study of Religion* 7, no. 2 (1968) 238–40.

the problems of the city. Unfortunately, this narrative severely undermines the long-standing work of indigenous leadership in the community.

Many white evangelicals feel called to plant churches in poor black communities. They see this effort as a mission that is necessary to spread the gospel message. These church planting efforts are seen as the best chance for these poor neighborhoods in desperate need for salvation. Lance Lewis, an African American church planter with an evangelical denomination, comments on attempts by evangelicals to plant churches in poor black communities that there are assumptions by white evangelicals that "there are no 'good' churches in black neighborhoods that could possibly meet the spiritual needs of the community in the same way that an evangelical church could." Lewis goes on to note that "it would be impossible for any evangelical denomination or ministry to plant a church in an all-black community that doesn't already have several active congregations serving that community. Since that's true, one must ask the question: why have we decided to plant here? The unspoken answer is: the existing black churches just aren't very good."[14] A warped perception of the city and assumptions about the success of the suburban churches led to a dysfunctional, paternalistic narrative about saving the inner city through the magic formulae employed by white suburban churches.

Jeremiah 29 opposes two of the options available to the exiles. They should not withdraw and hide from life (even in the heart of the wicked city of Babylon), nor should they seek the quick fixes offered by the surrounding culture. Jeremiah 29 commands the exiles to stay engaged in the life of the city but not to submit to the temptations of the city. In rejecting two key temptations for the exiles, the acceptable alternative becomes lament. Withdrawal from the world or seeking answers that one wants to hear reveals human effort or human problem-solving, while lament acknowledges who is ultimately in control. In the midst of a crisis Lamentations points toward God and acknowledges God's sovereignty regardless of the circumstances.

The Intersection of Suffering and Celebration

To grasp better the role of lament in the worship life of God's people, we must initially explore the distinction between praise and lament as uniquely presented in Hebrew poetry. Claus Westermann reduces the Hebrew poetic material into two categories: praise and lament. Westermann asserts that "the two modes of calling on God are praise and petition. As the two poles, they determine the nature of all

---

14. Lance Lewis, "Black Pastoral Leadership and Church Planting" in *Aliens in the Promised Land*, ed. Anthony Bradley (Phillipsburg, NJ: Presbyterian and Reformed, 2013) 27–28.

speaking to God."[15] Hymns of praise are psalms that express worship. Laments are prayers of petition arising out of a sense of need. To Westermann, praise and lament operate on opposite poles. They form discrete categories of Hebrew poetry. Under Westermann's categories the book of Lamentations would fall under the general category of lament, a category often ignored in triumphalistic expressions of Christianity.

In *Journey Through the Psalms* Denise Hopkins examines the absence of lament in the major liturgical traditions. Building on the work of Lester Meyer, Hopkins asserts that in T*he Lutheran Book of Worship*, the Episcopalian *Book of Common Prayer*, the Catholic *Lectionary for Mass*, *The Hymnal of the United Church of Christ*, and *The United Methodist Hymnal*, "the majority of Psalms omitted from liturgical use are the laments."[16]

This trend is found not only in the liturgical traditions but in other Protestant denominations as well. In *Hurting with God* Glenn Pemberton notes that in the Psalms, lament constitutes 40 percent of all psalms, but in the hymnal for the Churches of Christ, laments make up 13 percent, the Presbyterian hymnal 19 percent, and the Baptist hymnal 13 percent.[17] Christian Copyright Licensing International (CCLI) licenses local churches in the use of contemporary worship songs. CCLI tracks the songs that are consistently sung in local churches. CCLI's list of the top 100 worship songs in August of 2012[18] reveals that only five of the songs would even remotely qualify as a lament. Most of the songs reflect themes of praise: "How Great is Our God," "Here I Am to Worship," "Happy Day," "Friend of God," "Glorious Day," "Marvelous Light," and "Victory in Jesus."

The American church avoids lament. The power of lament is minimized, and the underlying narrative of suffering that requires lament is lost. The absence of lament in the liturgy of the American church results in the loss of memory. Absence does not make the heart grow fonder. Absence makes the heart forget. We forget the necessity of lamenting over suffering and pain. We forget the reality of suffering and pain.

---

15. Claus Westermann, *Praise and Lament in the Psalms* (Atlanta: Knox, 1981) 152.

16. Denise Hopkins, *Journey Through the Psalms* (St. Louis: Chalice, 2002) 5–6. See also Lester Meyer, "A Lack of Laments in the Church's Use of the Psalter." *Lutheran Quarterly* ns 7 (1993) 67–78.

17. Glenn Pemberton, *Hurting with God: Learning to Lament with the Psalms* (Abilene, TX: Abilene Christian University Press, Kindle Edition, 2012) Kindle Locations 441–45.

18. "CCLI Top 100 Christian Worship Song Trends," accessed September 18, 2013, http://www.praisecharts.com/ccli-top-100/.

A culture of American triumphalism that avoids lament results in amnesia about a tainted history. The reality of a shameful history undermines the narrative of exceptionalism; therefore, the shameful history must remain hidden. True reconciliation, justice, and *shalom* require a remembering of suffering, an unearthing of a shameful history, and a willingness to enter into lament. Lament calls for an authentic encounter with the truth. Lament must not be ignored for the sake of uplifting praiseworthy stories of success. Lament reintroduces necessary narratives of suffering.

Walter Brueggemann writes about the contrast between a theology of the "have-nots" versus a theology of the "haves." The "have-nots" develop a theology of suffering and survival. The "haves" develop a theology of celebration. Those who live under suffering live "their lives aware of the acute precariousness of their situation." Worship that arises out of suffering cries out for deliverance. "Their notion of themselves is that of a dependent people crying out for a vision of survival and salvation." Lament marks the story of suffering.[19]

Those who live in celebration "are concerned with questions of proper management and joyous celebration." Instead of deliverance they seek constancy and sustainability. "The well-off do not expect their faith to begin in a cry but rather, in a song. They do not expect or need intrusion, but they rejoice in stability." Praise marks the story of celebration.[20]

Praise seeks to maintain the status quo, while lament cries out against existing injustices. Christian communities arising from celebration do not want their lives changed because their lives are in a good place. Tax rates should remain low. Home prices and stocks should continue to rise unabated, while interest rates should remain low to borrow more money to feed a lifestyle to which we have become accustomed.

Lament recognizes the struggles of life. The status quo is not to be celebrated but instead must be challenged. Tax rates should not favor the rich, but instead hope should be offered to the least of our society. Redistribution of wealth would not be a catastrophe, but instead it would be a blessing. Lament challenges the status quo of injustice.

American Christians that flourish under the existing system seek to maintain the status quo and remain in the theology of celebration over and against the theology of suffering. Promoting one perspective over the other, however, diminishes

---

19. Walter Brueggemann, *Peace* (St. Louis: Chalice, 2001) 26–28.
20. Ibid., 28–32.

our theological discourse. To only have a theology of celebration at the cost of the theology of suffering is incomplete. The intersection of the two threads provides the opportunity to engage in the fullness of the gospel message. Lament and praise must go hand in hand.[21]

Walter Brueggemann asks the question: "What happens when appreciation of the lament as a form of speech and faith is lost, as I think it is largely lost in contemporary usage? What happens when the speech forms that redress power distribution have been silenced and eliminated? The answer, I believe, is that a theological monopoly is reinforced, docility and submissiveness are engendered, and the outcome in terms of social practice is to reinforce and consolidate the political-economic monopoly of the status quo."[22] For American evangelicals riding the fumes of a previous generation's Christendom assumptions, a triumphalistic theology of celebration and privilege rooted in a praise-only narrative is perpetuated by the absence of lament and the underlying narrative of suffering that informs lament.

Lament presents the opportunity to call out to God for his mercy. It acknowledges the need for God's justice and mercy that does not arise out of one's own strength and ability. Suffering challenges the church to acknowledge real suffering through lament and plead with God for his intervention. The desperate plea for God's intervention that arises out of lament reveals the thinnest shred of hope. Even after tasting God's fury and wrath, do we still have hope? Do we still have the ability to worship even as our faith is being tested? Or do we rush to praise, even in the absence of lament?

For those of us emerging out of the context of celebration, there is a need to hear the lament arising out of the context of suffering. For the complete biblical narrative to take root in our community, lament has to become a part of our story. Lament calls us to examine the work of reconciliation between those who live under suffering with those who live in celebration. Lamentations challenge our celebratory assumptions with the reality of suffering. The triumphalistic approach to urban

---

21. In *The Next Evangelicalism* I offer that evangelicals may "believe that those who currently have the wealth, power, and privilege will be the ones who will serve and lead those who are without. It is the assumption that the 'haves' have much to offer while the 'have-nots' have little to offer . . . To know only the theology of celebration is an incomplete theology . . . When we attempt to minister out of the theology of celebration to those under a theology of suffering—we discover that the intersection between the two theologies creates an important and necessary connection." Soong-Chan Rah, *The Next Evangelicalism* (Downers Grove, IL: InterVarsity, 2009) 144, 154.

22. Walter Brueggemann, *Psalms and the Life of Faith* (Minneapolis: Fortress, Kindle Edition, 1995) Kindle Location 102.

ministry that emphasizes the quick fix answers arising from successful suburban churches requires the corrective of lament.

The Genre of Lamentations and the Necessity of Lament

The book of Lamentations challenges the triumphalistic evangelical urban ministry narrative. Chapter one of Lamentations presents a funeral dirge that embraces a suffering narrative in order to engage the full story of God's people. Chapter one opens with the Hebrew word *'êkâ*, translated as "Alas" or "How." A more dynamic translation could yield "How tragic" or "How devastated." A confused cry of anguish, "How can this be?" is offered in response to a tragic death. This opening cry establishes the reality of Jerusalem's death and offers a funeral dirge in response.

Kathleen O'Connor summarizes the key characteristics of the funeral dirge. "These include a mournful cry for the one who has died, a proclamation of death, contrast with previous circumstances of the dead person, and the reaction of bystanders."[23] Lamentations 1 exhibits the characteristics of a communal funeral dirge. The opening cry of *'êkâ* in v. 1 is the mournful cry for the one who has died. Lamentations 1 repeatedly proclaims the reality of death through phrases like "deserted," "widow" (v. 1), "mourn," "desolate" (v. 4). The current state of death and desolation are contrasted with the previous circumstances of the dead person, "who was once so full of people . . . great among the nations . . . queen among the provinces" (v. 1). Lamentations 1 completes the pattern of the funeral dirge by revealing the reaction of the bystanders: "her priests groan, her young women grieve" (v. 4). Lamentations serves as "a poetic response to a national tragedy"[24]—the death of a city.

Another characteristic of the funeral dirge found throughout the book of Lamentations is the use of the *qinah* meter.[25] "In Lamentations, many sets of lines are of unequal length, producing a rhythm usually called *qinah* meter . . . The effect of . . . the rhythm of dirges is sometimes said to be more solemn than the effect of more

---

23. Kathleen O'Connor, "The Book of Lamentations," in *The New Interpreter's Bible* (Nashville: Abingdon, 2001) 1019–1020.

24. Ibid., 1013.

25. It should be noted that the dominance of the *qinah* meter in Lamentations (first offered by Carl Budde) has come under some scrutiny. Hillers notes that "Budde discovered in Lamentations chaps. 1–4 (5 is different) a poetic line of two unequal pats, the first one longer by at least one word. Moreover, Budde held that this unbalanced rhythm was specifically related to the lament and named it *qinah* meter. Budde himself recognized in Lamentations the presence of numerous lines diverging from this pattern, and others have argued for still more balanced lines in the book . . . In broad outline, Budde's discovery remains valid." Delbert Hillers, "Book of Lamentations," *ABD* 4:139–40.

evenly balanced rhythms."²⁶ The uneven rhythm of the poem reflects the imbalance felt by the author who mourns a tragic death.

Chapter one, therefore, follows the pattern of a funeral dirge, "but with national rather than personal application."²⁷ A funeral dirge is required because the city and the nation have died.²⁸ Lamentations mourns this historic event. "A *qinah* is an outpouring of grief for a loss that has already occurred, with no expectation of reversing that loss . . . The prophets' metaphoric use of *qinah* is entirely apt because they saw the demise of the nation as *a fait accompli*. They personify the nation as a corpse, over whom a dirge is recited."²⁹ Death has already occurred. The funeral dirge reflects a post-mortem grief over death rather than an anxiety over an impending death. The funeral dirge is not the appropriate time for a petition, but it is an appropriate time to mourn.

The genre of the funeral dirge reminds us that suffering and death are painful realities. To hide from suffering and death would be an act of denial. In contrast to the temptations addressed in Jer 29, the funeral dirge deals with reality. It allows for very real pain to be spoken. In the same way that we would express concern over a person in denial over the death of a loved one, should we not be concerned over a church that lives in denial over the reality of death in our midst? A funeral dirge emerges from reality and allows for the fullness of human expression in the context of very real grief.

The funeral dirge gives legitimation to the voice of the suffering. The dirge of Lam 1 layers elements of dialogical lament. The lamenter calls out for justice. Nancy Lee finds a challenge to the existing systems of power in a funeral dirge that utilizes

26. Adele Berlin, *Lamentations* (Louisville: Westminster John Knox, 2002) 2.

27. S. K. Soderlund, "Lamentations," *ISBE* 3:67.

28. Lamentations also falls under the genre of the city lament. The city lament was found frequently in the context of the ancient Near East, with the "Lamentation over the Destruction of Ur" and "The Lamentation over the Destruction of Sumer and Ur" presenting examples of this genre from ancient Mesopotamia. See "Lamentation Over the Destruction of Ur" and "Lamentation Over the Destruction of Sumer and Ur" in *Ancient Near Eastern Texts Relating to the Old Testament*, ed. James B. Pritchard, 3rd ed. (Princeton: Princeton University Press, 1969) 455–63 and 611–19. F. W. Dobbs-Allsopp notes that "a comparison of the generic repertoire of the Mesopotamian city laments with Lamentations reveals no less than nine important features held in common: subject and mood, structure and poetic technique, divine abandonment, assignment of responsibility, divine agent of destruction, destruction, weeping goddess, lamentation, and restoration of the city and return of the gods." F. W. Dobbs-Allsopp, *Lamentations* in *Interpretation* (Louisville: Westminster John Knox, 2002) 9. See also F. W. Dobbs-Allsopp, *Weep, O Daughter of Zion* (Rome: Editrice Pontificio Instituto Biblico, 1999). In employing the city-lament genre, Lamentations borrows a familiar ancient Near Eastern form to express the depth of sorrow that is experienced by both the community and the individuals in the community.

29. Berlin, *Lamentations*, 24.

dialogical lament. "The dirge serves a formal social function in a community by raising 'the voice of public justice'... when the dirge or funeral singer identifies and accuses the murderer who caused a death."[30] For Brueggemann the power of the lament is that the oppressed are given the right to speak and, by speaking, offered the possibility of redressing injustice. "The lament form thus concerns a redistribution of power."[31] Dialogical lament offers the hope that the grieving and the suffering have a right to speak, even if they are not in a position of power. Lament gives voice to the voiceless.

Lamentations, therefore, offers the possibility of a dialogue through the funeral dirge. This dialogue moves the theology of suffering into interaction with the theology of celebration. A theology of celebration has the luxury of being able to objectify God. Because suffering is a distant reality, it is not necessary for God to be immanent. God can remain a distant abstraction[32] and can be praised from a distance. Lament as dialogue challenges this abstraction. There is direct communication with God who is present in all circumstances, even in the very real experience of suffering. A theology of suffering must acknowledge the cry of distress in lament before moving to the psalms of praise. We praise the transcendence of God, but it is the immanence of God in our suffering that draws us to God.

The destruction of Jerusalem reflects a "central catastrophe in Israel's history that provides an illuminating backdrop for understanding the fury, grief, and disorientation that this book expresses... The book came to be seen as an expression of grief and outrage at heart-stopping tragedy—and the tragedy that provoked its composition was massive."[33] Lament, therefore, becomes the appropriate response of a people steeped in deep suffering, questioning their very survival, and wondering if they have been completely abandoned by their God. But in the lament we find the hope that God is present, even in our suffering.

---

30. Nancy Lee, *The Singers of Lamentations* (Boston: Brill, 2002) 35. See also Carleen R. Mandolfo, *Daughter Zion Talks Back to the Prophets: A Dialogic Theology of the Book of Lamentations* (Atlanta: SBL, 2007).

31. Brueggemann, *Psalms and the Life of Faith*, Kindle Location 1177 of 4119.

32. For example, Westermann notes that, "when Western theology speaks of God's salvation or of a God who saves, God thereby becomes objectively tied to an event, and thus emerges a 'soteriology.' The Old Testament cannot pin God down to a single soteriology. It can only speak of God's saving acts within a whole series of events... and that necessarily involves some kind of verbal exchange between God and man." Westermann, *Praise and Lament*, 261.

33. O'Connor, "The Book of Lamentations," 1015.

Toward the Integration of Lament in Urban Ministry

The genre of Lamentations provides the necessary corrective for the temptation toward celebratory triumphalism in urban ministry. The historical relationship between the church and the city points toward the emergence of a dysfunctional narrative. The suburban churches that had once fled the city now return to the city armed with a perspective that demonizes the city. The belief that the cities are places of need, devoid of the gospel, is linked to the success-oriented narrative shaped by suburban models of ministry. The cities need fixing and the suburban churches will do the fixing. A triumphalistic view of urban ministry by suburban transplants could generate the unintended negative consequence of diminishing the role of churches and Christian communities that have remained faithful over a prolonged time period in the urban context. As Patrick Miller observes, "The Christian community learns about the place and practice of lament from attending to the voices that lament."[34] Lamentations challenges the urban missionary who seeks to celebrate victory in the fallen city to hear instead the voices of lament that have faithfully served God in the city. I offer the following practical application of lament in the urban context.

First, urban ministry must embrace the theology of suffering in the face of great pressure to adopt exclusively the theology of celebration. Urban ministry requires the intersection of lament and praise. Lament requires a type of truth telling revealed in the funeral dirge of Lamentations. In the same way that the book of Lamentations opens with a funeral dirge because of the reality of death, our approach to urban ministry must acknowledge the painful story of the church's dysfunctional relationship with the city. In particular the white, suburban, evangelical church's dysfunctional relation to the city must be acknowledged. The church's flight from the city based largely upon racial prejudice and fear must be recognized. The dysfunctional triumphalisitc narrative that emerged from white flight and the subsequent growth of suburban churches must be challenged.

Second, in the intersection of lament and praise the celebratory suburbanite may be the ultimate beneficiary. Urban missions then becomes defined as the urban context ministering and reaching the suburban transplant. No longer should urban ministry be defined by the transplant who journeys to the city to save it. Instead, the relocator may find their redemption in intersecting with the city. Urban missionaries are not the saviors of the city. Rather, the churches in the city may provide

---

34. Patrick D. Miller, "Heaven's Prisoners: The Lament as Christian Prayer" in *Lament: Reclaiming Practices in Pulpit, Pew and Public Square*, eds. Sally A. Brown and Patrick D. Miller (Louisville: Westminster John Knox, 2005) 15.

redemption for those whose theology of celebration excludes the essential element of the theology of suffering. The deficiencies of a triumphalistic narrative should be exposed so that stories of suffering and pain (even for the success-driven suburbanite) would be allowed to emerge. Kathleen O'Connor points out that the recovery of lament and the suffering narrative would be an essential step toward justice.

> Lamentations can be a resource for the work of reclaiming our humanity, for breaking through the denial, personal and social, and for teaching us compassion. Lamentations urges us to do the difficult work of reclaiming our passion for life, for justice and empathy. Without such work we will never be able to hear the cries of the poor in our neighborhood or around the globe. Our own wounds, hidden and festering, will continue to enslave us, absorbing our energies in fruitless denial that blocks our ears and blinds our eyes.[35]

The urban church becomes the place where the fullness of suffering is expressed in a safe environment. The church has the power to bring healing. That power is not found in an emphasis on strength but in suffering and weakness.

A theological reading of Lamentations calls the church to make room for the stories of suffering. Space is created for healing to arise from the power of stories, particularly stories of suffering. The racial division and the racialized narrative that often emerges in the context of urban ministry cannot be solved with a triumphalistic mentality. As O'Connor states, "I am convinced that denial not of guilt but of pain contributes to the racial divide in the United States. When we cannot hear others' suffering and receive it without defensiveness or extreme fear, we perpetuate resentment and misunderstanding."[36] The exhortation to "get over it, we live in a post-racial America . . . We have a black President what more do you want" rings hollow to those in the urban context who live a racialized reality on a daily basis. The stories of suffering are shut out, crippling the potential and power of urban ministry.

In *The Sacrifice of Africa* Emmanuel Katongole presents stories of the church that exemplify a type of insanity that arises out of a deep-seated suffering but leads to profound reconciliation and healing. Each story reveals a type of revolutionary madness that arises out of a deep history of suffering. Yet this revolutionary madness finds expression in the narrative of the church and provides an "interruption of the social history shaped by tribalism, poverty, violence, and hatred."[37] The madness of suffering has found expression, not for further destruction but for reconciliation. In

---

35. Kathleen M. O'Connor, *Lamentations and the Tears of the World* (Maryknoll, NY: Orbis, 2002) xiv.

36. Ibid., 93.

37. Emmanuel, Katongole, *The Sacrifice of Africa* (Grand Rapids: Eerdmans, 2011) 195.

the same way Lamentations can interrupt a triumphalistic narrative of urban ministry with the stories of those who have suffered but have remained faithful to God's calling.

RESPONSE TO RAH

Jessica Rivera

I want to take this opportunity to thank Soong-Chan Rah for allowing me the opportunity to respond to his paper. Professor Rah's commitment to theological scholarship with an eye for the urban setting has always been a prophetic voice that should be heard. His critique of the American church is clearly heard throughout this paper. Both the historical background and the pressing issues the church in the United States faces are clear. Professor Rah challenges the American church as it seeks to bring urban transformation not to forget the importance of a theology of lamentation. As an urban pastor, I see the values and dangers in this proposal but also have questions and observations.

Who is the "American Church" addressed in this paper?

I feel the expression "American Church" was being used too generally in this paper. On a global level often times we use the term "American" to describe the North American church, forgetting that there are other people who call themselves American. We cannot forget that Central American and South American church experiences must be heard and explored as well. I know they are not the main focus in this symposium, but I wanted to make sure this point was at least mentioned.

On a national level, even within the North American church, we must be conscious that there are multiple subcultures and churches that encompass this group. There are urban, rural, and suburban churches. There are white, Asian, black and Hispanic churches. All of these churches are part of the North American church narrative, even though Professor Rah is not necessarily addressing all of them.

Specifically, as a Hispanic American pastor I often feel that my narrative is not perceived as the "American narrative." More often than not, "American" is defined as white, European people with no thought that colored people are Americans too. Professor Rah understands this reality, yet his paper does not transmit this message. Instead, it continues to show how easily the word "American" can be used to describe a specific group, while omitting other groups that are an integral part of the narrative. We must begin to be more intentional, especially within the academy with our responsibility for shaping the future generation, to speak of the American church as a church that is complex and composed of multiple realities, all of which are valuable and important if we want to be relevant in the urban setting. I suggest the term be adjusted and qualified. From my perspective this paper is specifically addressing the white, suburban, affluent church that is migrating back into the cities within the United States.

The Reality of Imperialistic Patterns of Church Planting Methods in Urban Centers

One of the highlights of this paper is the experience of the urban church with the proliferation of church plants. Within the last ten years there has been an intentional shift to church planting in the urban setting without any real effort to engage the religious leaders and the people that have been serving and struggling in the city. I agree that many white, suburban churches have the vision that they must redeem the city. Since they have experienced success in the past, they conclude their way is better. We might even begin to experience a form of Christian imperialism being demonstrated as they plant churches in urban settings.

I believe the underlying intentions are good as this shift has increased a desire for their presence in the city. We do not want to deem this effort merely as triumphalist nor diminish the heart of transformation that operates in many of these leaders. However, we need to discuss the methods and processes used to complete the mission. We want to caution the people involved to be sensitive to the needs of these communities and honor the pastors that have spent their lives sustaining the spirituality of this community.

In the past two years I have experienced two examples of this situation. Last year I was contacted by an out of state denomination that wanted to create a satellite church in our neighborhood. They requested that we allow them to use our church building on Saturdays to conduct their meetings. I suggested that instead of them creating a totally different church, perhaps we could collaborate. They discussed it with their board and replied, "We are not looking for a partnership. We just wanted to use the facilities." As a pastor who has been serving this community for over twenty-five years and pastoring this church for ten years, I felt this approach neither engaged nor honored the work we do in the city. I declined their request to use our facilities.

Currently on my desk I have a questionnaire from a suburban church that wants to plant a church in our neighborhood. They are asking me to provide them information concerning the needs of this community. Again the approach is not to come alongside to strengthen the work already being done. The approach is rather to fix the problems of the community with outside resources but without accountable and dynamic collaboration. This is not altogether bad, but it can be experienced as paternalistic and as a detached messiah complex that wants to come and save a community of which they have never been a part.

The Changing Setting of Urban Ministry

As the paper points out, there is a need to lament in the United States. In the book of Lamentations we see God calling people to lament over their sin. The result of the sin is the exile of the people. Although most North American people have never experienced territorial exile, many North Americans, especially in the urban settings, live in social, economic, emotional, and spiritual exile. This sin is perpetuated through constant segregation, even when it comes to worship. Lament cannot occur without there being brokenness. The question is how affluent Christians can begin to feel the pain of those who are suffering to the degree that they desire to come alongside the struggle and work together.

I also realized that we are coming to a time when the concept of urban ministry must be redefined. At one point the urban story was equated with the plight of the poor, but as white, middle-class families return to the city, the setting is changing. Now the affluent and the poor live side by side. Sometimes the only thing separating them is a street. The urban setting and urban approaches to ministry have become more complex and need to be developed in the context of humility and collaboration, lament and celebration. How should these changing communities face the realities? How does the urban pastor minister to the needs of such congregations? These are valid questions that we must ask ourselves.

How many Urban Churches already practice a Theology of Lament?

Finally, as an urban pastor I believe many churches have been operating under a theology of lament. Lament is sometimes inherent in our preaching due to the social, economic, and spiritual condition of those who live within the city. Being a church in the city does not guarantee that we will be sensitive to the pain and struggles of others. One can become desensitized as one is trying to survive. When one is exposed to so much brokenness and so much need constantly, he or she can easily forget the present hope that is found in the gospel. The altar calls often become the avenue of confession and repentance that lead to a point of celebration and liberation.

Some urban churches have become so accustomed to lament that we do not know how to celebrate. We have internalized lament. We see and hear the constant narrative of lament. The last thing we want to do is to keep the congregation in a state of lament. It is important that we create ways to move the people that lament to a theology of celebration. We must ask ourselves how the theology of lament, for those who are struggling, has become a crutch instead of a means of change and transformation. It is important that those who are suffering not lament forever.

Conclusion

Our theology is always rooted in our personal experience of God. We must understand that our urban settings are composed of two very distinct and opposite stories. We find in our urban settings the church of the affluent with its theology of celebration that reflects their current experience with God. Simultaneously on Sundays we find the church of those suffering with a theology of lamentation. Both are real and to impose either theology on either setting would not be incorrect as much as incomplete.

The real issue is not whether a theology of lamentation exists in the church; the issue is that there is no place for both of these forms of worship to encounter each other in deep transformational ways. The truth is that we need both forms of worship. We have constantly to be moving between both the moments of lament and the moments of celebration. It is important to invite the affluent, white, suburban church to lament, but we must also encourage the poor, urban church to celebrate. We must ask ourselves how we can engage both churches in the urban setting to bring down the racial, social, economic, and spiritual divides that still plague our churches in order to reflect one united body in Christ.

GOOD CITIZENSHIP: A STUDY OF PHILIPPIANS 1:27 AND ITS IMPLICATIONS FOR CONTEMPORARY URBAN MINISTRY

Dennis R. Edwards

A few days before I completed this paper, I attended a community gathering of outraged residents of my North Minneapolis community. The gathering was in the wake of several brazen, broad-daylight shootings over the previous two days. Some people used the gathering as an opportunity to fuss indirectly at elected officials, law enforcement, criminals, and those not attending the rally. Some of us, however, prayed with a few hurting people in the crowd, then withdrew a bit from the modest-sized gathering and asked ourselves how we can better connect with our neighbors. We concluded that connection is the key to transformation.

Having been an urban pastor for about twenty-five years, especially in economically disadvantaged communities, I have been struck by the challenges of ministry in the city, especially regarding the genuine transformation of lives and circumstances. Also, I have at times been jealous of thriving, suburban congregations in their ability to attract a crowd. Sometimes I have tried to do what those bigger churches appear to do in order to get more people in the door, but that really amounted to cosmetic changes. Those things did not necessarily enhance the church's ability to help transform lives for the better.

Additionally, in my study I found that often books written for urban ministry did not focus on biblical exegesis, but had more of a sociological bent. In fact, some have lobbed this criticism at those of us who practice urban ministry: our ideas are more rooted in sociology than theology. Further, I would often come across books on urban ministry that focused on personal success stories, but not always with principles that were transferrable.[1] This paper is an attempt to do exegesis on a particular passage and see how it informs our urban ministry. Yet we will not jettison helpful sociological analysis; that sort of study will help us to apply what we learn through exegesis of the biblical text.

---

1. See Timothy Keller, *Center Church: Doing Balanced, Gospel-Centered Ministry in Your City* (Grand Rapids: Zondervan, 2012) 14–15, who offers a breakdown of the "books ordinarily written for pastors or church leaders" with regard to urban ministry. He notes the proliferation of books "with personal accounts of successful churches, authored by senior pastors, distilling practical principles for others to use."

As I have studied and preached through Paul's letter to the Philippians on more than one occasion and in different settings, I have come to believe that the unity described in this letter was what would make healthy urban communities. When such healthy communities are formed, lives are enhanced as people work jointly for a common cause. The result is personal growth as well as betterment of families and neighborhoods. I was regularly struck by the image of citizenship offered in Phil 1:27 and 3:20. Then in more recent times I began to explore what community might mean in the urban contexts where I served. In doing such exploration I came across work by Peter Block who uses the image of citizenship as part of what it means to create healthy communities, and I will incorporate his thoughts below.

This paper offers an exegesis of Phil 1:27 focused on the image of good citizenship, and it also provides contemporary understanding of what it means to build healthy community. My hope is that urban ministers can explore this metaphor of good citizenship given by the apostle Paul and continue to see what it may mean in our contexts.

Philippians and Citizenship

Citizens Worthy of the Gospel

Paul's letter to the Philippians provides a framework for urban ministry, even in our contemporary American context. I hope to illustrate that the notion of community found in this letter may prove helpful in our present understanding of urban mission. This section of my paper explains the image of "citizenship" used uniquely in the letter to the Philippians.

Gordon D. Fee classifies Paul's letter to the Philippians as a "hortatory letter of friendship," given the letter's emphasis on mutual affection, moral exhortation, and unity.[2] Indeed, Paul stresses *koinōnia* ("partnership," "fellowship," "sharing") throughout the letter. The unity that the Philippians need to experience nourishes the soil of healthy community, out of which grows fruitful ministry. The unity that Paul admonishes is stimulated by the unique image of Christian community as consisting of good citizens. The Philippian readers and hearers of Paul's letter understood well the expectations of a good citizen. They were to apply that understanding to their Christian witness. In doing so, the Philippians would come to appreciate how their presence in the world could mirror the presence of Christ to the world, illustrated

---

2. Gordon D. Fee, *Paul's Letter to the Philippians*, NICNT (Grand Rapids: Eerdmans, 1995) 2–14.

so poignantly in the *carmen Christi* of Phil 2:5–11. The language of citizenship is introduced early in the letter (1:27) and returns powerfully at a later point (3:20).

After the typical opening, comprised of greetings, thanksgiving, and prayer, Paul shifts to personal matters, giving an update on his own situation. Immediately following at 1:27–30 Paul introduces instructions for the church in one long, complicated sentence, which contains one main verb. With that verb Paul offers a somewhat unusual command to the Philippians. The imperative, "conduct yourselves" (NIV), or "live your life" (NRSV), translates a word rarely found in the entire NT. The verb *politeuesthai* is found only here and in Acts 23:1 (interestingly, in the mouth of Paul). In the Philippians' context the verb suggests particular behavior on the part of Paul's audience but veers dramatically from Paul's typical language for ethical instruction.

Paul relies heavily on the verb *peripatein*, "to walk," to speak of lifestyle. In doing so, he continues in a long Jewish tradition of using the image of "walking" as a metaphor for living. The word "walk" is a shortcut for describing an entire way of life. That is true today, and it was true in Ancient Judaism. The Hebrew word *hālak*, ("walk") has often been used in the OT as shorthand for "living," especially with regard to ethical behavior.[3] There are copious examples, but I offer only one paradigmatic illustration, the famous opening lines of Ps 1: "Blessed is the man who does not *walk* in the counsel of the wicked or stand in the way of sinners or sit in the seat of mockers" (NIV, emphasis mine).

As it was extremely common in Judaism to speak about ethical behavior using the image of walking, the apostle Paul, being the good rabbi that he was trained to be, does the same thing.[4] Yet, as we would expect, Paul's usage is based upon his Christian faith. There are many instances where Paul continues the Jewish custom of speaking about lifestyles using the image of walking, and I hope a few examples will suffice:[5]

> Rom 6:4: Therefore we have been buried with him by baptism into death, so that, just as Christ was raised from the dead by the glory of the Father, so we too might *walk* in newness of life.

---

3. *Hālak* "is the verb most frequently employed to describe the act or process of living. It occurs more than 1500x in all, with several hundred examples of a figurative rather than literal meaning" (Eugene H. Merrill, "*halak*," *NIDOTTE* 1:1032).

4. *Peripatein* is not the only verb Paul uses to discuss ethical behavior, but it is very common. For a list of other Pauline vocabulary for ethical injunctions, see Raymond R. Brewer, "The Meaning of *Politeuesthe* in Philippians 1:27," *JBL* 73 (1954) 76–77.

5. The passages are taken from the NRSV, and the italicized words are the NRSV's translations of *peripatein*.

Rom 8:4: So that the just requirement of the law might be fulfilled in us, who *walk* not according to the flesh but according to the Spirit.

Rom 13:13: Let us *live* honorably as in the day, not in reveling and drunkenness, not in debauchery and licentiousness, not in quarreling and jealousy.

1 Cor 3:3: For as long as there is jealousy and quarreling among you, are you not of the flesh, and *behaving* according to human inclinations?

2 Cor 5:7: For we *walk* by faith, not by sight.

Gal 5:16: *Live* by the Spirit, I say, and do not gratify the desires of the flesh.

Given the significance of the image of "walking" for Paul and in the Bible generally, it is peculiar and noteworthy that Paul does not use this word as he begins a discussion of ethical behavior with the Philippians. Instead of using a favorite word, "walk," Paul switches and uses the rare word mentioned above, *politeuesthai*, which comes from the world of civics or social studies. It occurs here as a command, *politeuesthe*. We can see how this verb is related to *polis*, the Greek word for "city" or "state."

The verb *politeuesthai* literally means "to conduct oneself as a good citizen." The apostle Paul is deliberately playing off of the concept of citizenship in the Greco-Roman world. He does so with a group of people who were known for their devotion to Rome and their understanding of good citizenship.[6] The Philippians were urbanites who understood their elite status as a Roman colony. Paul takes an image that his audience understands and even celebrates, but applies it to their life together as Christian brothers and sisters.

The reason why the Philippians could understand Paul's image so well is that they were an important city and proud of their special status. Philippi was not an ordinary Roman city. In Acts 16:12 Luke calls Philippi a "leading city" and a colony of Rome.[7] Philippi was not the capital of the Roman Empire, but it was special and powerful.[8] Former soldiers made up the initial population of Philippi. These veterans were loyal to the empire and certainly could be expected to understand the concept of good citizenship. As a colony of Rome, Philippi enjoyed exemption from

6. Brewer, "The Meaning of *Politeuesthe*," observes that Paul's use of *politeuesthai* and the related word *politeuma* in 3:20 "conforms to the recognized tendency of Paul to adapt his language and his thought to the varied situations he confronted in his preaching and in the pastoral care of the churches in order that he 'might by all means save some'" (83).

7. See Joseph A. Fitzmyer, *The Acts of the Apostles*, AB (New Haven: Yale University Press, 1998) 584, for a discussion of Luke's use of *prōtēs* and the textual variant found in Acts 16:12.

8. Gerald F. Hawthorne, "Philippians, Letter to the," *Dictionary of Paul and His Letters*, ed. Gerald F. Hawthorne, Ralph P. Martin, and Daniel G. Reid (Downers Grove, IL: InterVarsity, 1995) 707–8.

certain taxes. Given the context of Paul's audience, when he says, "conduct yourselves as good citizens," we should understand that the Philippians knew just what that imperative would entail.

Expectations of Good Citizens

To the Philippians citizenship was about more than just voting, paying taxes, or participating in certain government holidays. Citizenship involved commitment to the community, to the *polis*. Aristotle wrote:

> Every state is as we see a sort of partnership, and every partnership is formed with a view to some good since all the actions of all mankind are done with a view to what they think to be good. It is therefore evident that, while all partnerships aim at some good, the partnership that is the most supreme of all and includes all the others does so most of all, and aims at the most supreme of all goods; and this is the partnership entitled the state, the political association.[9]

Gerald F. Hawthorne interacts with Aristotle's observations and offers the following summary:

> To the ancient Greek the state (*polis*) was by no means merely a place to live. It was rather a sort of partnership (*koinōnia*) formed with a view to having people attain the highest of all human goods (so Aristotle). Here in the state the individual citizen developed his gifts and realized his potential not in isolation, but in cooperation. Here he was able to maximize his abilities not by himself, or for himself, but in community and for the good of the community ... As a consequence, mutuality and interdependence were important ideas inhering in the concept of polis. "To live as a citizen" (*politeuesthai*), therefore, meant for the Greek (and later the Roman) rights and privileges but also duties and responsibilities.[10]

Notice the language: "partnership," "mutuality," and "interdependence." Life in the *polis* was meant to reflect genuine community. Yet Paul's admonition is not about citizenship in Philippi, per se, but citizenship with respect to the gospel. Indeed, Paul will say in 3:20 that, "our citizenship is in heaven." This is to say that one's ultimate allegiance is to God's heavenly city. However, it appears that Paul affirms the values of the Aristotelian city, yet wants those values to be energized by one's relationship to

---

9. *Politics* 1.1252a; The word translated "partnership" is the Greek *koinōnia*.
10. Gerald F. Hawthorne, *Philippians*, WBC 43 (Waco: Word, 1983) 55. (I transliterated Hawthorne's Greek.)

Christ. Paul evokes the image of citizenship in the earthly *polis* but modifies it with the expression "worthy of the gospel" (Phil 1:27).

Gordon Fee observes:

> By joining [*politeuesthe*] with the adverb "worthily," Paul now uses the verb metaphorically, not meaning "live as citizens of Rome"—although that is not irrelevant—but rather "live in the Roman colony of Philippi as worthy citizens of your heavenly homeland." . . . As Philippi was a colony of Rome in Macedonia, so the church was a "colony of heaven" in Philippi, whose members were to live as its citizens in Philippi. This suggests a missionary outlook on the one hand (they are "contending for the gospel" in Philippi; cf. 2:14–16), but a concern for the "welfare of the state"—the believing community itself—on the other.[11]

I propose that we borrow from Paul's exhortation to the Philippians for good citizenship and apply it to our urban contexts. The goal of urban ministry should be the formation of genuine, healthy, growing community. Rather than emphasize the "fixing" of particular problems that we associate with urban life, which seems to be the rationale for much of what we call urban ministry, the aim should be to generate good biblical "citizens." Good citizens will shape good communities that will in turn produce more good citizens.

An Image of Citizenship for Our Times

I suspect that in our times many people—even Christians—would value Aristotle's view of life in the *polis*. Despite the myth of American rugged individualism, we sense that it is right to be part of a healthy community. We also acknowledge that it is difficult to form healthy community; there is much that works against our role as good citizens. Peter Block, who works in the area of civic engagement, describes healthy community in a variety of ways.[12] Even though his work focuses on "secular" community, his observations are in sync with what Christians should desire. Block's analysis and proposals are especially relevant for urban areas where the sheer density of the population, as well as the likely diversity, magnifies the challenges that may be found in any other environment.

Early on in his *Community: The Structure of Belonging*, Block suggests that "to improve the common measures of community health—economy, education, health, safety, the environment—we need to create a community where each citizen has the

---

11. Fee, *Philippians*, 162.
12. Peter Block, *Community: The Structure of Belonging* (Cleveland: Berrett-Koehler, 2009).

experience of being connected to those around them and knows that their safety and success are dependent on the success of all others."[13] The creation of such communities should be a goal for urban ministries. Yet we who work in the city face an enigma. On one hand there are those who crave community, such as boys, girls, young men, and young women, who attach themselves to gangs, while the church appears irrelevant to them. The challenge seems to be creating welcoming spaces for such people who have written off the church.

On the other hand, it seems that at least in America, oftentimes people have been conditioned to resist being part of a community of interdependence and mutuality. They see the church as primarily a place for personal inspiration—and maybe even just entertainment—but not a place for connection. The challenge for the church seems to be emphasizing quality interactions even over quantity of attendees.

When I started a new church in Brooklyn, NY, about twenty-four years ago, a woman who joined us early on decided to leave at a pivotal point in our ministry, when we were about to move into a new space. The move may have signaled to her how much each person would be needed in the ministry because she left commenting, "Church is something that I go to, not something that I'm part of." The irony is that not many weeks later she became very ill and called me for help. My wife wound up running errands for this woman, checking in on her, and providing some practical help in her apartment. Despite the display of loving care from my wife, this woman seemed unable to make the connection that church is community.

Both behaviors—that of seeking belonging in an unhealthy group such as a gang, or avoiding personal connections by "going to" and not "being part of"—are indicative of consumer mentalities. Both groups seem to be saying, "I want something that you have," rather than, "we both have something to share." The consumer mentality works against citizenship.

"The antithesis of being a citizen is the choice to be a consumer or a client," writes Block, and he goes on to define consumers and clients as those who "believe that their own needs can be best satisfied by the actions of others."[14] In my experience some urban ministries have made the mistake of treating people like consumers and clients by trying to be the problem-solver for their lives, rather than helping them to become citizens. Consequently, churches and other ministries are known by what goods they give out. As the giver of goods, those ministries need tremendous resources—financial and otherwise. So then, to justify asking for more resources, ministry has to be described in terms of the problems of the city. Many of us have

13. Ibid., 5.
14. Ibid., 63.

seen the proliferation in some urban areas of churches and non-profit programs (including ministries), all needing tremendous resources, yet even with the flow of money into those agencies the problems of the city persist. In many cases there seems to be no transformation. Block notes that the institutions and programs built around a focus on the problems of cities are "just treating the symptoms."[15]

Some of our urban problems are not primarily about a lack of resources, but a lack of community. I agree with Block when he says, "our current context is a long way from one of gifts, generosity, and accountability. The dominant context we now hold is one of deficiencies, interests, and entitlement. Out of this context grows the belief that the suffering of communities is a set of problems to be solved." Block goes on to illustrate how we tend to elaborate on the problems of neighborhoods (e.g., housing, youth at risk, poverty, public education, etc.), and how those problems are studied by academics and discussed on talk radio, giving rise to a core belief that "an alternative or better future can be accomplished by more problem solving."[16] The goal, however, should not be a focus on problem solving, but an emphasis on transformation through good citizens who make up healthy communities.

Block further helps us to form an image of good citizenship for our times in his chapter, "What It Means To Be a Citizen."[17] He is quick to point out that citizenship is not primarily about the civic duties of voting or vowing to uphold the U.S. Constitution. Rather, citizenship consists of those willing to build community and who are committed to the building up of the whole. Block offers a list describing a citizen as one who is willing to do the following:

1. Hold oneself accountable for the well-being of the larger collective of which we are part.

2. Choose to own and exercise power rather than defer or delegate it to others.

3. Enter into a collective possibility that gives hospitable and restorative community its own sense of being.

4. Acknowledge that community grows out of the possibility of citizens. Community is built not by specialized expertise, or great leadership, or improved services; it is built by great citizens.

5. Attend to the gifts and capacities of all others, and act to bring the gifts of those on the margins into the center.[18]

15. Ibid., 34.
16. Ibid., 32–33.
17. Ibid., 63–72.
18. Ibid., 65.

I will not elaborate on this list, but any biblically literate person, giving even a cursory reading, will find some themes that resonate with a biblical view of community emphasized in Paul's language of citizenship. Block's image of a good citizen seems to fit with Aristotle's. Both emphasize partnership (*koinōnia*), mutuality, and interdependence.

Our goal in urban ministry should be to create a community of good citizens. In doing so, we will be honoring God by living out the "one another" admonitions of Scripture. We will also be working to alleviate some of the stereotypical problems associated with urban life. We will be working to activate the gifts and abilities of people—all people, regardless of social status, race, or ethnicity. When the gifts and abilities of a variety of people are activated, it will lead to increased energy in making life better in the city. Consequently, the emphasis for ministries will shift from creating programs designed by a few, then hoping for others to join, to instead creating ways for people to feel connected as citizens.

Good Citizenship's Contemporary Challenges

Creating community has become more challenging in our time. Prior to the advent of Facebook, Twitter, and other social media, Robert D. Putnam wrote *Bowling Alone: The Collapse and Revival of American Community*.[19] He followed up three years later with *Better Together: Restoring the American Community*, co-authored with Lewis M. Feldstein.[20] The latter offers several examples of creative efforts to build or restore community. Even though Putnam's analyses predate current notions of virtual community, it still can inform us regarding obstacles that work against building community.

Throughout his work Putnam employs the term, "social capital" to refer to the advantages gained through genuine community.[21] Social capital has at least two aspects to it: one focuses inward, describing efforts to form tight bonds among an "in" group. Putnam refers to this aspect of social capital with the adjective "bonding."[22] Additionally, there is "bridging" social capital, which seeks to connect people across diverse social locations. Putnam notes, "Bonding social capital constitutes a kind of sociological superglue, whereas bridging social capital provides a sociological

---

19. New York: Simon & Schuster, 2000.
20. New York: Simon & Schuster, 2003.
21. Putnam, *Bowling Alone*, 18–28.
22. Ibid., 22.

WD-40."[23] Interestingly, Putnam notes that some groups simultaneously build both bonding and bridging social capital. Among his examples is "the black church," which "brings together people of the same race and religion across class lines."[24]

Whether or not Putnam is correct about the "black church," he seems to recognize that both types of social capital can be part of healthy community. However, the research of Putnam and Feldstein concludes that "the problem is that bridging social capital is harder to create than bonding social capital—after all, birds of a feather flock together. So the kind of social capital that is most essential for healthy public life in an increasingly diverse society like ours is precisely the kind that is hardest to build."[25]

The trend over recent decades has been the decline in social capital as our society has witnessed a reduction in community engagement. Fewer people have chosen to become connected to other people in civic involvement, which often includes church involvement.[26] Indeed, with few exceptions, civic disengagement seems to affect most segments of society. "Civic disengagement appears to be an equal opportunity affliction. The sharp, steady declines in club meetings, visits with friends, committee service, church attendance, philanthropic generosity, card games, and electoral turnout have hit virtually all sectors of American society over the last several decades and in roughly equal measures."[27]

It is interesting to observe, however, that Putnam's research reveals a few notable exceptions to the trend toward civic disengagement. He notes: (1) a rise in volunteerism among youth, (2) increase use of the Internet, (3) growth among grassroots, conservative, evangelicals, and (4) the increase in support groups.[28] Reflecting on these exceptions may help us when we discuss how to create a community of good citizens, but it is still helpful to consider what Putnam's research revealed as to reasons for the decline of civic engagement.

As a result of much research, Putnam suggests that the following are the primary factors contributing to the decline of social capital: (1) pressures of time and

23. Ibid., 23.
24. Ibid.
25. Putnam and Feldstein, *Better Together*, 3.
26. David T. Olson, *The American Church in Crisis* (Grand Rapids: Zondervan, 2008), concludes that "the church in America is not booming. It is in a crisis. On any given Sunday, the vast majority of Americans are absent from church. Even more troublesome, as the American population continues to grow, the church falls further and further behind. If trends continue, by 2050 the percentage of Americans attending church will be half the 1990 figure" (16).
27. Putnam, *Bowling Alone*, 185.
28. Ibid., 180.

money facing many families, (2) suburbanization, commuting, and sprawl, (3) electronic entertainment (in that it "privatizes our leisure time"), and (4) generational change (i.e., "the slow, steady, and ineluctable replacement of the long civic generation by their less involved children and grandchildren"). [29]

Putman has offered a quantitative analysis of the decline of civic engagement. The overarching point is that the sort of community of citizens envisioned by Paul in his letter to the Philippians (and arguably in other places as well) is far from the reality in which Americans find ourselves. The disconnection between people in general seems acutely noticeable in urban areas.

Harvie M. Conn and Manuel Ortiz list what they refer to as "contemporary urban challenges."[30] Two items on their list seem to be particularly formidable in the work of building community: population explosion and socioeconomic gap. Conn's and Ortiz's concerns regarding the church's ability to keep up with significant population growth in our cities are similar to the questions raised by David T. Olson (n26 above). Urban areas represent a stark contrast between the economically rich and poor, with the poor being a significant percentage of the population.

Large numbers of people certainly make connectedness more difficult, and the contrasts between rich and poor works against the building of meaningful relationships. Ronald E. Peters offers a qualitative analysis of the impediments to ministry in an urban context, which are obstacles in the way of building community. Peters notes, "Realities that define the context in which urban ministry is carried out today can be summed up in three words: alienation, fear, and violence. These are relational realities that are found in all communities, but their characteristics are more obvious in urban society."[31]

Putnam's research demonstrates that people in our society are generally less connected to each other than in the past. This is especially true in urban settings with their unique challenges and has been noted by Peters, Conn and Ortiz, and others. We should note that most of the population of America lives in an urban setting, about 69 percent.[32] Since most people live in the city, urban ministry may no longer be a specialized focus but the basic agenda for the entire Christian church.

---

29. Ibid., 283. Putnam even offers suggested percentages for each of these factors' contribution to the overall decline of civic engagement.

30. Harvie M. Conn and Manuel Ortiz, *Urban Ministry: The Kingdom, the City, and the People of God* (Downers Grove, IL: InterVarsity, 2001) 17–23.

31. Ronald E. Peters, *Urban Ministry: An Introduction* (Nashville: Abingdon, 2007) 12.

32. The Henry J. Kaiser Family Foundation: http://kff.org/global-indicator/urban-population/ (accessed August 17, 2013).

Effective ministry in the city will impact ministry in other places as well, even if only by way of offering models.

A key goal for ministry—especially in urban settings—must be the creation of genuine communities of citizens. In doing so, the church will help to reverse the trend toward civic disengagement. As more people are connected to one another, the complications of life and ministry in the city will be diminished. The more interconnected we become, the greater our chances of seeing lives transformed by the gospel and neighborhoods improved for all.

How to Create a Community of Good Citizens

Creating Communities of Accountability and Commitment

In formulating a pathway toward a community of good citizens, it is helpful to return to Paul's letter to the Philippians. The one-sentence admonition of 1:27-30 highlights that unity is a key aspect of citizenship, as far as Paul is concerned. Unity is the theme that Paul emphasizes immediately after his imperative "live as citizens."

Earlier I argued that Paul's rhetoric, especially in 1:27, deliberately plays off of the Philippians' understanding of citizenship. They understood well the value and responsibility of citizenship. Paul's encouragement is for those believers to apply those concepts of citizenship in the *polis* to their life together. Yet what will enable them to do so is the awareness that their true citizenship is in heaven (3:20). The logic is that since Philippians know what being a good citizen entails, and since they also know that their true citizenship is in heaven, they are to live out heaven's values using the template of their citizenship in the earthly *polis*. So, for example, partnership (*koinōnia*) should become a more significant reality since it no longer merely depends on one's common allegiance to the *polis* but is now based upon the unifying work of Christ. Hawthorne describes Paul's challenge to the Philippians in this way:

> Through the gospel which proclaims Christ as Savior, the Christian is made a citizen of the heavenly Jerusalem . . . a partner in a spiritual fellowship, a member of a new community, the Christian commonwealth, the Church . . . To live worthily of the gospel, then, also means that the Christian lives as a good citizen of this new state, governing his actions by the laws of this unique *politeuma*—righteousness, peace, faith, hope, love, mutuality, interdependence, good deeds, service to one another, worship of the living God, and so on.[33]

---

33. Hawthorne, *Philippians*, 56.

In Phil 1:27 Paul elaborates on what living as citizens worthy of the gospel of Christ means. He urges unity described as standing "firm in one spirit, striving together as one for the faith of the gospel." Once again Paul appears to be alluding to a common understanding shared by the Philippians. That shared understanding relates to the history of the city of Philippi.

The hero in the founding of the city was Philip of Macedon, father to Alexander the Great. Philip developed the use of the phalanx in his military conquests, and Alexander borrowed that particularly effective technique. The phalanx required soldiers to fight and maneuver side-by-side, operating as a single unit. Paul's language in 1:27 seems to fit well the image of the phalanx. Paul commands a tenacious unity that would allow the gospel to flourish, even in the face of opposition. Verse 28 continues, "without being frightened in any way by those who oppose you."

Through the use of language skillfully employed to evoke a commonly understood image, Paul urges unity as the foremost characteristic of good citizenship. Unity may be thought of as mutual accountability and commitment to a common goal or common set of values. Peter Block asserts that, "To reclaim our citizenship is to be accountable."[34] Block elaborates on the notions of accountability and commitment, pointing out that entitlement works against accountability. "Entitlement is essentially the conversation, 'What's in it for me?' It expresses a scarcity mentality, and the economist tells us that only what is scarce has value . . . The cost of entitlement is that it is an escape from accountability and soft on commitment. It gets in the way of authentic citizenship."[35] Block goes on to accuse entitlement of being the viewpoint that drives people apart rather than uniting them. "It turns neighbor against neighbor. It denies that we are our brother's keeper. Every colonial and autocratic regime rises to power by turning citizens against each other."[36]

Block defines accountability and commitment in this way: "Accountability is the willingness to care for the well-being of the whole; commitment is the willingness to make a promise with no expectation of return."[37] Such unselfish thinking is part of Paul's notion of good citizenship. In the next long sentence following Phil 1:27–30, Paul emotionally urges a practical unity based on "being like-minded, having the same love, being one in spirit and of one mind" (Phil 2:2). The language of concord found in Phil 2:2 and continued in 2:3–4 echoes the language of the rhetoricians of the Greco-Roman world when they argued for concord rather than

34. Block, *Community*, 63.
35. Ibid., 70.
36. Ibid., 71.
37. Ibid.

factionalism.[38] So once again Paul borrows linguistically from the concept of good citizenship known to his readers.

Paul's joy even in the reality of his imprisonment is enhanced by the unity of his Philippian readers. Their identity as good citizens—a colony of heaven (3:20)—who live in the reality of the earthly colony called Philippi, is fundamentally characterized by unity.[39] The unity described here is recognized through shared love, shared purpose (i.e., "one in spirit and of one mind"), and genuine humility on the part of these citizens. The admonition of v. 3 ("Do nothing out of selfish ambition or vain conceit. Rather, in humility value others above yourselves") seems to militate against American—if not human—values. Our culture seems to celebrate humility with our lips, but in our actions laud those whose brash, self-centered, individualistic efforts gained them worldly success. Ancient Greco-Roman culture viewed humility negatively.[40] So although the Greco-Roman world valued concord, humility was apparently not an asset to achieving it.

The values of accountability and commitment, which make for good citizenship even in our modern context, are encouraged in the ancient Philippian context. Philippians 2:4 says that humility should be exercised by "not looking to your own interests but each of you to the interest of the others." Urban ministry will be more effective when we learn to become citizens, as good citizens are characterized by unity consisting of accountability and commitment. Peter Block shares a story illustrating a practical way in which the values of Phil 2:4 were demonstrated in a modern-day attempt to be good citizens. He tells of two married couples, described as "white overeducated adults," who worked at a neighborhood center in hopes of teaching young men what they "ought" to learn about relationships. Block describes how these young couples made no progress with their curriculum and decided to

---

38. See Margaret M. Mitchell, *Paul and the Rhetoric of Reconciliation: An Exegetical Investigation of the Language and Composition of 1 Corinthians* (Louisville: Westminster John Knox: 1991) 76–80. In her discussion of 1 Cor 1:10 Mitchell focuses on the expression, *en tō autō noi* ("united in mind"). Paul's language of unity found in 1 Cor is similar to that observed in Phil.

39. Dr. Martin Luther King Jr. employed the expression "colony of heaven" in his famous "Letter from a Birmingham Jail" to describe the impact that early Christians had in transforming their society. He writes: "Whenever the early Christians entered a town, the people in power became disturbed and immediately sought to convict the Christians for being 'disturbers of the peace' and 'outside agitators.' But the Christians pressed on, in the conviction that they were 'a colony of heaven,' called to obey God rather than man. Small in number, they were big in commitment. They were too God-intoxicated to be 'astronomically intimidated.' By their effort and example they brought an end to such ancient evils as infanticide and gladiatorial contests" (from the African Studies Center at the University of Pennsylvania; http://www.africa.upenn.edu/Articles_Gen/Letter_Birmingham.html [accessed August 19, 2013]).

40. See Hawthorne, *Philippians*, 69–70.

abandon it and instead simply hung out with the young men. Here's how Block describes what happened next:

> At first it seemed the young men were unreachable, and any attempt to "help" would be futile. Then, at some point the adults' listening made a difference. The adults and the young people began to trust one another. As one young man put it, "The reason I respect you so much is because you may be the only people who really listen. Everyone wanted to tell us to 'pull up our pants' and tell us how to live." Something valuable was built and in the end the "things" the adults wanted to teach about relationships were taught by simply changing the nature of the conversation.[41]

The story of listening rather than imposing a particular curriculum illustrates how the couples who sought to help practiced humility. In their humility they helped the young men in ways that they really needed help. The willingness to listen showed that the couples were trying to find some way to build accountability and commitment with the young men. One outcome of the effort was that the young men stayed in contact with the four adults even after the program ended and worked together on a joint venture to make a movie about young people in urban environments. Accountability and commitment made for unity, a characteristic of good citizens.

Focus on the Small Group

Earlier I pointed out some of Putnam's observations contradict his general findings regarding the demise of civic engagement. I will focus on two of those observations: (1) a rise in volunteerism among youth and (2) the increase in support groups.[42] Both of these phenomena relate to what may be key to fostering good citizens—the small group. My observations as a pastor are that young people both within and outside the Christian community are looking for opportunities to volunteer in ways that impact the common good and have often discovered some of those avenues through small groups. Similarly, some small groups function as support groups for people who are facing a potentially life-controlling challenge or are simply at a particular stage of life shared by others in the group (i.e., parenting small children, "sandwich" adults squeezed between parenting and simultaneously caring for elderly parents, people who are divorced, blended families, etc).

---

41. Block, *Community*, 89–90.

42. Putnam and Feldstein also noted that the rise in the use of the Internet might help to increase civic engagement. It is beyond the scope of this paper, but a study on the rise of social media and how it impacts growth in social capital, especially in urban contexts, would be very interesting.

Of course, for many evangelicals "small groups" are nothing new. My plea here is for small groups to be a fundamental aspect of urban ministry, being given at least as much attention as is given to the Sunday morning worship experience. Anecdotally, small groups appear to be ancillary, an "add on" to Sunday's main event. In order to develop good citizens who practice accountability and commitment, small groups must be central to the life of a church.

In *Better Together* Putnam and Feldstein offer models of successful attempts to restore civic engagement. All of these attempts attest to the value of small groups. For the sake of this paper, a look at three of the Christian groups featured in *Better Together* may serve as helpful illustrations.

Saddleback Church in affluent Orange County, California, is known for its pastor Rick Warren and his books *The Purpose Driven Church* and *The Purpose Driven Life*.[43] We know of the huge numbers in attendance. What is significant for the purpose of this discussion is their emphasis on small groups. In a recent personal conversation with a former attendee, I asked the man if he ever felt lost or overwhelmed in such a large congregation. The man said that he gets asked this question a great deal and indicated that the small group ministry of the church was so significant that he easily felt connected to people. According to Putnam and Feldstein, Saddleback "devotes extensive effort and attention to creating and supporting [small] groups."[44] An interview with a member of Saddleback revealed that participation in a small group is expected, not merely suggested. Rick Warren says that his first question to anyone coming to him with a problem is, "Are you in a small group?"

Small groups are not only within the purview of mega churches. Putnam and Feldstein highlight another California church, All Saints Church in Pasadena.[45] Although not a small church, it is nowhere near the size of Saddleback. Yet All Saints—different from Saddleback theologically, culturally, and in other ways—has also grown better connected through small groups.

Valley Interfaith in Pharr, Texas brings church and school groups together to improve schools through organizing parents and other residents.[46] Valley Interfaith's initiatives involved teachers making home visits and creating other face-to-face opportunities between teachers and parents. Eventually change came through parents and others who attended "house meetings," which involved the participants

---

43. *The Purpose Driven Church: Every Church Is Big in God's Eyes* (Grand Rapids: Zondervan, 1996); *The Purpose Driven Life* (Grand Rapids: Zondervan, 2002).

44. Putnam and Feldstein, *Better Together*, 130.

45. Ibid., 135–41.

46. Ibid., 11–33.

breaking into small groups of six to ten people. A local organizer related to Valley Interfaith pointed out, "Organizing is all about building relationships. It's not about meetings."[47]

In their conclusions Putnam and Feldstein point out how every group they featured had lofty goals and significantly broad ambitions. They note, "Yet to pursue these goals through connective strategies, organizers had somehow to reconcile them with the basic fact that smaller is better for social-capital creation. Researchers have repeatedly found that social capital is higher in smaller settings."[48]

Peter Block devotes an entire chapter to the power of the small group, observing, "The small group is the unit of transformation."[49] He goes on to make powerful observations about small groups that most Christians—especially we who work in environments that can be impersonal, such as the city—will find to be right on target:

> The small group is the bridge between our own individual existence and the larger community. In the small group discussion we discover that our own concerns are more universal than we imagined. This discovery that we are not alone, that others can at least understand what is on our mind, if not agree with us, is what creates the feeling of belonging. When this occurs in the same place and time, in the presence of the larger community, the collective possibility begins to take form and have legs.
>
> The power of the small group cannot be overemphasized. Something almost mystical, certainly mysterious, occurs when citizens sit in a small group, for they often become more authentic and personal with each other than in other settings.[50]

We should remind ourselves that Block's observations are made in a non-religious context. Yet, what he affirms are human realities described in biblical texts. Philippians is a letter that emphasizes some of the values that are highlighted in small group interactions. The authenticity and positive personal interactions that Block describes are enhanced through the practice of what Paul teaches in Philippians. The humility discussed earlier, based on a genuine concern for others, is the spiritual basis for what marks a good citizen.

Practically speaking, my appeal is that urban ministries make the creation of good citizens the main priority through the vehicle of small group gatherings, which can be of a variety of types. My observation is that many ministries give more time,

---

47. Ibid., 12.
48. Ibid., 275.
49. Block, *Community*, 93–99.
50. Ibid., 95.

energy, and financial and human resources to creating an "attractional" gathering. Even before the advent of hipster congregations—back in the 1980s, as a matter of fact—I recall a well-known African American preacher telling us emerging leaders that he was disappointed that most churches appear much more eager to hire a music minister than a youth minister. His point was that the Sunday event took precedence over building up the youth, who are among the most vulnerable members of the community. Our efforts to build community must take priority.

Rachel Held Evans has written on the alleged exodus of young adults—Millennials—from the church, particularly the evangelical church.[51] In her "Why Millennials are Leaving the Church," for CNN's *Belief* blog she notes that young people crave more substance. She observes:

> Time and again, the assumption among Christian leaders, and evangelical leaders in particular, is that the key to drawing twenty-somethings back to church is simply to make a few style updates—edgier music, more casual services, a coffee shop in the fellowship hall, a pastor who wears skinny jeans, an updated Web site that includes online giving. But here's the thing: Having been advertised to our whole lives, we millennials have highly sensitive BS meters, and we're not easily impressed with consumerism or performances. In fact, I would argue that church-as-performance is just one more thing driving us away from the church, and evangelicalism in particular.

Held Evans goes on to suggest what a more substantive church experience for young adults might look like:

> We want an end to the culture wars. We want a truce between science and faith. We want to be known for what we stand for, not what we are against . . . We want to be challenged to live lives of holiness, not only when it comes to sex, but also when it comes to living simply, caring for the poor and oppressed, pursuing reconciliation, engaging in creation care and becoming peacemakers.

Some of what Rachel Held Evans describes seems to relate to Putnam's observation that the voluntcerism of young adults is at variance with the trend toward civic disengagement. The type of faith that Millennials want to experience includes a

---

51. CNN Belief Blog; http://religion.blogs.cnn.com/2013/07/27/why-millennials-are-leaving-the-church/ (accessed August 21, 2013). We should note that some have challenged the notion that Millennials are leaving the church. For example, Scot McKnight's Jesus Creed Patheos Blog; http://www.patheos.com/blogs/jesuscreed/2013/08/03/millennials-and-leaving-church-really/ (accessed August 21, 2013).

more activist component. Many Millennials have taken up residence in the city; they are a factor in any description of urban ministry.[52]

Of course, for any ministry—and perhaps especially urban ministry with its unique challenges—building good citizens is difficult. The difficulty is due in part to values such as mutuality and interdependence sometimes being undermined by stereotypical American values of individualism and self-empowerment. Philippians offers a spiritual challenge to the status quo. The climax of Paul's letter to the Philippians is the hymn to Christ, the *carmen Christi*, found in 2:5–11. In this passage the incarnation of the Lord Jesus is offered by way of an example of how we should live out the values of a good citizen of heaven:

> In your relationships with one another, have the same mindset as Christ Jesus:
> Who, being in very nature God, did not consider equality with God something to be used to his own advantage; rather, he made himself nothing by taking the very nature of a servant, being made in human likeness. And being found in appearance as a man, he humbled himself by becoming obedient to death —even death on a cross! Therefore God exalted him to the highest place and gave him the name that is above every name, that at the name of Jesus every knee should bow, in heaven and on earth and under the earth, and every tongue acknowledge that Jesus Christ is Lord, to the glory of God the Father.

Conclusion

Life in urban environments can be challenging. In light of this, ministry to people living in urban environments can be difficult. Yet what is important for all people, perhaps especially people in the potentially alienating, fear-laden environment of densely populated cities, is to make interpersonal connections. Those connections increase social capital, which is a term that describes the benefits of civic engagement. The call for urban ministries is to give chief effort to increasing social capital. The best way to do that is through small groups. I have not emphasized how those small groups should be conducted.[53] It appears that those details can be worked out to fit the particulars of a given context. The point is to have small groups and make them a priority.

---

52. *The Atlantic*; http://www.theatlanticcities.com/jobs-and-economy/2012/09/next-big-question-facing-cities-will-millennials-stay/3229/ (accessed August 21, 2013).

53. A helpful resource for small groups is Joseph R. Myers, *Organic Community: Creating a Place Where People Naturally Connect* (Grand Rapids: Baker, 2007).

The admonition to increase social capital through small groups comes through an understanding of the notion of citizenship. The image of good citizenship may come to us through the political arena, but the image fits for our ministry goals. The image is not one that just happens to be chosen at random; it is actually a Pauline metaphor used by the apostle to motivate the urban disciples of ancient Philippi. The citizen image carried significant weight in the Greco-Roman world and is one that we can recapture for our current times.

When we understand and appreciate what citizenship means, then fortify those notions with what biblical discipleship entails, then we will be further on the road to impact our urban settings for good.

RESPONSE TO EDWARDS

Kurt N. Fredrickson

This is a helpful paper using the image of the church as *citizen* to encourage our thinking about transformative ministry in urban settings through the intentional development of connections between people. We live fragmented, disconnected, and individualized lives. That is true in urban settings and often very apparent in those settings. It is also true, though masked, in suburban settings. Human beings hunger to belong. We are created for relationship. Belonging is an issue of identity: Who am I? Where am I? Whose am I?[1] Yet, we thwart this slant toward relationality in our cultural settings and in the church with rugged individualism, harmful relationships and communities, and consumerist mindsets.[2]

But there is another way. Edwards points us to Phil 1:27:

> The one thing I would stress is this: your public behavior must match up to the gospel of the king. That way, whether I do come and see you or whether I remain elsewhere, the news that I get about you will indicate that you are standing firm with a single spirit, struggling side by side with one united intent for the faith of the gospel.[3]

This passage emphasizes the theme of citizenship. We are to live differently. We are citizens of heaven (Phil 3:20). We belong to the king; therefore we must act like it. In this is the hope of transformed lives, a transformed church, and transformed communities. Edwards expands on the biblical description of God's people as citizens through the writings of Aristotle, Robert Putnam, and Peter Block, emphasiz-

---

1. Diana Butler Bass, *Christianity After Religion: The End of Church and the Birth of a New Spiritual Awakening* (New York: HarperOne, 2012) 171–72.

2. See Scott Peck, *A World Waiting to Be Born: Civility Rediscovered* (New York: Bantam, 1993). There is a story about life characterized by isolation and disconnection, which sadly is often the state of our lives in urban settings and in the church. A man was stranded alone for thirty years on a little island. He finally waved down a ship, and when the first mate came ashore in a lifeboat, he saw three huts at the edge of the jungle. "What are those huts?" he asked. "Well," the castaway replied, pointing to the first hut, "That one is where I live," and, pointing to the third, "that's where I go to church." "What about the middle hut?" the first mate asked. "Oh," the man said, "that's where I used to go to church." See Cameron Lee and Kurt Fredrickson, *That Their Work Will Be a Joy: Understanding and Coping with the Challenges of Pastoral Ministry* (Eugene, OR: Cascade, 2013) 51.

3. N. T. Wright, *The Kingdom New Testament: A Contemporary Translation* (New York: HarperCollins, 2011).

ing the importance of being connected to others. He sees this being lived out well in small groups.

I appreciate and agree with the general thrust of this paper. Small groups are an essential component of healthy ecclesial communities and can lead to healthy and more vibrant neighborhoods. In this response I will draw our attention to three themes that can get overlooked by using the church image of citizen.[4]

First, it is important to develop a robust ecclesiology. Drawing from sociology or political theory can have the unintended consequence of minimizing a broad understanding of church. The image of citizen potentially misses the essential communal nature of the church captured in the biblical images: the people of God, the body of Christ, and the temple of the Spirit.[5] The citizen image too easily suggests individuals being connected to a concept or an ideal without the necessary element of being vitally connected to each other. The church is more than "partnership, mutuality, and interdependence," more than "mutual accountability and commitment." An ecclesial understanding of small groups sees community as something larger than the sum of its parts.[6]

Beyond the words "accountable and committed" to describe the work of transformative small groups in a particular context, I would also employ the biblical concepts of witness (proclaiming good news), hospitality (reaching out to the stranger), and generosity (sacrificial kindness and mercy). These characteristics are only possible in an ecclesial small group because of an underlying sense of humility (Phil 2). The practice of humility within community itself is a work of God and a gift from God.

Second, we must stress the essential work of the Spirit. The church is not simply another volunteer organization like a Rotary Club or a gardening group. These groups certainly can create a sense of belonging, of bonding, and of bridging, but ecclesial groups are more than just an assembling of like-minded or like-focused

---

4. Paul S. Minear, *Images of the Church in the New Testament* (Philadelphia: Westminster John Knox, 2004) 60–61.

5. For more on these images see among other sources Kurt N. Fredrickson, "An Ecclesial Ecology for Denominational Futures: Nurturing Organic Structures for Missional Engagement," PhD diss., Fuller Theological Seminary, 2009. Available in Kindle format at Amazon.com.

6. *Koinōnia* is more than a partnership. It is closer to Victor Turner's anthropological concept of *communitas*. For an outworking of this in church contexts, see Alan Hirsch, *The Forgotten Ways: Reactivating the Missional Church* (Grand Rapids: Brazos, 2006). He writes: "*Communitas* in his view *happens* in situations where individuals are driven to find each other through a common experience of ordeal, humbling, transition, and marginalization. It involves intense feelings of social togetherness and belonging brought about by having to rely on each other in order to survive" (221). Jesus said: "For where two or three gather in my name, there am I with them" (Matt 18:20).

individuals. Ecclesial small groups ultimately are units of transformation because of the work of the Spirit. Our ministries seek to see people changed by God (2 Cor 5:17) through transformative ecclesial groups that lead to healthy and more vital neighborhoods. This type of group must ultimately acknowledge a dependence on the work of the Spirit of God.

Unity is not primary a characteristic of good citizens; it is the work of God. The unity of the church is not merely a goal we set out to achieve, nor is it simply agreeing to work toward a common good. We are connected to each other because God binds us together (Eph 2). Unity in the church emerges from the heart of God, and it is derived directly by the work of the Spirit of God (1 Cor 12:12–13).[7] We are one *in Christ* (Gal 3:28).

Third, we must recognize that a robust ecclesiology and an essential pneumatology by definition lead to a vibrant missiology. The goal of transformative small groups reaches beyond the formation of a genuine, healthy, and growing community, the generating of good biblical citizens who shape good communities and produce more good citizens, an emphasis solely on the transformation of good citizens, and even the creation of genuine communities of citizens. Ecclesial groups, empowered by the Spirit, missionally extend good news into neighborhoods.[8] Dietrich Bonhoeffer reminds us, "The church is only the church when it exists for others."[9]

Small groups become transformative because people, changed by the Spirit of God and united to each other in Christ by God, are able to influence their neighborhoods for good in the name of Christ. Scott Boren puts it this way: "Instead of doing groups for the sake of experiencing community, groups experience community for the sake of participating in God's redemption of creation."[10]

This commitment to mission was a key emphasis of the early Covenanters who formed the denomination North Park serves. "Mission Friends" was one of the earliest designations of this group emerging from the nineteenth-century revival movements in Sweden. The name signifies a commitment to extending the good news of Jesus Christ through evangelistic outreach and to the importance of Christ-centered fellowship.[11]

---

7. Wesley Granberg-Michaelson, *From Times Square to Timbuktu: The Post-Christian West Meets the Non-Western Church* (Grand Rapids: Eerdmans, 2013). See especially chap. 4.

8. For more on engagement in a neighborhood, see Alan Roxburgh, *Missional: Joining God in the Neighborhood* (Grand Rapids: Baker, 2011).

9. Dietrich Bonhoeffer, *Letters and Papers from Prison* (New York: Touchstone, 1997) 282.

10. M. Scott Boren, *Missional Small Groups: Becoming a Community That Makes a Difference in the World* (Grand Rapids: Baker, 2011) Kindle Locations 200–201.

11. Kurt Fredrickson, "The Evangelical Covenant Church as Mission Friends: Missional

Missional extension is a key element to the life of the church. It happens locally, in neighborhoods. Lesslie Newbigin says, "How is it possible that the gospel should be credible, that people should come to believe that the power which has the last word in human affairs is represented by a man hanging on a cross? I am suggesting that the only answer, the only hermeneutic of the gospel, is a congregation of men and women who believe it and live by it."[12]

Transformative ecclesial small groups empowered by the Spirit of God that extend into the neighborhood are essential. Our gatherings are very ordinary, though intentional and relational. It makes a difference. We are citizens of heaven. Desmond Tutu said: "Do your little bit of good where you are; it's those little bits of good put together that overwhelm the world."[13] This work of God among the people of God offers hope and change for a fragmented world.

Imaginations for a Denominational Future," *The Covenant Quarterly* 66, no. 2 (2008) 16.

12. Lesslie Newbigin, *The Church in a Pluralist Society* (Grand Rapids: Eerdmans, 1989) 227.

13. Attributed to Desmond Tutu in an issue of *Guideposts Magazine; see* Allister Sparks and Mpho Tutu, *Tutu: Authorized* (New York: HarperOne, 2011) 310.

LOVE YOURSELF: URBAN MINISTRY AND THE CHALLENGE OF SELF-LOVE

Chanequa Walker-Barnes

Attend a conference on urban ministry or Christian community development, and you are quite likely to hear someone talking about burnout. The consensus seems to be that burnout is an occupational hazard, and a common one at that, among Christian leaders who minister in under-resourced urban communities. Conversations often revolve around how to sustain oneself in ministry over the long haul and how to prevent one's family from becoming collateral damage in the quest for vocational faithfulness. It is ironic that few texts on urban ministry treat the issue of burnout with any depth. Instead, articles and books on urban ministry focus upon how to identify good candidates for ministry and strategic approaches for planting and growing urban congregations. The authors of these texts usually acknowledge the existence and pervasiveness of burnout, including the contextual factors that make ministry in urban settings particularly difficult, but rarely do they discuss whether there are theological teachings that raise the risk of burnout among urban ministry practitioners.

In this paper I argue that Christian leaders laboring in under-resourced communities often endorse and embody a theological understanding of selfhood that predisposes them to neglect themselves and their families for the sake of ministry. I utilize a feminist/womanist pastoral theology to argue that urban ministers often suffer from the church's distorted theologies of self-love and self-sacrifice. I draw upon Luke's travel narrative as a scriptural resource to aid urban ministers in developing a healthy view of selfhood.[1]

---

1. Material in this article is adapted from a chapter in my forthcoming book, *Too Heavy a Yoke: Black Women and the Burden of Strength* (Eugene, OR: Cascade). In that text, I draw upon womanist/feminist scholarship to argue that the church's equation of Christian love with selflessness and self-sacrifice is a particularly dangerous teaching for African American women whose lack of coherent sense of self and whose identity has been shaped largely by the confluence of racism and sexism.

Urban Ministry and the Problem of Burnout

Authors who address issues of burnout in urban ministry contexts tend to focus on two issues that place Christian leaders at risk: (1) the contextual challenges of urban communities and (2) poor training and development of leaders.

It is important to note that, while the economic and cultural shifts over the past decade are forcing reconceptualization of the term "urban," in the context of Christian community development, the term is often a code word referring to densely populated city centers marked by high levels of poverty, unemployment, drug use, violence, and family breakdown. Individuals and families living within these communities experience a broad spectrum of social, economic, and healthcare needs for which there are few resources. The urban ministry that offers services in these settings is likely to feel pressed on every side.

Stone and Wolfteich identify six challenges that are common to ministering in urban contexts: (1) continual and rapid transition, especially related to issues of suburban flight, gentrification, diversity and immigration, closing of manufacturing plants, and shifting economic centers; (2) the comprehensive social need of the individuals and communities living in the city; (3) negotiating pastoral and congregational identity, particularly in the light of declining denominationalism, pressures to be relevant, and commuter congregations; (4) issues of diversity and immigration; (5) social division and isolation; and (6) scarcity of economic and spatial resources.[2] They note that pastors and congregations in urban settings

> often find themselves attending to a wide range of social issues that are virtually impossible to summarize easily, including poverty and widespread economic disparity; crime; unemployment; drugs; industry closings; homelessness; gang violence; lack of affordable health care; racism and segregation; immigration; the treatment of seniors, of those who are mentally ill, and of ex-offenders; teen pregnancy and lack of family and social support for teenage parents; inadequate support systems for preteens, which often leads to violent crime; overworked or absent parents; and substandard public schools.[3]

For congregations and parachurch ministries in these contexts, pastoral care is not limited to visiting the sick and shut in, counseling people through transition and loss, and conducting funerals and weddings. It may also include food and clothing pantries, educational enrichment programs, job training, healthcare clin-

---

2. Bryan P. Stone and Claire E. Wolfteich, *Sabbath in the City: Sustaining Urban Pastoral Excellence* (Louisville: Westminster John Knox, 2008) 5–8.

3. Ibid., 9–10.

ics, legal aid, and community organizing.[4] Urban churches that are genuinely concerned about meeting the social needs of their communities are seven-days-a-week churches.[5] It is not surprising that ministers in urban contexts report spending 20 percent more time each week in pastoral work than do their rural counterparts.[6] The number is likely much higher for those ministers—ordained and lay—who are actively engaged in Christian community development and who typically live in the neighborhoods that they serve.

Indeed, urban ministry has unique challenges for those who are ministers-in-residence. For them, John Perkins notes, working in the city not only requires bearing witness to the suffering of others, it also entails personal risk for them and for their families. Perkins counts the following as the costs of urban ministry: culture shock, the risk to one's possessions, threats to one's personal safety and that of one's family, and the emotional stress and pain associated with ministering among the marginalized.[7] He stresses that the emotional costs of ministering in urban contexts are particularly high: "Many aspects of urban ministry are emotionally draining and demanding. Urban activists are likely to be barraged with the entire spectrum of human need. The emotions will be taxed beyond normal experience and in time, one is likely to become exhausted, depressed, and even despairing."[8] Together, the combination of comprehensive community need, the amount of time and energy devoted to ministry activities, and the personal risk of living and working in under-resourced communities is a recipe ripe for burnout. Thus, while burnout is a hazard common to ministry and to the helping professions broadly, it is more prevalent among individuals serving in urban ministry because of the frequency, severity, and diversity of problems that they encounter as well as the likelihood that they will be personally impacted by the very problems that they are seeking to remediate.

In addition to the contextual challenges described above, urban ministry scholar-activists have identified poor leadership training and development as a factor predisposing urban ministers to burnout. Elliston and Kauffman, for example, declare that: "One of the serious problems facing urban ministries today is the high dropout rate . . . Many Bible college and seminary graduates drop out of effective leadership, not because God has called them elsewhere, but because of serious prob-

---

4. Ibid., xi.
5. Ibid., 13–14.
6. Ibid., 24.
7. John M. Perkins, *Beyond Charity: The Call to Christian Community Development* (Grand Rapids: Baker, 1993) 151–55.
8. Ibid., 155.

lems in their ministries which could have been addressed developmentally early in their ministry formation."⁹ They assert that many ministers develop "destructive habits" early in their careers that sabotage their capacity for long-term service, particularly problems related to faith development and discipleship. As an antidote they emphasize the importance of spiritual maturity as a desired characteristic of Christian leaders, and they prescribe ongoing spiritual formation.¹⁰ Interestingly, however, they do not explain the specific role of maturity in urban ministry.

Given the authors' emphasis on the importance of contextualization in the development and training of urban ministers, it is striking that they do not contextualize the need for spiritual and personal formation. Nowhere do they attend to the hazards of urban ministry and its heightened risk for burnout. Neither do they discuss the toll that urban ministry takes upon physical and psychological health, financial stability, and marriage and family relationships.

Instead, their recommendations for equipping Christians for urban ministry largely center upon strategic skills for understanding their contexts, building relationships and ministry teams, and identifying and addressing the needs of the community.¹¹ In the final pages of their book, they offer some recommendations that are geared toward the personal and spiritual development of the urban minister, including: (1) "equip emerging leaders with the essential skills for spiritual warfare"; (2) "intentionally focus on the spiritual formation of emerging leaders"; (3) "develop leaders who are committed to remain faithful to the end of their lives."¹² These recommendations seem anemic at best, unlinked as they are to the remainder of the text and to the specific challenges faced in urban ministry settings.

In his book *Urban Impact*, which aims to provide "a practical how-to book on growing a successful urban ministry," John Thompson addresses the issue of burnout with more specificity than do Elliston and Kauffman.¹³ Thompson's prescriptions for preventing and curing burnout include: (1) finding rest and encouragement through prayer; (2) finding a spiritually mature believer, preferably one with an understanding of ministry, to serve as a prayer partner; (3) taking regular time off for vacations as well as for personal relaxation and recreation with one's spouse and children; (4)

---

9. Edgar J. Elliston and J. Timothy Kauffman, *Developing Leaders for Urban Ministries* (New York: Lang, 1993) 242.

10. Ibid., 11.

11. Ibid., 211–49.

12. Ibid., 230, 242, 243.

13. John L. Thompson, *Urban Impact: Reaching the World Through Effective Urban Ministry* (Eugene, OR: Wipf and Stock, 2011) xix.

getting adequate sleep and exercise; (5) learning to prioritize and to say no; and (6) maintaining a regular devotional.[14] Still, with the exception of a brief table differentiating burnout from stress and making recommendations for preventing burnout, Thompson does not really address why burnout is more common among urban ministers.

Perkins points out that unrealistic expectations about the realities of living and working in under-resourced communities are common factors leading to burnout. He states that the high costs of urban ministry are often underestimated by eager young activists: "In my experience, too many young activists have rushed into the inner city without regard for the cost. The normal, natural hardships that ensue come as a complete surprise, often leaving them embittered and cynical concerning ministry to the poor."[15] He goes further, however, by declaring that the challenges faced by Christian community developers are essentially spiritual battles. Like Elliston and Kauffman, Perkins emphasizes the importance of ongoing spiritual formation for the Christian urban minister. Specifically, he urges the urban ministry practitioner to tend to the care of their own souls by maintaining a rich life of prayer, studying the Scriptures, and being rooted within communities of faith that can enrich their faith and support their vocation.[16] However, he does not limit his prescription for vocational sustenance to practicing spiritual disciplines. He also emphasizes the importance of support networks and disciplined recreational time away from one's ministry context for maintaining one's emotional and vocational vitality in urban ministry.[17]

Like Perkins, I believe that the challenges faced by urban ministers are a form of spiritual warfare. Our struggle against the systemic evils—classism, racism, xenophobia, and sexism—that characterize U.S. culture and plague urban communities is not "against enemies of blood and flesh, but against the rulers, against the authorities, against the cosmic powers of this present darkness, against the spiritual forces of evil in the heavenly places" (Eph 6:12, NIV). As Perkins and Elliston and Kauffman suggest, it is almost certainly the case that some urban ministry leaders burn or drop out because they have been ill-prepared for the battle, because they lack the spiritual fortitude that will sustain them over the long haul. However, I also believe it to be the case that there are Christian leaders with very rich spiritual lives who are at elevated risk for burnout precisely because of the theological beliefs that

14. Ibid., 152–54.
15. Perkins, *Beyond Charity*, 151.
16. Ibid., 169–76.
17. Ibid., 155.

shape and ground their commitment to urban ministry. Specifically, I am talking about the problematic understanding of self-love that I have observed among many friends who are in urban ministry.

A Tripartite Vision of Love

While urban ministers draw upon a wide variety of Scriptures in both the Hebrew canon and the New Testament as inspiration for their vocation, the Great Commandments (Mark 12:28–34; Matt 22:34–40; Luke 10:25–37) are undoubtedly key. Perkins explicitly identifies the Great Commandment as the primary scriptural foundation for ministry that has practical implications for daily life in marginalized contexts: "This idea of relevance becomes clear when we see that *God's will is summed up in the two great commandments:* to love God with all that we have and are, and to love our neighbor in the same way we love ourselves."[18] Likewise Elliston and Kauffman argue that urban ministry "rests on two different, but complementary, biblical imperatives: 1) making disciples of all nations and 2) loving one's neighbor."[19] Based particularly upon the Great Commandment, at the outset of their text, they identify three key relationships for urban ministers that must be aligned in order to enhance ministry effectiveness: the minister's relationship with God; the minister's relationship with his/her neighbors; and the minister's relationship with the local context.[20] Further, they identify two critical traits of urban Christian leaders: love of God and neighbor and integrity.[21]

Like many practitioners of urban ministry, Perkins and Elliston and Kauffman quickly make the move from love of God to love of neighbor, excising the implicit command to love oneself. For example, Perkins states:

> Christians can, in fact, give themselves to the most grueling and costly forms of service, to the point of spending their lives for the poor and giving themselves to being burned at the stake. But if our acts of service are done out of some other motivation and not done in love, 1 Corinthians 13 tells us it is in vain . . . Make no mistake. It is this love for God that moves us into this neighborly action. There is no duty or work to which the Christian is called outside of the two great commands that we love the Lord our God with all our soul, mind, and strength and that we love our neighbor as ourselves (see Luke 10:27). Jesus said that on these two commands hang all the requirements of

18. Ibid., 140.
19. Elliston and Kauffman, *Developing Leaders*, 6.
20. Ibid., 5.
21. Ibid., 72–74.

the law and the prophets. This is the essence of our Christianity. Love is the common denominator: a *love* for God and a *love* for neighbor.²²

Perkins does not seem to consider burnout to be a ministry hazard to avoid. Rather, he seems to affirm it as the cost of discipleship. However, if we consider the text more carefully, we see that the love demanded of us is tripartite: a love for God, a love for self, and a love for neighbor.

This tripartite vision of love, in which devotion to God, love of self, and caring for one's neighbor are held in balance, is perhaps most fully explicated in Luke 10:25–42. This pericope contains two incidents that occur in the context of what is commonly known as the Lucan travel narrative, a series of encounters occurring as Jesus and the disciples journey from to Jerusalem. The first is Jesus' encounter with a Torah scholar (Luke 10:25–37), and the second is Jesus' visit to the home of Martha and Mary (Luke 10:38–42).

The pericope begins when the Torah scholar poses the question, "What must I do to inherit eternal life?" (Luke 10:25).²³ Christ immediately recognizes it as disingenuous question, an attempt to challenge his knowledge and authority. Characteristically, he responds with a question of his own, forcing the impertinent scholar to concede the answer: "You shall love the Lord your God with all your heart, and with all your soul, and with all your mind; and your neighbor as yourself" (Luke 10:27). The scholar's response echoes Christ's Great Commandment (cf. Matt 22:34–40; Mark 12:28–31). As with urban ministry practitioner-scholars, Christian tradition broadly has tended to focus upon the first two elements of the response, namely that we are to love God and our neighbors. Little emphasis has been placed upon the final two words of the passage: "as yourself." Yet, both here and in the Great Commandment, self-love is assumed. Further, while love of self appears as the final theme in the sentence, it is not seen as being less important than love of one's neighbor. Rather, it is assumed to take place alongside, perhaps even in advance of, love of neighbor. That we are to love our neighbor in the same way that we love ourselves presumes that we already love ourselves. What is especially noteworthy in Luke's account is that self-love is implicated in one's salvation. The question posed by the scholar was not "What makes me a good person?" but rather "What must I do to inherit eternal life?"

Love of self, then, is a biblical injunction and is not to be equated with sinfulness or selfishness. The critical issue is how we understand the self. Moessner notes

---

22. Perkins, *Beyond Charity*, 147.
23. All Scripture quotations in this article are from the NRSV translation, unless otherwise noted.

that "the loved self is a self-in-relationship-to God. Persons have absolute value because they have been created to receive God's presence. The absolute value of a person is based on God, who alone is wholly good."[24] This is a liberating message for urban ministers, who often feel as though they need permission to exercise self-love. As Stone and Wolfteich found in their study of pastoral leaders of ninety-six urban congregations across the United States:

> Urban pastors are drawn to the command to rest. They particularly appreciate having a religious rationale for rest because many feel that they need "permission" to take time apart from ministry. Indeed, sabbatical and other Sabbath practices are an important corrective to the exhaustion, burnout, over-functioning, and even trauma experienced by many urban pastors. Sabbatical often serves as liberation from habits of overwork and as an invitation to self-care. At the same time, the call to rest competes against strong cultural pressures toward productivity.[25]

The pressure to be productive is particularly pronounced among urban ministers. There is a common, often unstated, perception among persons in ministry that caring for one's self is, at best, equivalent to wasting time that could be more usefully spent serving others and at worst, selfish. Individuals who minister in under-resourced communities may be further hindered from practicing self-care because of their ardent embrace of Christ's incarnational example, which compels them to live among and suffer alongside the people in under-resourced communities. They often experience a form of survivor's guilt in which they feel that taking regular time off from ministry to practice self-care is a luxury to which they should not be entitled. Stone and Wolfteich noted the presence of this sentiment among their study participants: "As vital as sabbatical is, however, urban pastors sometimes feel guilty for taking time apart from ministry. Their parishioners' crises continue unabated. Their parishioners and their spouses do not get similar time off from work."[26] The biblical affirmation of self-love teaches urban ministers that knowing, valuing, and caring for their authentic selves is as vital to vocational longevity as is love of the neighbors whom they serve.

Feminist pastoral theologian Jeanne Stevenson Moessner argues effectively that Luke carries the love-of-self theme through the parable of the Good Samaritan. Dissatisfied with Christ's subversion of his test, the Torah scholar pushes his chal-

---

24. Jeanne Stevenson Moessner, "Preaching the Good Samaritan: A Feminist Perspective," *Journal for Preachers* 19, no. 1 (1995) 22.

25. Stone and Wolfteich, *Sabbath in the City*, 42.

26. Ibid., 44.

lenge one step further: "Wanting to justify himself, he asked Jesus, 'And who is my neighbor?'" (Luke 10:29). Again, Jesus does not provide a direct answer but responds with a lesson and a question of his own. The merciful behavior of the Samaritan exemplifies the neighbor-love that is paradigmatic of Jesus' ministry and that he expects from his disciples.[27] As Wayne Gordon demonstrates in *Who is My Neighbor?* the parable has rich implications for urban ministry.[28] However, Moessner argues the parable of the Samaritan is also about self-love. The idea that one's self is worthy of love and care is borne out in two characters in this pericope: that of the man who has been beaten by robbers and left to die and that of the Samaritan who extends care to a person who has been abused and neglected by others. Moessner argues that in the moment of being cared for by the Samaritan, the beaten man realizes that he is loved by God:

> It is only from the periphery of the parable, from the side of the road, wounded and devalued, as one receives the mirroring of God's perfect love through the compassion of the Good Samaritan, that a person has a kairotic moment of understanding that she/he is of cosmic concern and immense worth to God. This is the foundational understanding of a loved self. Love of self in this biblical sense is always interconnected with love of God and neighbor, thus avoiding the dangers of narcissism, ontological individualism, selfishness, utilitarian individualism, egotism, and romantic individualism which posits the isolated self as the only valid reality in the universe with the maximization of self-interest.[29]

Moessner's interpretation of the text underscores that Christian self-love is not narcissistic but stems from the love that we receive from others out of their love of and obedience to God. The Samaritan, in tending the wounds of the beaten man, affirms that his bruised and broken body is worthy of love by God and by the neighbors who journey along the same road. What a powerful image for the urban minister who believes that urban ministry is a call to martyrdom. It affirms Baker-Fletcher's assertion that "God does not demand that we be burnt-out workers. God provides grace and rest not only for others but for the self. It is important to love oneself, accepting God's love in one's own life, in order to remain alive long enough to share God's love with those who are within reach of the full life-span God intends

---

27. Stephanie Buckhanon Crowder, "The Gospel of Luke," in *True to Our Native Land: An African American New Testament Commentary*, ed. Brian K. Blount et al. (Minneapolis: Fortress, 2007) 170.

28. Wayne Gordon, *Who Is My Neighbor? Lessons Learned from a Man Left for Dead* (Ventura, CA: Gospel Light, 2010).

29. Moessner, "Preaching the Good Samaritan," 21.

for us."³⁰ In submitting himself to be loved and cared for by another, the beaten man commits an act of radical self-love, refusing to acquiesce to the culture's expectation that he die.

Moessner points out that the Samaritan also embodies self-love. As a feminist pastoral theologian she highlights an aspect of the parable that is particularly salient for women, but that I also find applicable for urban ministry practitioners, namely, that the Samaritan finished his journey:

> The Samaritan finished his journey while meeting the need of a wounded and marginal person. The Samaritan did not give everything away; in this enigmatic parable, he did not injure, hurt, or neglect the self. He relied in a sense on the communal, on a type of teamwork as represented by the host at the inn. For women who have excelled at self-denial, self-abnegation, and self-sacrificial care of others, an understanding of the shared responsibility and the networking in pastoral care is a liberating perspective.³¹

In contrast to the priest and the Levite who crossed to the other side of the road so as to avoid encountering the beaten man, the Samaritan accepts the plight of the beaten man as his personal responsibility. Yet, he does not assume that he has to bear the entire responsibility for the man's care. He takes care of the man's most immediate needs and then places him in the hands of another before continuing on his journey. That is a profound lesson for urban ministry practitioners. The Samaritan does not assume that his own journey should stop. Remember that he encounters the beaten man while traveling. Presumably, he has a destination and goal in mind. By caring for the wounded man he has delayed his journey, but he does not allow caring for another to bring his own journey to a halt. Neither does he assume that the man has become his long-term responsibility. His promise to return and repay the innkeeper demonstrates that he does not assume that the innkeeper should care for the man without reciprocity and that he expects the innkeeper's caregiving, like his own, to be time-limited. In other words, he expects the victimized man to resume his own journey.

Thus, the parable of the Good Samaritan has several "journey mercies" that are instructive to urban ministry practitioners. "The journey mercies that are received from the parable of the Samaritan in Luke 10 are these: love of self as interconnected with love of God and neighbor; shared responsibility and networking in pastoral care; the experience of community; and the finishing of one's journey while car-

---

30. Karen Baker-Fletcher and Garth Kasimu Baker-Fletcher, *My Sister, My Brother: Womanist and Xodus God-Talk* (Maryknoll, NY: Orbis, 1997) 250.
31. Moessner, "Preaching the Good Samaritan," 323.

ing for others."[32] The urban minister has a lot to learn from the Samaritan, who interrupts but does not terminate his life's journey in order to care for one who is wounded. The text teaches the urban minister that he should not live only for others; he must live for himself.

Following the encounter with the Torah scholar, Jesus and the disciples continue their journey, traveling to the home of Martha and her sister Mary. There is a tendency by biblical scholars to treat these texts as though they are unrelated. Interpreters of Jesus' visit with Martha and Mary rarely focus upon the interaction between this pericope and the broader context of Luke's travel narrative. Several scholars though argue that the positioning of the narrative and its language indicate that it is closely connected to the rest of the chapter.[33] After all, Luke's travel narrative starts with Jesus' commissioning the seventy-two disciples, providing these instructions:

> Carry no wallet, no bag, and no sandals. Don't even greet anyone along the way. Whenever you enter a house, first say, "May peace be on this house." If anyone there shares God's peace, then your peace will rest on that person. If not, your blessing will return to you. Remain in this house, eating and drinking whatever they set before you, for workers deserve their pay. Don't move from house to house. Whenever you enter a city and its people welcome you, eat what they set before you. (Luke 10:4–8)[34]

In welcoming Jesus into her home Martha fulfills the type of hospitality that Jesus has instructed his disciples to expect. Jesus is a guest at the home of Martha and Mary. Martha, who appears to function as the head of household, is busy making preparations. The text does not specify what sort of preparations, and there is debate over the exact nature of Martha's busyness. The traditional reading is that she is busy preparing a meal for Jesus, thus fulfilling her role as a woman and a host.[35]

---

32. Ibid.

33. Warren Carter ("Getting Martha out of the Kitchen: Luke 10:38–42," *CBQ* 58 [1996] 264–80, esp. 267) notes the continued use of several words that appear throughout the travel narrative, specifically *poreuesthai*, "go," *eiserchesthai*, "enter," and *kōmē*, "village." Christopher R. Hutson ("Martha's Choice: A Pastorally Sensitive Reading of Luke 10:38–42," *Restoration Quarterly* 45 [2003] 139–50, esp. 143) notes that whereas the transition to a different setting with different characters leads many interpreters to treat the story of Mary and Martha as unrelated to Jesus' encounter with the Torah scholar, Luke deliberately juxtaposes the two narratives so that Mary and Martha serve as further illustration of the themes in the encounter between Jesus and the Torah scholar.

34. This is the second time in Luke's Gospel that Jesus provides such instructions to disciples as he commissions them for the journey, the first being the commissioning of the twelve in Luke 9:1–6.

35. For an example of this traditional reading of Martha's role, see R. Alan Culpepper, "Luke," in *New Interpreter's Bible* (Nashville: Abingdon, 1995) 9:230–32.

Other scholars reject this interpretation, noting that the text does not mention a meal and that, in fact, the language used to denote Martha's "serving" is that used to describe diaconal ministry.[36] Elisabeth Schüssler Fiorenza notes: "The text does not say that Martha is in the kitchen preparing and serving a meal but that she is preoccupied with *diakonia* and *diakonein*, terms that in Luke's time had already become technical terms for ecclesial leadership."[37]

If Martha's activity epitomizes Good Samaritan service, as Sook Ja Chung claims, why does Jesus rebuke her when she requests that he direct Mary to help her?[38] Why does Jesus affirm the responses of the scholar who is deliberately challenging and testing his authority, but reject the plea of Martha who opens her home to him and is providing sustenance for his continued ministry? If we read Luke 10:38–42 as a continuation of the tripartite vision of love espoused in Jesus' encounter with the Torah scholar, we can discern a continuing interplay between devotion to God, love of self, and care for the neighbor. That is to say, Jesus does not rebuke Martha because she embodies Good Samaritan service; he rebukes her because she does not.

In contrast to the Good Samaritan's capacity to care for another while also remaining faithful to his own journey, Martha's caregiving results in a fragmented sense of self.[39] In her hospitality Martha represents a faithful doer of the word and not merely a self-deceptive listener of the sort described in James 1:22. The problem, however, is that she is so consumed with *doing* that she is incapable of *listening*. She has failed to choose "the better part." Mary's acts of sitting and listening, in contrast,

36. Carter ("Getting Martha," 270) suggests that readers understand Martha's serving as a missional, rather than domestic activity. He states, "The nature of the 'go-between' activity or agency which distracts Martha can be clarified by investigating the use of the noun *diakonia* in Luke-Acts. By the end of Acts Luke's audience has encountered the noun *diakonia* eight times in contexts that concern not kitchen activity but participation with others in leadership and ministry on behalf of the Christian community." For a similar interpretation, see Jane D. Schaberg and Sharon H. Ringe, "Gospel of Luke," in *Women's Bible Commentary*, edited by Carol A. Newsom et al., 3rd ed. (Louisville: Westminster John Knox, 2012) 507–9.

37. Elisabeth Schüssler Fiorenza, "A Feminist Critical Interpretation for Liberation: Martha and Mary: Lk. 10:38–42," *Religion & Intellectual Life* 3 (1986) 30.

38. Sook Ja Chung, "Bible Study: Women's Ways of Doing Mission in the Story of Mary and Martha," *International Review of Mission* 93 (2004) 12.

39. Mary Rose Bumpus ("Awakening Hidden Wholeness: A Jungian View of Luke 10:38–42," *Journal of Psychology and Christianity* 29 [2010] 229–39, 230–31) does a Jungian reading of Luke 10:38–42 and argues that "Martha and Mary represent two dimensions of the one Christian life, and both are essential for discipleship and transformation. We experience fragmentation in personality and discipleship when we fail to integrate these two dimensions. The aim, then, from Jungian psychology is to draw these two components of the self together into a single, integrated sense of self, such that we can 'experience the fullness of life promised by Jesus Christ.'"

are acts of radical self-care. In her seemingly passive act of devotion before Christ, Mary receives the physical rest and spiritual nourishment needed to sustain her ministry. Martha, distracted from the very source of her life and ministry, becomes anxious and overwhelmed. Despite being in the presence of both her kin and her Lord and Savior, she feels abandoned and alone. Thus, her plight is not unlike that of the urban minister who is on the path to burnout, whose love of God, neighbor, and self perennially lean away from the latter, such that she becomes spiritually, physically, and emotionally ill-nourished while caring for the needs of others. The remedy for Martha and for the urban minister is to partake of the spiritual sustenance and physical rest that will help her to develop and maintain a coherent sense of self.

Loving Self, Keeping Sabbath

In their study of urban pastoral leadership Stone and Wolfteich suggest several spiritual practices that are particularly vital for pastors in urban contexts: seeking and maintaining holy friendships, cultivating silence and solitude, daily disciplines of prayer and devotions, reading the Scriptures, theological study and reflection, laughter, and taking care of one's personal health and family relationships.[40] They found that many urban pastors had learned the lesson that excellence in ministry was not to be measured by the busyness of one's schedule.

> One pastor suggested that if we can use the term excellence to describe Christian pastors, it is an excellence that is more about brokenness and cruciform discipleship than about "doing more." There is a death to self that pastors reported to us in various ways as being at the core of pastoral excellence. But it is not a death *of* self that comes through busy-ness, depletion, exhaustion, and overextending oneself. On the contrary, it is a death *to* self in the sense of letting go, being able to say no, and releasing the stranglehold pastors sometimes think they need to keep on their congregations and ministries.[41]

This statement implies that excellence in urban ministry requires kenosis of a different sort than is typically thought of by urban ministers.[42] It is not the self-emptying that requires us to ignore, repress, or deny personal needs and desires for the

---

40. Stone and Wolfteich, *Sabbath in the City*, 64–76.

41. Ibid., xvi.

42. Kenosis is Christ's voluntary act of self-emptying that is described in Phil 2:1–11. A number of feminist theologians have noted the dangers of utilizing this text to mandate self-sacrifice, most notably Sarah Coakley in *Powers and Submissions: Spirituality, Philosophy, and Gender* (Malden, MA: Blackwell, 2002).

sake of doing more to minister to God's people. Rather, it is the emptying of the self that tempts us to assume that the salvation of the city is dependent upon our efforts.

Further, in contrast to the tendency of urban ministry texts to focus upon organizational strategies, these pastors had learned that excellence is not about programs or ministry strategies.

> Pastoral excellence is instead a virtue shaped and nurtured by practices that continually bring a pastor into connection with the source of all holiness. Virtuous pastors recognize and affirm as sacred their own longing for spiritual nurture, for community, for knowledge, and for time simply to be. They incorporate practices of prayer, renewal, friendship, presence, Sabbath, and study into the particular demands of their context. These practices are not distractions from ministry, luxuries to be tolerated, but rather key dimensions of what it means continually to grow into the life of disciple and pastor."[43]

However, even among those who practiced Sabbath rest regularly, there was a temptation to do so in a mechanistic and utilitarian way. Pastors often misunderstood Sabbath practices to be techniques for enhancing productivity and maintaining longevity in ministry.

> Too often pastors described Sabbath in instrumental terms as a tool to increase their effectiveness and efficiency. We would resist that utilitarian sense of Sabbath—common as it might be. Practices of Sabbath keeping are indeed foundational to ministry. Yet this is so not because Sabbath keeping is a self-help tool or leadership strategy; rather, it is a practice that embodies and rediscovers right understanding of God as creator, our own identity as created beings, and the gift of freedom from unceasing work.[44]

Sabbatical disciplines are not simply about increasing productivity or even self-care; they are acts of obedience that are critical to helping pastors rediscover and reconnect with their authentic sense of self, which often gets lost in the day-to-day chaos of ministry.[45] They are embodied spiritual practices that create alternative rhythms of time and relationship in urban contexts that are marked by chaos, busyness, fear, and disconnect. In taking time to nurture the person whom God has created, urban ministers proclaim "Anathema!" to the spirit of darkness that tries to convince them that human worth is measured by economic productivity and material acquisition and that God has abandoned the city to human hands.

---

43. Stone and Wolfteich, *Sabbath in the City*, xvii.
44. Ibid., 39–40.
45. Ibid., 43.

PROPHET, PAGAN, PRAYER: URBAN THEOLOGY OF REVERSAL IN THE STORY OF JONAH

David Leong

Growing up in the evangelical South, one of my favorite Sunday school stories, especially on flannelgraph, was the book of Jonah. Like many other children, I suspect it was a combination of the miraculous and seemingly absurd that drew my attention to this action-packed narrative. A rebellious prophet, a disastrous storm, a giant human-swallowing fish, an evil empire of a city, super plants that grow and wither—what's not to like about this well-worn "whale of a tale"?

My real interest in the book of Jonah, however, began a few years ago when I preached a sermon about the importance of alternative narratives, about stories in which the traditional character roles and moral expectations are overturned or rearranged. In all the biblical canon there are few stories as puzzling and surprising as that of the prophet Jonah, son of Ammitai. The book's four brief chapters have been the source of a tidal wave of interpretive work across the theological and cultural spectrum. The story of Jonah is "a particularly buoyant sliver of biblical text . . . a tiny text that is virtually capsizing under the weight of interpretation . . . Jonah has demonstrated an extraordinary capacity for cultural survival."[1]

So why read the book of Jonah with an urban hermeneutic? Why add to the already rich and varied mix of midrash and exegesis on this ancient text? I believe the story of Jonah is particularly poignant when read from the perspective of the cultural and theological realities of the modern city. In some ways the increasingly globalized, pluralistic, multicultural, and post-industrial North American city is seemingly light years away from the word of the LORD that came to Jonah and sent him to the ancient city of Nineveh. In many other ways the dynamics of inclusion and exclusion, the practices of ethnocentrism and religiosity, and the questions of agency and vocation in God's plan of liberative salvation all make the story of Jonah a relevant text for urban theology and ministry. Theological interpretation of Scripture always requires a fresh and dynamic reading of the text that roots its

---

1. Yvonne Sherwood, *A Biblical Text and its Afterlives* (Cambridge: Cambridge University Press, 2000) 3.

meaning in the covenantal community of faith. May this reading, informed by the Spirit, be a revelatory word of God's scandalous grace and participatory commissioning to the church.

I intend to read the story of Jonah through three related motifs in the text: prophet, pagan, and prayer. First, the vocation of the prophet prompts questions of identity for the church in mission. What is the role of the prophet in mediating the word of YHWH? How is a faithful prophet obedient to the saving work of YHWH in the world, especially in the city? Second, the place of the "pagan" sketches a portrait of those on the supposed receiving end of God's word. How do the pagans in the story of Jonah reveal an unexpected perspective on those we have considered outsiders and enemies? What parallels do we find in urban communities? Third, the practice of prayer is the formative and praxeological center of the text. How is the belly of the fish a crucial setting for reflection and repentance? How can cries of lament, petition, and worship shape our understanding of compassion and prophetic witness in the city?

Through each theme is a common thread of reversal and surprise; things are not always as they seem. These somewhat unusual observations keep the reader attuned to the layers of irony and multivalent meaning for the church. For the people of God in the city, an upside-down community of cruciformity, an awareness of the gospel that is attentive to the surprising beauty of reversal often reveals important and "unexpected news."[2]

The "unprophet"

Like the *ekklesia* a prophet is *called* and *sent*. Jonah's call begins like many other prophets; the word of the LORD comes to him with an instructive mission. It is the destination that is unusual, given Nineveh's reputation as Assyria's "center of savage and often sadistic power."[3] God wants Jonah to go and deliver a message of judgment, not to his own people, but to a foreign people in a hard place—the center of empire in a land of Israel's sworn enemies. Is it any wonder that Jonah immediately flees in the opposite direction? The prophetic vocation is never a call to the smooth sailing of sentimental religiosity; rather, the office of the prophet by definition takes the messenger into harm's way to confront the brokenness of fallen people and the injustices of empire.

---

2. Robert McAfee Brown, *Unexpected News* (Philadelphia: Westminster, 1984).
3. Miguel De La Torre, *Liberating Jonah* (New York: Orbis, 2007) 11.

To be fair to Jonah, this mission must have felt a bit overwhelming, to say the least. How could one man with a message of doom and gloom confront the terrifying Assyrian empire and escape with his life? So Jonah departs for Tarshish in quite a hurry and begins a pattern of behavior that echoes throughout the story. The prophet Jonah, *ben Ammittai* ("son of faithfulness"[4]), has an ironic proclivity to proclaim God's character as true without living in accordance to who he knows God to be. In other words, Jonah has "good theology" but poor practice; too often "his credo is belied by his actions."[5] He is a surprisingly unfaithful prophet in this regard and, therefore, serves as a kind of "unprophet," from whom faithful readers must learn *not* to follow.

How is Jonah's call to Nineveh like the church's call to the city? Urban pastor and theologian Eric Jacobsen contrasts the allure of suburban ideals with the fear of the city in ways that parallel Jonah's flight to Tarshish.

> For the past two decades ... we have been abandoning our strategic locations within city cores and traditional neighborhoods, and we have tried to create for ourselves a new kind of society in the form of suburban megachurches. And as individual Christians, we have marched right along with the rest of our culture and moved our homes outside of the urban core into the sanitized world of the suburbs. Even when we have not participated directly in this radical shift, we have come to view the particularities of functioning in the midst of the city (restricted parking, unsympathetic neighbors, and pushy transients) as inconveniences rather than as opportunities for ministry ... Unfortunately, if we were to take a hard look at how Christians in this country have come to view their cities, we would have to conclude that our views have not necessarily been shaped by the Bible, prayer, or meaningful discussions among fellow Christians. It might be more accurate to say that the fear of cities, or the fear of one another, or possibly the love of convenience has been the actual basis of much of our current perceptions about the city.[6]

Nineveh is a hardship post, an oppressive place that "came to symbolize violence and cruelty."[7] Yet this is the prophetic destination, a place of uncertainty and risk where the prophet must rely on God's sovereignty and common grace, especially in the midst of structures and institutions that exclude and oppress. Before we rush to judgment of the urban context as characterized solely by evil and brokenness, we must also recognize that the city cannot be painted in such broad strokes, especially

---

4. Ibid., 13.
5. Frank Spina, *The Faith of the Outsider* (Grand Rapids: Eerdmans, 2005) 101.
6. Eric Jacobsen, *Sidewalks in the Kingdom* (Grand Rapids: Brazos, 2003) 16.
7. De La Torre, *Liberating Jonah*, 11.

in consideration of the significant cultural and socioeconomic transitions occurring in the urban geography of emerging and post-industrial cities.[8] As the landscape shifts toward a "mixed multitude" of immigrants, gentrifiers, refugees, hipsters, and "nones" (the "spiritual but not religious"), we must continue to press for more nuance and sophistication in our perception of "the city."

As it turns out later in the story, Nineveh is not at all the place of violent terror and evil Jonah expects it to be. Jonah allows his fear to dictate his disobedience, and on the way to Tarshish, God intervenes to teach Jonah about the consequences of abandoning his prophetic vocation. Notably, the teachable moment extends to the reader as well as we first encounter the surprising pagan motif in the sailors who are caught up in the storm of Jonah's predicament.

The "Godly Pagan"

In contrast to the unfaithful prophet, these "pagan" sailors exhibit godly virtues: humility, repentance, and reverence. Ironies abound as the narrator sets the scene in vv. 5–7. Chaos has enveloped the ship, the crew is hurling cargo into the sea, and prayers of desperation are being flung in the general direction of any god who will listen. Yet Jonah, who went *down* to Joppa to board the ship, *down* below deck into the belly of the boat to lie *down*, has fallen into a deep sleep (and this still is not the bottom of how low he will go). Clearly he is concerned about the calamity that has consumed the entire ship as a result of his disobedience.

As the crew's attention turns to Jonah in v. 8, Jonah responds to their interrogation with a simple but pointed affirmation: "'I am a Hebrew,' he replied. 'I worship the LORD, the God of heaven, who made the sea and the dry land.'"[9] In one fell swoop Jonah addresses their emphatic questions with a declaration of the identity of the Hebrew God. YHWH, in contrast to the pagan's competing gods, is Creator of all and over all. Here Jonah demonstrates his ironic "knowledge" of YHWH in the midst of his futile attempt to flee the all-powerful, all-knowing, ever-present Hebrew God. Sadly, the unprophet's theology falls short in the area of praxis and is especially thin in contrast to the pagan sailors' righteous reaction to Jonah's explanation.

Even after Jonah takes the blame for their collective disaster and invites the sailors to cast him into the sea to appease the Lord, the crew refuses to lay a finger on Jonah and continues the struggle to reach land. After rowing in futility against

---

8. See Peter Dreier and Todd Swanstrom, *Place Matters* (Lawrence: University Press of Kansas, 2013).

9. Jonah 1:9, NRSV.

the still raging storm, they finally relent and cry out to YHWH for mercy. In humility, they petition the Lord for forgiveness and offer a simple affirmation of the Hebrew God's identity and power: "You are the LORD: whatever you want, you can do."[10] Once they throw Jonah overboard and witness the efficacy of his request in the calmness of the sea, they continue their theological conversion through their actions: "The men worshipped the LORD with a profound reverence; they offered a sacrifice to the LORD and made solemn promises."[11] Thus the "pagans" exhibit a genuinely surprising outcome in their penitent and worshipful encounter with the living God.

Implications for Urban Ministry

This profound reversal of prophet and pagan is the first episode of irony in the story of Jonah, but it is a significant development for those who have fallen prey to the mischaracterization of the city as full of godless paganism in desperate need of a righteous, prophetic deliverer. Too often, urban ministry has been cast as the noble enterprise of "incarnational" Christians on whose shoulders the integrity and salvific truth of the gospel rests. In the process those on the receiving end of urban ministry can be unintentionally portrayed as poor, helpless souls and victims of their own alleged immorality. The prophet-pagan dynamic in the story of Jonah reminds the church that not every prophet lives their theology, and not every pagan is godless. The urban minister, even as a herald of God's kingdom reality, is still in need of rescue as a broken vessel of grace and truth. Those on the margins of urban communities, poor and needy as they may often be, are also bearers of God's image and goodness. Those who are attentive to YHWH's surprising economy of prophetic encounter as revealed in the story of Jonah may find themselves on the receiving end of God's mercy at the hand of pagans who have responded in faithfulness to YHWH.

To be clear, this reversal is not a binary switch in which those who identify with a prophetic vocation are somehow as praxeologically flawed as Jonah, and those who are considered pagan are subsequently pure exemplars of moral virtue. To romanticize the urban poor as paragons of righteousness simply makes the opposite error of colonialism.[12] Yet the story of Jonah is an essential canonical reminder that "the

---

10. Jonah 1:14b, CEB.

11. Jonah 1:16, CEB.

12. In the sense that imperial colonialism, broadly speaking, failed to recognize the full humanity of those they colonized, to romanticize the urban poor is similarly to caricature their existence in objectifying or essentializing ways.

elect," those "chosen out of all the peoples on earth,"[13] often have the tendency to drift into an exclusivity that precludes the possibilities of "the faith of the outsider"[14] as essential to God's plan of salvation. Themes of reversal in Jonah offer a corrective to the cultural tunnel vision that was all too common in the life of Israel, and they remind the reader that when it comes to covenantal qualifiers in the community of God, a healthy dose of humility is in order.

Bounded and Centered

In the context of the city, where diverse cultures and worldviews inevitably collide, it may be simpler for the church to operate with more of a rigid, "bounded set"[15] identity. In this kind of bounded ecclesiology the barriers to entry are tightly controlled by gatekeeping qualifiers that can be explicit or implicit. Such qualifiers may be cultural, theological, or socioeconomic, and they comprise the intrinsic, essential characteristics of the group. Those on the inside of the boundary can assume the role of prophet with the confidence that with such an office comes a clear distinction between those appointed to deliver the word of God and those tasked with receiving the word of God. As a mediator of divine truth or judgment, the bounded set prophet speaks to "the other" on the outside of the community with a message of invitation to consider crossing the boundary through cultural conformity, theological ascent, or behavioral modification. For example, the old "inner-city rescue mission" model of ministry may require that people in need of a meal or shelter first sit through a chapel service or respond to particular theological affirmations. This "pray to play" approach, though fading in popularity in many urban ministries, can still rely on the implicit coercion of power disparity, even when language or implementation is softened. For the prophet operating out of a bounded set community, the "pagan" can too easily become a kind of essentialized target—more an issue or demographic than a person with God-given humanity, dignity, and agency.

In contrast to the bounded set, Hiebert proposes a "centered set" paradigm as a category in which individuals are identified, not in terms of a rigid either-or boundary, but instead by their relationship to the center.[16] From this perspective

---

13. Deut 14:2, NRSV.

14. Spina's book, *The Faith of the Outsider*, highlights texts that, like Jonah, demonstrate the critical role outsiders play in Israel's story and identity.

15. The "bounded set" has clear boundaries established by essential characteristics, as opposed to a "centered set" perspective. See Paul G. Hiebert, "The Category 'Christian' in the Mission Task," *International Review of Missions* 72 (1983) 421–27.

16. David Livermore, *Cultural Intelligence* (Grand Rapids: Baker Academic, 2009) 166.

the center may be a covenant community or even the person of Jesus Christ, but the crucial identifier is not a set of intrinsic qualities that are shared with the center. Rather, individuals are defined by their relationship to a common reference point. "For example, a son and a daughter are children of a father and mother. If they are children of the same parents they are brother and sister, not because of what they are intrinsically, but because of their relationship to a common reference point."[17] In this case, neither a prophet nor a pagan is essentially righteous or sinful in and of themselves, but what defines their prophetic or pagan nature is their affinity with and connections to the people of God, centered in a covenantal relationship with YHWH.

The centered set prophet is one who recognizes a close connection to the particularity[18] of YHWH, but also sees the permeability of both the mantle of prophet and the boundary markers of God's people. As one who identifies with YHWH based on covenant-keeping practices,[19] the centered prophet must be rooted in the community of God, but not so deeply submerged in the religious community that the social logic of exclusivity becomes dominant. The prophetic vocation calls individuals and the church into a delicate balance of rootedness and openness, confidence and humility. Only an acute awareness of this balance can lead to a genuinely hospitable encounter with "paganism" in the world. If the prophet's posture toward the outsider or other is too essentialist and "bounded," then the pagan becomes objectified and dehumanized. When the centered prophet is truly rooted in the "ḥesed, mišpāṭ, and ṣĕdāqâ"[20] of YHWH, then new possibilities for those who bear witness to the love and compassion of God open up in surprising places, even (or especially) in the lives of pagans.

For the urban church that is open to the irony throughout the story of Jonah, permeable boundaries may be an essential characteristic of faithful, prophetic ministry in the city. About three years ago, a friend and United Methodist church planter in my neighborhood began a community committed to three ideals: deep listening, creative liberation, and radical hospitality.[21] Along the way he has occasionally faced criticism from parties across the theological and denominational spectrum. I have

17. Ibid.
18. YHWH is the Hebrew God, a deity with particular identifiable characteristics as Creator, deliverer, the God of Abraham, etc.
19. E.g., adherence to Torah, observance of the Sabbath, etc.
20. Jer 9:24. "Mercy, justice, and righteousness" are central characteristics of YHWH, and those who "understand and know" YHWH.
21. Rev. John Helmiere of Valley and Mountain Fellowship in Seattle, WA.

heard evangelical murmurs that he is inclined toward Unitarianism and agnostic suggestions that he is a yet another proprietor of organized religion. Some Wesleyans think he is too United Methodist, and my neighbors—well, sometimes they are not quite sure what to think. If there's anything they all seem convinced of, it is that this peculiar community, whatever it may be, is committed to seeking a God whose plan for salvation includes some unusual people. Urban ministers must be drawn to the odds and ends, the eclectic and outcast, or as Simon and Garfunkel put it in their very loose paraphrase of the Beatitudes, "Blessed are the sat upon, spat upon, ratted on."[22] The story of Jonah has a few of these characters, but before we get to Nineveh, there is a fish to deal with.

A Fishy Prayer

As Jonah one ends with an unusual "rescue" inside a fish, the second chapter begins with a prayer. Eugene Peterson sums up the entirety of the story with this prayer at the heart: "[T]he book of Jonah is a parable at the center of which is a prayer."[23] Just as Jonah encountered numerous obstacles in the journey of discerning his prophetic vocation, so must the church enter into a place of dark reflection and hardship, a place where "we become what we are called to be. We become what we are called to be by praying. And we start out by praying from the belly of the fish."[24]

Like the rest of the book, numerous interpretations of Jonah's prayer have been offered based on its context, literary structure, and historical setting. What we do know is that the basic form of the prayer is a psalm of thanksgiving, and its language is borrowed heavily from all across the Psalter.[25] In preparation for his impending mission to Nineveh, Jonah's prayer spans a range of emotions and declarations, from distress and despair to remembrance and worship. However, this arc of thanksgiving that moves from lament to praise is not a singular movement in the story of Jonah; though the prayer catalyzes Jonah's mission, it does not remain as a triumphant overtone in the book. This prayer, however momentarily gratifying it is to the reader, also foreshadows the challenge Jonah will later face in accepting that deliverance belongs to YHWH and YHWH alone.

Regardless, the prayer of Jonah is both a cry for help in a place of darkness and a word of gratitude for the goodness of God. In this sense, it is an appropriate liturgy

---

22. Paul Simon and Art Garfunkel, "Blessed," *Sounds of Silence*, 1966.
23. Eugene Peterson, *Under the Unpredictable Plant* (Grand Rapids: Eerdmans, 1992) 7.
24. Ibid., 74.
25. James Limburg, *Jonah* (Louisville: Westminster, 1993) 63–65.

for the urban church that must acknowledge and verbalize the pain of the depths while somehow moving toward the hope of God's salvation in the midst of suffering. Praying with Jonah may not result in the kind of quick fixes and easy solutions that North American evangelicalism is prone to pursue, but it can provide a framework for hopeful lament and thanksgiving, rooted in the Psalms, for urban prophets and pagans alike.

Moving Downward

As the prayer begins, Jonah, who has been moving—both literally and metaphorically—*down* is on his way to hit bottom. Cast "into the depths in the heart of the seas," Jonah cries out "from the belly of the underworld."[26] Flooded by waves and rushing waters, Jonah is "at the base of the undersea mountains," sunk down "to the point of death," and imprisoned in the underworld "with no end in sight."[27] The repeated downward movement presses Jonah to his limit and takes the reader into the deep pain of abandonment and despair. In the tradition of the Psalter, the author does not shy away from emphasizing Jonah's anguish, pain that is expressed "not in the reflectively managed and manicured form of a confession, but as a pre-reflective outburst from the depths of the soul."[28] How can the urban minister "mourn with those who mourn"[29] by going to the depths with Jonah?

Too often North American Christianity has been stricken with a pathological avoidance of pain and suffering, and the deficit of lament in our communal prayer lives is merely one among many indicators of this tendency to "look on the bright side." Though its popularity was relatively short-lived, the infamous *Prayer of Jabez*[30] is an example of the prayerful positivity that plagues comfortable congregations with a theological veneer of blessing and prosperity.[31] The "Jabez effect" of one-dimensional prayer afflicts both the rich and the poor in different ways, but its damage is nonetheless distressing. For the "haves," those with privilege, power, and access to

---

26. Jonah 2:2–3, CEB.

27. Jonah 2:5–6, CEB.

28. Miroslav Volf, *Exclusion and Embrace: A Theological Exploration of Identity, Otherness, and Reconciliation* (Nashville: Abingdon, 1996) 124. Though Volf in this passage is referring more specifically to expressions of rage and hatred, the raw emotion of the Psalms is still relevant to Jonah's pain.

29. Rom 12:15.

30. Bruce Wilkinson's short book (Multnomah, 2000) was an international bestseller and to date has sold more than nine million copies worldwide.

31. Given the global distribution of wealth and resources, praying for "an enlargement of our territory" is probably the last thing for which North American Christians should be earnestly praying.

resources, the Jabez effect feeds a sense of divine entitlement in which the blessed are somehow led to believe that their current state of blessing is not enough. Must God in his infinite riches give more to those who already have much? On the other side, the poor who pray like Jabez cry out for blessing in the hopes of winning a divine lottery ticket, sometimes convinced by a prophet who has assured them of success if they simply enlarge their faith. This over-emphasis on blessing and prosperity is part and parcel of the greedy and consumptive syncretism that has infected much of North American Christianity, but one of its primary effects on the prayer life of the church is the exclusion of pain, the silencing of suffering, and the masking of deep hurts.

Jonah's prayer in the belly of the fish is in part a cry of agony from a broken prophet who is finally beginning to see his own paganism, an idolatry of self and disobedience that has led to his current predicament. By verbalizing this pain as an integral part of this psalm of thanksgiving, Jonah is acknowledging the depths out of which hope can again see the light of day. Rather than glossing over the anguish of his circumstances, Jonah lingers in the questions of God's absence and names the abandonment he feels. This naming of and lingering in the suffering of his situation is a critical pastoral skill for urban ministers who often face hardship and despair in their own lives and the lives of the communities they serve. No urban minister is prepared to offer words of truth or comfort unless they are willing and able to fully enter into the depths of distress that come with "the cost of discipleship."[32] This distress may be the kind of "aquatic exile" that Jonah is facing under the discipline of YHWH or the pain that accompanies the daily challenges of urban poverty and violence.

Thankfully, it is not the intensity or extremity of suffering that urban ministers have personally experienced that qualifies them to identify with those who are in pain, but rather their humility and openness to being broken before God and a willingness to cry out in the absence of God's goodness. Urban ministers would be wise to make prayerful space for the suffering that comes as a result of brokenness in the people, systems, and structures of the city. Before we pray for blessing and before we move to hope, the belly of the fish is first a place of lament, and that lament lays the foundation on which God's salvation can stand firm.

---

32. Bonhoeffer's emphasis on "costly grace" that calls the Christian to "come and die" is essentially a call to the suffering and self-emptying of a cruciform life. See Dietrich Bonhoeffer, *The Cost of Discipleship* (New York: Touchstone, 1995) 43–78.

Remembering Hope

Even as Jonah names his distress throughout his prayer, there is also an underlying confidence in God's presence with him. Jonah calls out to the Lord and YHWH answers; from the depths Jonah declares, "You heard my voice."[33] At the lowest point of the prayer in v. 6, as Jonah feels trapped in the deep waters forever, the tide finally turns and Jonah remembers, "Yet you brought up my life from the Pit, O LORD my God." Verse seven continues, "As my life was ebbing away, I remembered the LORD; and my prayer came to you, into your holy temple." How does Jonah make this turn, and what prayerful practices might help to inform the urban church on its way to declaring, as Jonah did before his dramatic exit from the fish, that "deliverance belongs to the LORD"?

Though we obviously cannot be certain as to Jonah's particular experience and thought process in the belly of the fish for three days and nights, I want to suggest that the role of memory, specifically the practice of *active remembering*, is an essential component of Jonah's prayer and the work of the church in the city. Throughout the narrative of the Pentateuch (and beyond), memory plays a crucial role in the worshipping life of Israel. Innumerable variations of Moses' instruction to "Remember this day on which you came out of Egypt, out of the house of slavery, because the Lord brought you out from there by strength of hand,"[34] are woven into Israel's story of deliverance, wandering, judgment, and restoration. It is precisely Israel's inability to remember, their seemingly reoccurring collective amnesia, that causes their various hardships in the desert, in defeat, and eventually exile. The memory of the Exodus, of God's great rescue from oppression, was one of the singularly defining identity-markers of God's people. Without that memory, without its vivid and consistent reproduction in story, song, and prayer, Israel had no anchor in forming who they were, and more importantly, *whose* they were. As a repository for communal liturgies, the Psalter served as a cultural memory bank for Israel. Its prayers and poetry enlivened the imagination of God's people and reminded them again of God's grand story of election and salvation from Abraham to the present.

These Psalms are the memories that shape Jonah's prayer in the belly of the fish. At his lowest point, the structure and language of lament and thanksgiving come rushing in, and the words of both pain and hope rehearse the arc of God's saving work in his life. Jonah remembers YHWH, the God of the Exodus, and his confidence that he will not remain in the depths forever is restored. In v. 9 Jonah vows

---

33. Jonah 2:2, NRSV.
34. Exod 13:3, NRSV.

to sacrifice with thanksgiving to the Lord, for YHWH is the God of deliverance. In an ironic turn of events Jonah's vows finally mirror those of the "pagan" sailors who earlier bore witness to YHWH's saving power. Just as the sailors were spared from the calamity of the storm, now Jonah is rescued from further digestion as the fish spits him out onto dry ground at the Lord's command.

In the same way that Jonah's prayerful remembrance of the Lord and acknowledgment of YHWH as the agent of salvation brings about his deliverance, so must the urban church pray with an active memory of God's saving work—past, present, and future. This active remembering is eucharistic and imaginative in its essence, yet also concrete and commonplace in its implementation. The Eucharist is the centerpiece of the church's liturgy; it is the work of the people that is done in remembrance of Jesus Christ. Each time the people of God partake of the bread and the wine, these gifts of God are instruments for the making-present of *Yeshua*, the Messiah. As mysterious means of grace, these common elements deliver a living memory of Christ's presence, and the prayers of the people around the Lord's Table create a community for the Spirit of God to inhabit. In remembering Christ's broken body and shed blood, people come to the table as humble sinners in need of God's grace, and the forgiveness that is offered reconciles people to God and one another. This old story has too often been rehearsed with stale and somber rituals that rob the Eucharist of its imaginative beauty. As the early church gathered for the love feast, remembering Jesus in the breaking of the bread was an occasion for both serious reflection and radical hospitality. It would take the early followers of the Way a considerable leap of faith to imagine that the particular people God was forming was a community where "Jew and Gentile, slave and free, and male and female"[35] could be reconciled at the table. Yet this is exactly the function of the bread and the wine that the church consumes as we remember Jesus and his disciples in the upper room.

Praying with this eucharistic imagination does not necessarily have to be an elaborate, "high-church" liturgy for the urban congregation. Every time the church gathers at the table in remembrance of Jesus, whether in the formality of eucharistic liturgy or the spontaneity of a casual "love feast," the people of God must simply reenact the hospitality and reconciliation of the gospel story. It is a story that begins (and ends) with YHWH, centered in Jesus, and is given to the church for its commissioning. Just as Jonah's remembering of YHWH in the belly of the fish brought his life up from the depths of despair, so must the urban church remember God's

---

35. Gal 3:28.

saving and reconciling work that culminates in the new life graciously offered to all through Christ's body and blood.

Thus, a congregation that lives in remembrance of this story prays—whether liturgical, charismatic, meditative, or communal—through "psalms and hymns and spiritual songs"[36] that are rooted in hope. This hope is not a naive optimism that is blind to the suffering that is all too visible in the racial and socioeconomic disparities plaguing our cities. Rather, hope persists in the face of suffering because YHWH is present with those in pain, and Jesus creates belonging wherever there is exclusion. As a community of hope, the urban church can become a eucharistic presence in the city by living into the hopeful story that "God is forming a family out of strangers."[37] Though we often find ourselves estranged from one another in the urban environment, an active and prayerful remembering of the Lord's Table builds fellowship and community through block parties, barbeques, potlucks, and common meals.

It is in remembering YHWH that Jonah's prayer enters into the presence of God, and his hope of God's deliverance is rekindled. Moving up from the depths with thanksgiving and out of the fish with such emphatic momentum, his confidence in his prophetic task seems restored. Is Jonah prepared to get it right the second time? Will his prayerful conversion be sufficient preparation for such an intimidating urban mission?

Nineveh's Penitent Pagans

As we saw in the first chapter of Jonah, ironies abound in this story of an "unprophet" and the "Godly pagans" he encounters. As the narrative turns to Jonah's arrival in "the great city" of Nineveh, surprising revelations of Nineveh's devout citizenry develop very quickly. In this third chapter Jonah plays a somewhat minor role in contrast to the Ninevites. We know simply that the word of YHWH comes to him a second time, and fresh off of his own conversion experience in the fish, Jonah responds in faithful obedience and begins his journey into the city. As an itinerant preacher of sorts, Jonah's message is short and to the point: in forty days Nineveh will be overthrown. Generally speaking, proclamations of doom and destruction, especially devoid of further context, are easy to ignore, but much to Jonah's surprise and the surprise of the reader, the reaction of the Ninevites is anything but dismissive.

---

36. Eph 5:19.
37. Stanley Hauerwas, *Resident Aliens* (Nashville: Abingdon, 1989) 83.

Like the allegedly pagan sailors that precede them in the text, the people of Nineveh—from top to bottom—act with righteous and repentant hearts by believing in God, proclaiming a fast, and mourning in sackcloth. Though the sailors acted in response to the imminent danger they faced in the stormy sea, the Ninevites take Jonah at his word, acting on faith. The king of Nineveh himself, in a profound display of humility, removes his royal clothing and drapes himself in sackcloth while sitting in ashes.[38] To drive the point home even further, Nineveh's penitent piety does not stop with humans. By royal decree both people and animals are commanded to fast from food and water while covered in sackcloth as they cry out to God for forgiveness for their evil and violent ways. No half measures would suffice; the people of Nineveh fully committed themselves to seeking God's mercy.

In sum, "all the Ninevites have to go on is Jonah's ambiguous and truncated five-word oracle, something they could just as easily have been inclined cavalierly to dismiss. Who even knew what it meant? Yet the Ninevite response epitomizes sincerity. Has any Israelite city ever responded to a prophetic utterance so immediately, so thoroughly, and so admirably? Nineveh has just become a model for how to respond to the prophetic words of the Israelite prophets."[39] Again, the poignant reversal of the expected insider-outsider dynamic is striking. Jonah, obedient but perhaps still less than enthusiastic about his mission, preaches what must have been the shortest message of his prophetic career, and the very people we expect to be evil, angry, and vindictive are in fact just the opposite. Things in this great city are not at all as they seem.

In the critically acclaimed television series *The Wire*,[40] David Simon creates a surprising and complex portrait of the American city in Baltimore, Maryland. As the series unfolds, the viewer encounters an unusual cast of characters. Where one expects to find clearly defined ethics in a crime drama genre that typically pits criminals against authorities, there is significant moral ambiguity and a consistent role-reversal when it comes to the numerous antagonists in the city. Instead of characterizing drug dealing and gang violence as solely dark, immoral choices made by sociopathic individuals, *The Wire* brilliantly demonstrates the many shades of gray that exist in complex urban systems, all while shedding new light on the full humanity of those we have often considered pathological in the urban environment. As we

---

38. This nameless Ninevite king stands in stark contrast to the evil and idolatry of King Jeroboam of Israel in 1 Kgs 13–14.

39. Spina, *The Faith of the Outsider*, 112.

40. *The Wire* was a crime drama broadcast on HBO from 2002–2008. Noted for its urban realism, critics have long affirmed its complex portrayal of the American city.

learn in the story of Jonah, things are not only as they seem, and urban paganism often has another side to its idolatry.

Where *The Wire* most excels in its urban realism is its blurring of traditional moral categories and recognition of the unique interdependencies that exist in the (post)modern city. The cop is a crook, the politician is a thief, the dealer a victim, the user a hero, and the gangster a loyal friend. This is more than a mere reversal of moral roles, for the cop is also a protector, the politician is also a benefactor, the dealer is also a criminal, the user is also a pawn, and the gangster is also a ruthless killer. *The Wire* defies the simple, one-dimensional characterizations of heroes and villains in its blurring (but not eradication) of the lines between "good" and "evil," leaving both the protagonists and antagonists to muddle through their moral ambiguity in an endless series of nested ethical compromises.

At first glance, it may seem like the story of Jonah lacks this moral complexity, and its brevity, along with a tendency to (on the surface) reverse the roles of prophet and pagan, may seem simplistic. Yet a deeper reading of Jonah reveals a more subtle gradient of morality throughout the narrative; despite the strong overtones of reversal, there is a considerable range of nuance within each of those reversals. Jonah, disobedient from the beginning, is also honest and confessional in his encounters with the sailors, even knowing the potential cost to his well-being. Though his actions were unfaithful, his theology was soundly orthodox. The sailors, though quick to respond to YHWH's power, could also be construed as merely self-serving and outcome-oriented. Who can say what later came of their pragmatic paganism? Even Jonah's prayer has been subject to considerable criticism; it lacks a clear confession, and given how quickly his attitude reverses, the genuine nature of his transformation from the depths seems questionable. The Ninevites, also quick to respond to Jonah's oracle, are not known to have persisted in their repentance. Many scholars suggest that "Nineveh's deliverance lasted as long as their repentance. At the end of 40 days, they returned to their sinful ways and Jonah's prophecy overtook them."[41] Much like *The Wire,* Jonah's cast of characters is hardly flat and predictable. Even as the prophet's flaws are magnified while the pagans' virtues come to the fore, considerable complexity remains.

Urban ministry is nothing if not unpredictable and complex. The socioeconomic stereotypes and racialized categories that define urban existence are constructed powerfully by social norms and pervasive media. Notions of safety, trustworthiness, and integrity are juxtaposed with subtle (and at times, not so subtle) impressions of

---

41. James Nogalski, *Hosea-Jonah* (Macon, GA: Smyth & Helwys, 2011) 402.

aggression, duplicity, and criminality. Navigating these concerns across the cultural perceptions of race, class, and gender is no easy task in the city. The story of Jonah reminds the church to hold loosely to the boundaries we construct and the characters we assume to know in our neighborhoods. Again, a centered-set approach to cultural engagement helps to dismantle more binary implementations of "prophet-pagan" encounters that are inherently oppositional. Nineveh, it seems, was not at all what Jonah expected, and as we see in the final chapter of the story, his inability to process constructively his unmet expectations kept him from seeing the real fruit of his ministry.

Jonah Refuses God's Mercy

As the third chapter closes with God's change of heart in the wake of Nineveh's repentance, the fourth and final chapter of Jonah concludes with a disturbing reaction to the mercy of YHWH on the part of the prophet. The window we get into Jonah's rationale is a sad picture of a myopic and petulant man whose full understanding of YHWH was simply too parochial to account for God's gracious love extended to all. At the root of Jonah's cognitive dissonance is the *ḥesed* of YHWH, the steadfast mercy and loving kindness that disrupts Jonah's logic of retribution. Jonah's hypocrisy comes to a head in an ironic prayer that affirms God's gracious nature and yet refuses to accept its implications.

In what amounts to a prayerful outburst that closely resembles an emotional tantrum, v. 2 highlights what Jonah "knows," but does not truly know. "I knew that you are a gracious God and merciful, slow to anger, and abounding in steadfast love, and ready to relent from punishing."[42] The language of the Psalter is attributed to God's true character, and in response to this creedal confession of God's goodness Jonah wishes to die. What a way to end a prayer! Jonah's despair once again evokes the Lord's voice, and YHWH confronts Jonah's desperate wish for his life to be taken. As Jonah ponders all that has happened, he sulks off to the outskirts of the city and waits to see what God will do. Seeing the opportunity to take advantage of a teachable moment, God begins yet another vivid object lesson with Jonah. The plant that God appoints to provide shade for Jonah covers him with protection and lifts his downtrodden spirit. Just as Jonah begins to enjoy this newfound shelter, God uses a worm to attack the plant that then quickly withers away. To make it worse,

---

42. Jonah 4:2, NRSV. *Ḥesed* is translated here as "steadfast love."

God next prepares an oppressive, scorching wind that—in combination with the hot sun—leads Jonah back to where he was the day before: wishing to die.

In the final scene of the story, God once again confronts Jonah's anger over the plant, an episode that clearly demonstrates the sovereignty of YHWH's agency over life, death, and judgment. Jonah simply cannot see beyond his immediate circumstances, and even though his theological understanding of YHWH is adequate at times, his lived theology is found more than lacking again and again. The book closes in the same way that it began—with the great city of Nineveh. The people living in this imperial stronghold, the center of all that Israel finds detestable, are in fact the cherished concern of YHWH. These helpless souls are "like sheep without a shepherd,"[43] unable to make righteous choices and without a moral foundation. Even the animals are deserving of God's deep compassion, and their inclusion that mirrors their earlier repentance demonstrates both the depth and breadth of God's concern for the city and all of creation that sustains the city.

Overall, the dramatic reframing of Nineveh as deserving recipients of God's mercy reminds the reader of the complex meaning of *ḥesed*. More than mere relenting of judgment, *ḥesed* has a covenantal meaning that is infused with the steadfast love of YHWH that is continually shown to Israel. God desires for Israel to extend this same mercy to its pagan neighbors, and yet Jonah demonstrates the difficult nature of this responsibility. In the end, "Jonah has a complex purpose. On the one hand, it is steeped in the traditions of Israel's prophets. On the other hand, it is critical of the narrow nationalistic use of the traditions from which it draws ... the book holds Jonah's bigotry up to the light of day so that its readers see how ludicrous that bigotry appears against God's desire to reconcile with all."[44]

Toward Urban Reconciliation

The interwoven themes of prophet, pagan, and prayer give the reader an eclectic and varied perspective across the terrain of the text of Jonah. Adding the recurring motif of reversal and surprise along with an urban hermeneutic provide further points of connection for the meaning of this story in the city. No singular summary can bring neat resolution to such a layered text, but the conclusion of the story does leave the reader with an important question: Should not God be concerned about the city, especially the people, institutions, and systems that we have often written off as immoral or beyond hope of redemption?

43. Matt 9:36.
44. Nogalski, *Hosea*-Jonah, 406.

Jonah's tragic inability to reconcile God's gracious character with the actual outcome of that compassion in the world is an important lesson for the church's concern for the city. Gone are the days of prophetic ministry in which declarations of judgment are offered in only one direction (if ever such an approach was even merited to begin with). The urban prophet that too clearly distinguishes the guilt of the pagan and their own fallen nature is not only blind to humility, but also ignorant of the complicity that prophets and pagans often share in the city.

One of my former students now works in a homeless shelter in downtown Seattle, a shelter that shares many partnerships with churches in the area. For years these churches have volunteered to donate clothing, help serve meals, and conduct chapel services. Leading chapel was a particular favorite of several churches as it provided opportunities to share the good news of salvation to the poor and needy men who are looking for "three hots (meals) and a cot." My student noticed something right away about the nature of these chapel services, namely, that the interaction—or lack thereof—amounted to what seemed like "drive-by preaching." Cheery volunteers from across town would pop in for a song and sermon routine and then take off as quickly as they had arrived, sometimes pausing to hand out a piece of bread. The messages, though not overtly condemning, were somewhat "bounded-set" in their approach as to who was saved and who needed saving. Prophetic ministry was little more than naming the vices and moral failings that lead to poverty, and then concluding with some charitable but distant gestures of kindness.

Like Israel's expectations of their exclusive status as God's chosen people, these homeless shelter preachers had—however kindly—identified the paganism in "the other" without making much space for a recognition of their own idols: safety, security, certainty, and self-determination. My former student decided to redesign completely the church partnership program from "chapel and charity" to "reconciliation between the rich and the poor." Rather than drive-by, drop-in assistance, interested churches could come to the shelter for a ten-week Bible study based on *Friendship at the Margins*.[45] After completing the study these church volunteers would commit to returning each week for a time of unstructured conversation and fellowship with the men at the shelter for the purposes of building friendship and mutual understanding. Sadly, of the dozens of churches once eager to volunteer at the shelter, there was only one church that agreed to make the transition to this new kind of partnership.

---

45. Christopher Heuertz and Christine Pohl, *Friendship at the Margins* (Downers Grove, IL: InterVarsity, 2010).

The clarity that comes with rigid prophet-pagan categories may be inaccurate, but it sure is comfortable.

Christian reconciliation is a journey and not a destination, a process and not a product. Prophets and pagans coming together to share words of truth and confess mutual brokenness will not turn the city around in an instant, but it does have the potential to bear witness to the kingdom of God, a reality that breaks into the present when theologies of reversal run their course in God's surprising economy of who is first and last. Though the language of reconciliation continues to be contested ground for many,[46] the story of Jonah in all of its reversals teaches us to hold loosely to our prophetic expectations and to remain open to the virtues of the other who may have more to offer and teach us than we assume. Prayer, lament, memory, and hope surround the ambiguity of reconciliation with concrete practices for urban ministry. The church that prays in the tension between suffering and deliverance can surely become adept to the uncertainty of the city and the challenges therein. Jonah's story continues as we encounter and pursue the sailors and Ninevites in our midst with genuine compassion and concern. May the people of God respond to the word of YHWH with humility, faithfulness, and hope.

---

46. "Reconciliation" can often be used as a cipher for other agendas or further negotiation of power when those with privilege are the facilitators of the process. See Willie Jennings, *The Christian Imagination* (New Haven: Yale University Press, 2010) 9–10.

RESPONSE TO LEONG

Daniel White Hodge

Jonah was an unusual "prophet,"[1] to say the least. His message to the city of Nineveh was in an unusual form of patronizing hermeneutic with a singe of judgment and condemnation. Jonah's narrative, while told in the prose of joy and the "following of God's word," presents a troubling theological dilemma, a dilemma that creates a top-down, hierarchal, and paternalistic status to that of the missionary, youth worker, and messenger of God in any context. Moreover, this dilemma of a theological nature is interestingly close to a neocolonialist worldview that argues for *its way* being the correct way to live and work out "God's law."[2] Further, if Jonah's overall character is to be followed as a prime example of a missionary, then we have to examine critically what God is actually calling us to and where to "go forth" because Jonah presents problematic ontologies that by the end of the book are revealed in the discourse God is having with him.

David Leong presents us with a challenge as he views Jonah from the perspectives of prophet, pagan, and prayer. The story of Jonah, while short and brief, presents missiological issues that we as the body of Christ must take into consideration. Leong argues well that "things are not always what they seem" and that Jonah does in fact fall short of God's intent for Nineveh.

In response to Leong's paper I have found five contemporary socio-theological tropes in the Christian faith that connect with the story of Jonah and also with what Leong raises in his paper and that affirm my argument that Jonah was practicing a form of neocolonialism.

---

1. In this sense, it should be asked, can Jonah even be called a prophet? A prophet is one who speaks for God and contains divine inspiration for a people, place, or object. It could be argued that, in one sense, Jonah did neither of these to the fullest; while he did have a "message" and eventually fulfilled God's call on his life, it was done, arguably, in a space in which he almost wanted the people to perish—thus negating the very essence of what a prophet should and can be. See John MacArthur, "Jonah," in *The MacArthur Topical Bible: New King James Version* (Nashville: Word, 1999).

2. For an examination of such concepts, see Zygmunt Bauman, "Postmodern Religion?," in *Religion, Modernity, and Postmodernity*, ed. Paul Heelas (Oxford: Blackwell, 1998); *Liquid Modernity* (Malden, MA: Polity, 2000); J. Kameron Carter, *Race: A Theological Account* (New York: Oxford University Press, 2008).

First, *fear generated by a culture of ontological fear*. Barry Glassner, sociologist and author of *The Culture of Fear*, reminds us that as Americans, we fear the wrong things; fear, which at times is constructed in media frenzies over terrorism, killer teenagers, wicked bowling alleys, and the like, is amplified in the U.S. and thus a development of a culture of fear is established.[3] This type of fear does not limit itself to the doorsteps of "secular" America; it is well entrenched within religious institutions such as the Christian church and Western Evangelicalism.

Fear is rooted in many of our Christian ecclesiologies: fear of terrorism, fear of our nation being "lost," fear of the loss of "values" and "morals," fear of "those people," and fear of the other.[4] Generations of seminary students receive heavy doses of this fear only to pass it along to the next generation. Fear causes groups to create laws. Fear causes people to create borders. Fear also creates an inner desire for safety. Leong is correct in stating, "Jonah allows his fear to dictate his disobedience," and we see this pattern in Jonah's story.

In Jonah's instance fear of heading into an urban complex and people who were, as one commentator wrote, "a godless people" was overwhelming and causes Jonah to flee. A fear like Jonah's is also present today: fear of the city, fear of things such as Hip Hop or rap music, and fear that people will influence us to sin. Fear keeps missionaries captive in their work. People fear the actual work God has called us to do, and potentially they fear that God's message might actually change a group into something we were not expecting them to be, or even more culturally shocking, into a space and place that is foreign to the norms, beliefs, values, and language we revere as "the right way."

This fear of the other and "secular culture" is a crucial area of discussion for those who consider themselves "missionaries." This fear has direct implications for how we interpret and live out the Great Commission and the mandate Jesus gave us to "go forth" into the nations to those who are different from us in culture and tongue. Just as with Jonah, fear will keep us at bay and will not allow us truly to engage and allow God to do God's work.

Second, *the "unprophet" concept: safely living in the suburbs yet proclaiming "truth" for the city from a securitized zone*. This concept is critical and an area that deserves much more attention, research, and scholarship. Who is it that gets to tell the

---

3. Barry Glassner, *The Culture of Fear: Why Americans Are Afraid of the Wrong Things* (New York: Basic, 1999) xi–2.

4. In this sense "the other" refers to ethnic minority groups, first generation ethnic minority immigrants, and anything or anyone who does not adhere to a conservative American Evangelical Christianity, thus creating a sense of the other.

story of God and how are their own racial, gender, and class biases already embedded in the theological DNA?[5] Moreover, in Jonah's case he was approaching Nineveh from a top-down, paternalistic, hegemonic perspective; in other words, I have the "truth" and ultimately these people will burn when they do not follow God. We see Jonah's intent and mindset similar to this in the dialog that ensues in chapter 4.

Being safe, wanting to be secure, and the desire for protection has tended to take a racial, cultural, and religio-hegenomic stance in post-9/11 America. This concept of safety within "our borders" or "within our home" is one that has nationalism and pious discourse laced throughout. Jonah's worldview led him to flee, flee not only from God's calling on his life but for safety and escape. Even after Jonah had preached God's message, the people repented, and God's wrath was averted, he left. Jonah left the city. He did not stay and contextualize himself, as missiologist and renowned missionary Wilbert Shenk encourages people to do.[6] He did not help the people and walk with them, as Daniel Shaw and Charles Van Engen challenge missionaries to do.[7] Instead, he leaves, which can be interpreted as a fleeing back to safety as Nineveh's reputation was known as a "bloody city."[8] This safety and securitized missiology must be challenged as it is not the way of the *missio Dei*, nor is it part of the Great Commission.

This brings us to our third socio-theological trope, *refusal to go into the city, with the result that the city continues to deteriorate*. With the advance of gentrification, white flight, and a mindset from those "outside" the city that it is dangerous, urban contexts continue to deteriorate. We seek safety and security, so why would anyone want to go to a gang, drug, and violent zone?

The city is not for the weak at heart. With such a context, with so much nihilism, and with diminished hope of success, who would want to do "God's work" in such a place? This is exactly the type of work to which the gospel calls us, which

---

5. Race and ethnicity play a large role in how missionaries carry out their mandate and calling with a people group. Conservative, rigid, liberal, or progressive ideas all affect the way the gospel is ultimately received, and when there is a superiority complex already infused within a racist bias (even if unknown), the gospel can be tainted with that and with a continuing neo-urban colonialism. For more on this subject and the conversation about race and God, see Michael Barkun, *Religion and the Racist Right : The Origins of the Christian Identity Movement*, rev. ed. (Chapel Hill: University of North Carolina Press, 1997); Carter, *Race*; and Soong-Chan Rah, *The Next Evangelicalism: Releasing the Church from Western Cultural Captivity* (Downers Grove, IL: InterVarsity, 2009).

6. Wilbert R. Shenk, *Write the Vision: The Church Renewed*, Christian Mission and Modern Culture (Eugene, OR: Wipf and Stock, 2001).

7. Daniel R Shaw and Charles E. Van Engen, *Communicating God's Word in a Complex World: God's Truth or Hocus Pocus* (Lanham, MD: Rowan & Littlefield, 2003).

8. MacArthur, "Jonah."

Jonah failed to see. Yes, it is difficult and sometimes full of misery, but it is what God is calling some to do. Jonah tried to avoid the tough call altogether, and when he eventually did heed God's call, why did he? Was it to appease his own pain in the belly of the beast? Was it to make himself feel better after doing "God's work?" These are difficult questions, but even more so for the missionary who feels called to urban ministry. We must remember David Bosch's words regarding the city: "[T]he adjective 'poor' was increasingly used to qualify the noun 'heathen.' It appears times without number in the literature . . . The patent needs of the 'poor heathen' became one of the strongest arguments in favor of mission . . . God's love had deteriorated into patronizing charity."[9] This seems to describe Jonah and many other urban missionaries.

It is imperative that we examine motives behind our efforts. Jonah did not do that well, and Leong is correct in asserting that those called often have the tendency to drift into exclusivity and miss out on the possibilities on "faith from the outsider." This creates walls and barriers, and the city itself is not truly reconciled to God nor are its systems of oppression ever overthrown.

Fourth, *a centered set prophetic word* was part of Jonah's message. Leong pointed to Paul Hiebert's idea of bounded and centered set theology, which applies to Jonah. Jonah approached Nineveh with a bounded set message, a message of the gospel with boundaries. You are either in *this way* or out *that way*. Jonah expected the people of Nineveh to be and act a certain way. After all, Christians *should* reflect good Christian behavior, correct? But what does that actually mean and how has that been socially constructed?

Today we see a similar spirit in those entering spaces to "bring the gospel." There are clear markers of what is accepted and what is not. The initial knee-jerk response is "Shouldn't there be boundaries? Doesn't God clearly say what *sin is* and what *isn't*?" I would argue we should sit in the tension of that question. For too long we have jumped at the opportunity to "preach" to people without ever engaging real issues; now we have a generation that desires to push past a "just pray about it" response and desires a much more complex engagement with God. Ambiguity and mystery are okay. As Anthony Pinn reminds us, we need to get into the "nitty-gritty hermeneutic" and move out past a simplistic response and bounded set theology.[10]

---

9. David Jacobus Bosch, *Transforming Mission : Paradigm Shifts in Theology of Mission*, American Society of Missiology (Maryknoll, NY: Orbis, 1991) 290.

10. Anthony B Pinn, *Why Lord? Suffering and Evil in Black Theology* (New York: Continuum, 1995) 114–17.

Fifth, *patronizing charity and a disdain for the "other"* was at the heart of Jonah's message. Jonah leaves Nineveh frustrated and angered that God did not destroy the people. Why should he have gone at all? What was the real reason behind his mission? Did Jonah actually expect God to burn down the city and the people in it?

In my own research on apocalyptic and eschatological themes in popular culture, I found a number of Christians and religious people who, in fact, anxiously wait for God to kill, burn, and maim the "wicked." People expressed a sense of joy in thinking about those who were in the world being burned and given what they "deserved" for a life without God. This is not that far from Jonah in chapter 4. This chapter reveals a type of patronizing charity and a true disdain for those who are considered to be "other" or outside what is socially acceptable for Christians. Such attitudes are one of the main reasons this generation of young people is turning away from Christian faith.

Leong is correct to reject such judgmental attitudes, such lack of humility, and a one-way approach to evangelism. Jonah's example makes a strong case to move beyond simply "proclaiming" God's truth to living it among the people. Guilt, shame, emotional arm twisting, and top-down authoritative missiology are not the call of the Great Commission.

Jonah's four chapters illustrate a mixed, multifaceted, and complex message that can be construed in different ways. On the one hand, this story is told to children in churches as a heroic narrative, one of valor and "following God's call." Yet, when we push further into chapters 3 and 4, we see a different side to Jonah, a side that is both patronizing and prejudicial toward the people of Nineveh. This is why it is important to discuss the motives of each person entering a mission field. Are you doing what you are doing because you want to help "those people"? Is it because you feel that this place "needs Jesus"? Or, is it out of a genuine call from God to enter in? If the latter, then the serious work of intercultural communication, racial awareness, gender consciousness, and class mindfulness needs to be done and continued throughout life. If not, missionaries will assume that *their way* of Christianity is *the right way* to do things without considering the complex and rich narratives of what God has been doing in other cultures and societies. This is also why we must give attention to cultures and people groups such as Hip Hop as they provide prophetic messages for people about God and life with God that cannot be ignored. Moreover, spaces like Hip Hop Culture offer room for mystery, ambiguity, and doubt—a key tenet in the Mosaic Generation.[11] Leong presents us with strong challenges to missions, urban

---

11. This is a term that the Barna Research group assigned to the group of young adults between

missions, and the city of God. We must carefully consider his contribution and move past a singular modality of viewing God[12] and engage in the multicultural richness that God's kingdom truly is.

---

the ages of nineteen and twenty-nine.

12. Which all too often is a western, white, conservative, evangelical message; there is nothing wrong with that in and of itself, but it is not the only road to Christ nor the only form of Christianity.

THE MINISTERIAL SIGNIFICANCE OF EARLY SYRIAC THEOLOGY

Vince L. Bantu

Since the Civil Rights Movement, Islam has experienced increasing growth in the African American community, and it shows no sign of slowing down. As a native of the Bible Belt, this phenomenon came as somewhat of a surprise to me when I first became involved in ministry in the urban Northeast a decade ago. Escalating numbers of African Americans (especially young men) have joined movements such as Sunni Islam, Nation of Islam, Five Percent Nation, and traditional African (often Yoruba) religious groups. Perhaps the most interesting aspect of this phenomenon from a missiological perspective is that the vast majority of African American converts to Islamic and other religious movements have some degree of a Christian background. Dissatisfied with the relatively mild response to white racism from the black church, many African Americans have found Islam a more empowering platform as black Islam in the U.S. has been characterized since its inception by vehement social critique.[1]

Common among black Muslims is the belief that Christianity is a "white man's religion" and that Islam was the religion of American slaves.[2] It is also of interest that the identity of black Muslims is largely motivated by social, as opposed to theological, concerns. When one listens, for example, to the speeches of Malcolm X, there is an apparent lack of intimate acquaintance with the Qur'an or hadith but, rather, a sociologically-centered message that is agreeable to many black Christians. The frequent lack of actual knowledge of Islamic belief and practice among many African American Muslims becomes even more evident when engaging in ministry in the urban, black community. Over the years I have encountered countless young black men who want nothing to do with Christianity for reasons of their religious identity as a Muslim, often simultaneously citing dissatisfaction with Christianity. Yet so

---

1. C. Eric Lincoln, *The Black Muslims in America*, 3rd ed. (Grand Rapids: Eerdmans, 1994) xx.
2. Glenn Usry and Craig S. Keener, *Black Man's Religion: Can Christianity Be Afrocentric?* (Downers Grove, IL: InterVarsity, 1996) 8.

many of the same young men will still smoke weed, drink alcohol, use profanity, and engage in behavior unbecoming of a devout Muslim.

This is not to diminish the same kind of inconsistent behavior common in many Christian and other religious communities. However, it is significant that so many urban blacks will display such an obvious lack of acquaintance with Muslim teaching while still strongly asserting a Muslim identity through certain gestures such as wearing a kufi or having a crescent tattoo on their cheek. The baffling reality is this: while Islam's chief critique of Christianity has historically been the doctrine of the Trinity, African American Islam's primary qualm with Christianity is not theological at all, but racial. This phenomenon has severe implications for the mission of the church. Christians have created the single greatest stumbling block to non-Christians coming to faith in Christ: the Western captivity of the church.[3] European Christians have for centuries communicated the idea that the message of the gospel is truly expressed only through Western, eurocentric media, and non-western Christians have swallowed this nonsense wholesale.

Whether in the form of Scandinavian depictions of Jesus, individualistic theology or racial demographics in Christian higher education, the Western captivity of the church has thoroughly permeated the Christian tradition and is the single greatest reason non-Western people have no desire to participate in a religion that is perceived as American, Western, white, or all of the above.[4] The example outlined above is one of many people groups that feel culturally alienated from Christianity. Countless Native American, Asian, African, and Middle Eastern communities share the sentiment that to be a Christian is fundamentally at odds with their cultural identity. Even as Christianity is increasingly perceived as a global religion whose center is now the Global South,[5] the Christian communities of Africa, Asia, and Latin America often experience an imported version of Christianity that continues to empower Western cultural captivity.

For the gospel to take firm root among all peoples, the idea of the superiority of Christianity laden with Western cultural values must be rejected. Conversely, non-Western expressions of Christianity should be cultivated and promoted in order to reflect a church that is truly for all peoples. Though necessary, this task becomes

---

3. Soong-Chan Rah, *The Next Evangelicalism: Freeing the Church from Western Cultural Captivity* (Downers Grove, IL: InterVarsity, 2009) 18.

4. Randy Woodley, *Living in Color: Embracing God's Passion for Ethnic Diversity* (Downers Grove, IL: InterVarsity, 2001) 45.

5. Philip Jenkins, *The Next Christendom: The Coming of Global Christianity* (Oxford: Oxford University Press, 2002) 2.

increasingly difficult for non-Western Christians whose Christian history is inextricably bound to racism, slavery, and colonialism. As in the case of black Muslims, the idea that Christianity is the religion of the white man will persist. It is, therefore, necessary for modern Christians to understand the rich history of the church in the non-Western world beginning in the early period. The Coptic, Syriac, Armenian, Ethiopian, and other Christian communities of the Near East serve as a powerful testimony that Christianity is not *becoming*, but has always been a global, multiethnic religion.

Acquaintance with Christian tradition that developed free of Western cultural captivity will further empower the modern church in moving away from Eurocentrism and toward becoming a house of prayer for all nations. The following study will analyze one of the greatest examples of indigenous, non-Western Christian tradition—the Syriac Christian community and its most significant figure, Ephrem the Syrian. Ephrem was a fourth-century deacon, poet, monk, and teacher who devised a captivating theological method that utilized indigenous cultural methods to express orthodox Christian belief, thereby transforming the Syriac Christian world. With a specific focus on the contextualized theological method that developed through Ephrem, consideration will also be given to contemporary efforts at cultivating multiethnic expressions of Christianity.

Historical Background of Syriac Christianity and Ephrem

Over the centuries there have been many Christian communities from various ecclesiastical, national, and ethnic affiliations that shared a common heritage rooted in the Syriac-speaking world. A few prominent examples include the Syrian Orthodox Church (also called Jacobite, after Jacob Baradaeus, sixth-century bishop of Urhoy), the Assyrian Church of the East (often erroneously labeled "Nestorian"; including a substantial constituency in China during the medieval period), the Maronite Church, the Chaldean Catholic Church, and the various Saint Thomas Christian communities of Kerala, India. Over two millennia across the continent of Asia various Christian communities have expressed diverse forms of worship grounded in different (and often opposing) theological positions, united primarily in their shared heritage of a dialect of Aramaic called Syriac.

Though the Syriac language, as well as the Syriac-speaking Christian tradition, eventually spread throughout the continent of Asia, they both originally developed in an ancient city named Urhoy (often called by its Greek name "Edessa"; modern Urfa in southeast Turkey). The culture of Urhoy has always been cosmopolitan as there have been several ruling powers over the centuries.[6] Although Urhoy does not enter the written record until the Hellenistic period, it is of little doubt that this well-watered site was frequently visited and possibly settled during the Persian Achaemenid Empire (550–330 BCE).[7] Following the conquest of the region by Alexander the Great in 334 BCE, Urhoy was officially settled in the Hellenistic Seleucid kingdom and named Edessa after a city of the same name in the Macedonian homeland.

At the end of the second century BCE the Persian Parthian Empire took advantage of the increasing internal rivalries between the Seleucid, Ptolemaic, and ascendant Roman kingdoms and assumed control of the region. During Parthian rule Urhoy, including its surrounding region Osrhoene, established a local kingship system called the Abgarid dynasty.[8] During Parthian hegemony Urhoy developed a friendly relationship with Rome, though there was no attempt at incorporating Urhoy into the Roman empire until the second century CE, Urhoy/Osrhoene's incorporation into Roman territory was a century-long process that began with Trajan's campaign against Parthia in 114 CE and culminated with the last native king of Urhoy, Abgar X, becoming a Roman consul in 242 CE.

The *Teaching of Addai* is an early fifth-century Syriac text that narrates the legend of how Christianity came to Urhoy through a personal correspondence between King Abgar Ukkama ("Black") and Jesus that resulted in the apostle Thaddeus[9] evangelizing Urhoy and establishing the first Syriac-speaking church.[10] Although the historicity of the Abgar legend is largely dismissed by contemporary scholarship,[11] an earlier account of the same story appears in Eusebius' *Ecclesiastical History*.[12] It is generally accepted that Christianity came to Urhoy no later than the late second century and to the neighboring city of Nisibis soon after.[13] Likewise, the Syriac ver-

---

6. The Antiochene orator Malalas reports that Seleucus I referred to Urhoy as a "half-barbarian Antioch." See Steven K. Ross, *Roman Edessa: Politics and Culture on the Eastern Fringes of the Roman Empire, 114–242 CE* (London: Routledge, 2001) 8.

7. Ross, *Roman Edessa*, 5; J. B. Segal, *Edessa: "The Blessed City"* (Oxford: Oxford University Press, 1970) 3.

8. After the royal name that appears most often during this dynasty, "Abgar."

9. Saint Addai, or Thaddeus of Edessa, alleged to be one of the seventy apostles; not to be confused with Thaddeus of the twelve apostles.

10. *The Teaching of Addai*, ed. George Howard (Atlanta: SBL, 1981).

11. Ross, *Roman Edessa*, 136. Walter Bauer, *Orthodoxy and Heresy in Earliest Christianity*, eds. Robert A. Kraft and Gerhard Krodel, trans. Philadelphia Seminar on Christian Origins (Philadelphia: Fortress, 1971) 11.

12. Eusebius, *Ecclesiastical History* 1.12, ed. Paul L. Maier (Grand Rapids: Kregel, 1999).

13. Ross, *Roman Edessa*, 117; Bauer, *Orthodoxy and Heresy*, 13; Wilhelm Baum and Dietmar Winkler. *The Church of the East: A Concise History* (London: Routledge, 2003) 8. An inscription attributed to Bishop Aberkios attests the existence of Christianity in Nisibis no later than the late second century.

sions of both OT and NT were most likely translated in the first century but certainly no later than the second.[14] Like the majority of the Roman Empire, Christianity in Urhoy was theologically varied, and orthodoxy was not clearly defined before the fourth century. Christians of Urhoy were strongly influenced by the writings of Marcion, Bardaisan, and Mani, all of whom were declared heretics later by the greatest Syriac champion of Nicene orthodoxy, Ephrem. Not until the fourth century did orthodox theology as represented by figures such as Aphrahat and Ephrem (whose background is discussed in greater detail below) become the mainstream doctrine.[15]

During the second and third centuries, while Roman Christianity lived under frequent waves of persecution, the East Syriac Christians living in the Persian Parthian Empire experienced a much more peaceful existence. It is most likely that Syriac Christianity came to the Persian Empire through Jewish merchants traveling the Silk Road.[16] Greek-speaking Christian refugees from the Roman Empire also arrived at Persia in large numbers in the third century and were called "Christians" (*krestyane*) as opposed to the native, Syriac-speaking Christians who were called "Nazarenes" (*nasraye*). The Syriac Christians of the Persian Empire (the Church of the East) became independent in 410 CE[17] and were declared heretics shortly after the Council of Ephesus (431 CE) because of their close association with the teachings of Theodore of Mopsuestia. The exegetical training institution called the

---

See Kathleen E. McVey and John Meyendorff, *Ephrem the Syrian: Hymns* (New York: Paulist, 1989) 6.

14. M. P. Weitzman, *The Syriac Version of the Old Testament: An Introduction* (Cambridge: Cambridge University Press, 1999) 2. The standard Syriac Bible today is the Peshitta ("simple," "straightforward") and results from the combination of the standard OT and NT, which took place no later than the ninth century in order to distinguish them from contemporary translations. See Sebastian Brock, *The Bible in the Syriac Tradition* (Piscataway, NJ: Gorgias, 2006) 23.

15. Robert Murray argued (*Symbols of Church and Kingdom: A Study in Early Syriac Tradition* [Cambridge: Cambridge University Press, 1975] 6–9) that what later was declared orthodox Christianity developed first in the Syriac-speaking world in Nisibis and not Urhoy. This argument is based largely on the fact that Nisibis produced orthodox Syriac Christianity's earliest figures in Aphrahat and Ephrem, whereas the earliest Christian figures of Urhoy were heretics such as Bardaisan, Marcion and Mani. See also Segal, *Edessa*, 62. This view is rooted in Bauer's thesis (*Orthodoxy and Heresy*, 229) that orthodox Christianity developed in Rome while heretical movements came from exterior territories of the empire. This Eurocentric view fails to account for the presence of heretics in Rome such as Valentinus, as well as early pillars of orthodoxy in Syria and Egypt such as Tatian and Clement of Alexandria. It is most probable that Nisibene Christianity was as theologically varied in the second century as Urhoy.

16. Wilhelm Baum and Dietmar Winkler, *The Church of the East*, 8. The same theory is advanced for the beginning of East Syriac Christianity in China in the mid-sixth century (p. 47) while the introduction of Christianity to India seems to have been the result of direct missionary activity in the early fourth century (p. 53).

17. As opposed to the more common date of 424 CE; see Baum, and Winkler, *The Church of the East*, 19.

School of the Persians was forced out of Urhoy by emperor Zeno in 489 CE because of its allegiance to the teachings of Theodore (as well as to Diodore of Tarsus and Nestorius). Led by renowned East Syriac scholar Narsai, the school moved to Nisibis and flourished as the School of Nisibis for several centuries.[18]

Shortly after the Council of Ephesus, the Council of Chalcedon (451 CE) caused mixed reactions among the West Syriac Christians in the Roman empire and many West Syrians were greatly influenced by the anti-Chalcedonian teachings of Severus of Antioch and the missionary work of John of Tella. The imposition of Chalcedonian doctrine by the Byzantine Emperor Justinian and his convening of the Second Council of Constantinople (553 CE) marked the permanent separation of the majority of Syriac-speaking Christians from European Christendom and the official formation of the Syrian Orthodox Church.[19] The Christian communities of India during this period were predominately affiliated with this community, and even today the largest constituency of the Syrian Orthodox Church is in India. Meanwhile the Christian communities of Central Asia and China were predominately affiliated with the Church of the East.[20]

While the Syriac Christian communities of the Roman and Persian empires continued to flourish despite the former being cut off from Roman imperial Christendom and the latter suffering persecution under the Sasanid Empire, the dawn of Islam radically changed the fates of Syriac Christians in both empires. The career of the prophet Muhammad as well as the composition of the Qur'an took place in a milieu where Syriac-speaking Christians and Jews already had a historical presence.

However, as a result of the Arab conquest immediately followed by the Rashidun and Umayyad Caliphates during the seventh and eighth centuries, the entire Syriac-speaking world now found itself under Muslim rule. While Christians who accepted the Council of Chalcedon (Melkites) expressed hope for a Byzantine recovery of Mesopotamia, those who rejected Chalcedon (Miaphysites and Church of the East)

---

18. The School of Nisibis modeled itself closely after the School of the Persians in Urhoy. See Adam H. Becker, *Sources for the Study of the School of Nisibis* (Liverpool: Liverpool University Press, 2008) 5. Becker demonstrates the way the School of Nisibis founded much of its identity and character on its immediate predecessor, the School of the Persians in Urhoy. See his *Fear of God and the Beginning of Wisdom: The School of Nisibis and Christian Scholastic Culture in Late Antique Mesopotamia* (Philadelphia: University of Pennsylvania Press, 2006) 74.

19. Volker L. Menze, *Justinian and the Making of the Syrian Orthodox Church* (Oxford: Oxford University Press, 2008) 249.

20. However, the Church of the East died out in Central and East Asia in the mid-fourteenth century due to China's cutting itself off from the West; see Baum and Winkler, *The Church of the East*, 104.

expressed no loyalty to either Byzantine or Muslim rule.[21] In fact, it is probable that Christians living under early Islamic rule did not perceive the conquest initially as religious in nature.[22]

Syriac literature immediately following the Islamic conquest portrayed Islam and Muhammad in nonpolemical terms, and only in the early eighth century was literature critical of Islam composed.[23] Syriac Christians began to produce literature both in Syriac and Arabic engaging in cultural, social, and theological conversations with their Muslim rulers. Bilingual figures such as Theodore Abu Qurrah, who wrote both in Arabic and Syriac,[24] represented a new age of Arabic-speaking Christians rooted in the Syriac heritage. The story of Syriac Christians under Muslim rule is characterized by steady marginalization; today the language's current form (Neo-Aramaic) is spoken by small minorities in modern Syria, Iraq, and Turkey. However, out of the long, rich heritage of Syriac Christianity the figure who stands out as most significant is Saint Ephrem.

Because Ephrem's biography was written two centuries after his lifetime, it is more useful to consult his own writings and those of his contemporaries for historical information regarding his life. The dates for Ephrem's life are commonly agreed upon as 306–373 CE; while the date of his death is fairly certain, his birth date is an approximation.[25] Ephrem's writings indicate that he was born to Christian parents in the city of Nisibis where he served as a deacon and theological instructor under various bishops.[26] Because the Syriac-speaking community existed along the frontiers straddling the Roman/Persian border, political tension between these two empires was a highly influential factor in the lives of Syriac Christians.

After the reforms of Constantine in which Roman Christians were afforded unprecedented autonomy, the Roman emperor sent a letter threatening that Persian Christians would be loyal to Rome in the event of war.[27] Persian Christians such as

---

21. G. J. Reinink, *Syriac Christianity under Late Sasanian and Early Islamic Rule* (Aldershot, NH: Ashgate, 2005) 157.

22. Ibid., 166.

23. Ibid., 182.

24. Although only his Arabic corpus survives. See Sidney H. Griffith, *The Church in the Shadow of the Mosque: Christians and Muslims in the World of Islam* (Princeton: Princeton University Press, 2008) 60.

25. Sebastian P. Brock, *The Luminous Eye: The Spiritual World Vision of Saint Eprhem the Syrian* (Kalamazoo, MI: Cistercian, 1985) 16.

26. Sebastian P. Brock, *St. Ephrem the Syrian: Hymns on Paradise* (Crestwood, NY: St. Vladimir's Seminary Press, 1990) 9.

27. Sebastian P. Brock, "Christians in the Sasanian Empire: A Case of Divided Loyalties," in *Religion and National Identity*, ed. S. Mews, Studies in Church History 18 (Oxford: Oxford University

Aphrahat expressed vehement distaste for the Persian king in favor of the Roman emperor.[28] Whether or not a direct result of such statements, the fourth century saw the beginning of wide-scale persecution of Christians in the Persian empire, as well as increasing interest in political expansion following the death of Constantine. During Ephrem's life in Nisibis the Persian Empire made three incursions into Nisibis, the third resulting in the Persian king Shapur II damming the local river in order to flood the city. However, the most significant historical event in Ephrem's lifetime was when the Roman emperor Julian was killed during an incursion into Persian territory and Nisibis came under Persian authority.

Ephrem attributed the fall of Nisibis to the pagan practices of the Roman emperor in his *Hymns Against Julian*.[29] A result of Nisibis's annexation to Persia was the evacuation of the region's Christian population. This resulted in an exile of Nisibene Christians, including Ephrem.[30] Ephrem is most often depicted iconographically in monastic habit, and he is often labeled as "the prince of the monks."[31] This is due to his association with a form of protomonasticism native to the environs of Urhoy and Nisibis, as opposed to the Egyptian style of monasticism that became influential in Syria after Ephrem's lifetime.[32] Syriac Christians committed to living in simplicity in small communities serving the needs of the local church were called *ihidaye*

Press, 1982) 1–19, 7.

28. Ibid., 8. Despite the common belief that all Persian Christians held such an attitude, many Christians under Persian rule actually maintained patriotic loyalty to the shah despite religious differences. See S. J. McDonough, "A Question of Faith? Persecution and Political Centralization in the Sasanian Empire of Yazdgard II (438–457 CE)," in *Violence in Late Antiquity: Perceptions and Practices*, ed. H. A. Drake (Aldershot: Ashgate, 2006) 67–82, 78.

29. McVey and Meyendorff, *Ephrem the Syrian*, 23.

30. Although Ephrem initially found the conditions of Perisan Nisibis agreeable and encountered no opposition, he eventually made his way to Urhoy. See Arthur Vööbus, *Literary Critical and Historical Studies in Ephrem the Syrian* (Wetteren, Belgium: Imprimerie Cultura, 1958) 51.

31. Ibid., 112.

32. This has led Brock to oppose vehemently the labeling of Ephrem as a "monk." This is rightfully out of a desire to avoid confusion with that later system that would be introduced from Egypt that would employ the more technical term *monachos*. See Brock, *St. Ephrem the Syrian*, 26; also Vööbus, *Literary Critical and Historical Studies*, 129. However, this is based largely in the false dichotomization of Egyptian monasticism as a solitary, desert phenomenon in contrast to the more urban/village movement that sprang up in Mesopotamia. James E. Goehring has demonstrated that early coenobitic monasticism as it developed in the Pachomian communities of Upper Egypt were intricately involved with, if not located within, urban centers. See his *Ascetics, Society and the Desert: Studies in Early Egyptian Monasticism* (Harrisburg, PA: Trinity, 1999) 46. Because monasticism has taken so many forms in various places over the centuries, it is not necessary to assume that calling Ephrem a "monk" is to equate him with the coenobitic tradition of Egypt. It is an accessible label that describes devout Christians who formulate a specific ministerial community characterized by profound spiritual piety, sexual purity, and service of the poor, as was the case for the *ihidaye*.

("single," "celibate," "straightforward," "single-minded"). By Ephrem's lifetime, the *ihidaye* consisted of both single people, *bthule* ("virgins"), and married people, *qaddishe* ("sanctified"), who had renounced marital intercourse.

Ephrem's concern for the poor is demonstrated in the report given in Palladius's *Lausiac History* of Ephrem's leadership during a famine in Urhoy, during which he challenged the wealthy to share resources with the poor and supervised the distribution of food and shelter.[33] This story, along with general praise for Ephrem's monastic and theological contributions, is recorded in other historians contemporary to Palladius such as Sozomen and Jerome.[34] During the final decade of his life while in Urhoy, Ephrem lived in a monastic cell in the mountains but made frequent visits to the city.[35] In the sixth century the composition of the Syriac *Life of Ephrem* began the legend of Ephrem's meeting with the Egyptian monastic leader Bishoi and the Cappadocian bishop Basil (at which time Ephrem is said to have been miraculously endowed with the ability to speak Greek).[36]

Ephrem served under various bishops as a theological instructor in Nisibis for the local church before going to Urhoy. The East Syriac scholar Barhadbshabba, in his *The Cause of the Foundation of the Schools*, attributes the beginning of what would eventually be called the School of Nisibis to Ephrem's early teaching career in Nisibis.[37] After the flight from Nisibis following the death of Julian, Ephrem began teaching at the School of the Persians in Urhoy. The arrival of Ephrem and the Nisibene Christians dramatically increased the literary activity and reputation of the School of the Persians as new theological skills arrived in Urhoy.[38] Much of Ephrem's theological focus during the last decade of his life spent in Urhoy was combating the theological views of the followers of Bardaisan, Marcion, and Mani, three heavily influential predecessors of Ephrem whom he vehemently opposed as heretics.

---

33. Palladius, *Lausiac History*, ed. Robert T. Meyer (Mahwah, NJ: Paulist, 1964) 116 17.
34. Brock, *St. Ephrem the Syrian*, 15.
35. Vööbus, *Literary Critical and Historical Studies*, 53.
36. Brock, *St. Ephrem the Syrian*, 21.
37. Becker, *Sources for the Study*, 149–50. Becker's edition contains an English translation of the text with an introduction and notes. Becker also demonstrates the manner in which Ephrem's description of God as the teacher became influential among the School of the Persians two centuries later. See Becker, *Fear of God*, 26.
38. Becker, *Fear of God*, 41.

Ephrem's Theological Method

Although there are many texts attributed to Ephrem that are of doubtful authenticity (especially Greek texts), the texts that are generally accepted as genuine can be divided into four categories.[39] First, there are many straight prose works, which consist of polemical works and biblical commentaries, one of the most significant being the commentary on Tatian's *Diatessaron*, which is the principal source for this four-part Gospel harmony. Second, there are also texts written in artistic prose, including letters and treatises. The latter are highly significant literary forms specific to the Syriac Christian world. Third, there is a literary style called *memre* in which authors expound on a biblical story or a historical figure or event. Often thought of as prose "homilies," *memre* are actually poetic constructions written in seven plus seven syllable couplets. Fourth, there is a literary form that exists mainly in the writings of Ephrem. Often written for special occasions (like *memre*), *madrashe* are stanzaic poems written in over fifty different syllable patterns with assigned melodies. The names of the melodies survive, but the original melodies are unknown. It is the symbolic complexity and theological depth found in the *madrashe* that have earned Ephrem, also called the "Harp of the Spirit" by his contemporaries, the reputation as the most significant figure in the history of Syriac Christianity, as well as the greatest poet-theologian, equaled only by Dante.[40] The best-known figure to utilize this literary form before Ephrem was Bardaisan, a second-century native of Urhoy whom Ephrem vehemently condemned as a heretic.[41]

Ephrem ingeniously appropriated this indigenous art form to polemicize against one of its greatest figures (Bardaisan) while promoting Nicene orthodoxy. This rhythmic medium captured the attention and imagination of the citizens of Urhoy. While Bardaisan preceded Ephrem in his use of *madrashe*, Ephrem is generally considered the master of this literary art form.[42] The collection of various *madrashe* into liturgical cycles dates back to at least the fifth century, but whether Ephrem organized the *madrashe* into cycles is uncertain.[43] *Madrashe* are often

---

39. Brock, *The Luminous Eye*, 18. Brock also points out that many works attributed to Ephrem in Greek, as well as Latin, Arabic, and Slavonic, were never originally composed in Syriac at all. See Brock, *St. Ephrem the Syrian*, 36.

40. Murray, *Symbols of Church and Kingdom*, 31.

41. Whose name literally means "son of the Daisan," the river of Urhoy. See Segal, *Edessa*, 35.

42. Murray, *Symbols of Church and Kingdom*, 30.

43. Brock, *St. Ephrem the Syrian*, 35. Brock here points out that it seems evident that Syriac poetry was based principally on syllabic patterns from the start.

equated to hymns;⁴⁴ however, a more apt modern equivalent are Negro spirituals due to the shared characteristics of call and response, repeated chorus, high reliance on scriptural allusion, and references to contemporary events or significant religious figures.

Nisibis and Urhoy were cosmopolitan centers with multiple cultural influences, and so the writings of Ephrem exhibit several sources of cultural influence. Ephrem is heir to ancient Mesopotamian traditions that were maintained in his day. He employs the ancient Sumerian literary technique of the precedence dispute in which an author will set two participants in a debate, each arguing for superiority. In Ephrem's *madrashe* on Nisibis for example, the precedence dispute sets Death and Satan in opposition.⁴⁵ Ephrem also employs many ancient Mesopotamian themes and symbols such as the term *sam hayye* ("medicine of life") in reference to Christ or the Eucharist.⁴⁶ Ephrem is also an heir to Judaism not only in his use of the Jewish Bible, a practice common throughout Christian tradition, but also by his intimate knowledge of nonbiblical Jewish tradition and practice.

As there is no evidence for Ephrem's direct consultation of targumim or midrashim, it is likely that such Jewish material reached Ephrem through oral tradition. An example of Jewish influence on Ephrem's thought is his frequent use of the imagery of the balance of God's grace (*taybuta*) and righteousness (*kenuta*), an image used commonly in rabbinic literature. Ephrem's poetry also bears a striking resemblance to the form of Hebrew poetry and synagogue hymnody.⁴⁷ It is significant that such Jewish influence is not found in Christian literature outside of Ephrem and other Syriac writers.⁴⁸ This attests to the close association of Syriac Christianity with

---

44. While "hymn" is the most frequent English rendering, scholars remain divided on how to translate *madrashe*. Kees den Biesen calls them "teaching songs." Kees den Biesen, *Simple and Bold: Ephrem's Art of Symbolic Though* (Piscataway, NJ: Gorgias, 2006) vii.

45. Brock, *The Luminous Eye*, 19.

46. Ibid., 20.

47. Sidney H. Griffith, *"Faith Adoring the Mystery": Reading the Bible with St. Ephraem the Syrian* (Milwaukee: Marquette University Press, 1997) 10.

48. Brock, *The Luminous Eye*, 20. Yet despite Ephrem's clear indebtedness to Judaism, the frequent anti-Jewish polemic found in his writings has resulted in Ephrem being depicted as harboring racism against Jews. While it is clear that Ephrem participated in a system of marginalization common in early Christianity that cannot be dismissed as only religious with no racial or ethnic implications, it should be noted that Ephrem's anti-Jewish rhetoric should be understood in the context of his concern with establishing Nicene orthodoxy in the face of Arian and Judaizing presence. See Murray, *Symbols of Church and Kingdom*, 68; and Christine Shepardson, *Anti-Judaism and Christian Orthodoxy: Ephrem's Hymns in Fourth-Century Syria* (Washington, DC: Catholic University of America Press, 2008) 20.

Judaism and is further evidence that Christianity and Judaism cannot, especially in Late Antique Mesopotamia, be treated as isolated, homogeneous movements.[49]

Although Ephrem probably did not read Greek, his writings nevertheless exhibit Greek influence. It is likely that he had access to many Greek Christian texts translated into Syriac and that many of his biblical allusions came from the Greek Bible rather than Syriac.[50] It is true that Ephrem "expresses contempt for Greek thought."[51] However, Ephrem finds use of Hellenistic culture and philosophy where it is compatible with and subject to Scripture in a manner common to early Christians such as Tatian and Basil of Caesarea.

Ephrem's theological method has often been described as symbolic, as opposed to a philosophical or systematic approach to theology.[52] Whereas the Hellenistic theological method of Ephrem's day sought out definitions or boundaries (Greek *horoi*) with which to speak of God, this approach appeared to Ephrem as dangerous, if not blasphemous. Rather, Ephrem uses his *madrashe* to speak of God by means of symbols and paradox. By avoiding the attempt to define the indefinable, symbolic theology allows for a method of speaking of God that remains constantly dynamic. Ephrem and Syriac literature as a whole have been met, unfortunately, with not a small amount of Eurocentric condescension labelling Semitic modes of theology as demonstrating "little profundity or originality of thought . . . turgid, humourless, and repetitive."[53] Fortunately, recent scholarship has developed an increasing appreciation of Ephrem and Syriac literature in general:

> Our difficulty in understanding Ephrem is due to two related factors: our inability to appreciate any form of intelligence different from rational thought and our tendency to underestimate the tremendous power of language and of art in general. Theology seems to have suffered from a typical Western superiority complex and has far too long looked down upon "primitive" authors such as Ephrem, surmising that whatever quality it could discern was a matter of either uncompromising orthodoxy, accomplished poetics, or unconscious performance. In reality, we have only just begun to perceive and appreciate Ephrem's art of symbolic thought. Ephrem is indeed an accomplished poet, yet his specific form of orthodoxy employs the art of language in such a way as

---

49. Weitzman, *The Syriac Version of the Old Testament*, 2. As further evidence for this point, Weitzman points out the significance of the Peshitta OT being translated directly from the Hebrew, as opposed to the more common use of the Septuagint in many other communities of the Christian Near East.

50. Brock, *The Luminous Eye*, 21.

51. Murray, *Symbols of Church and Kingdom*, 30.

52. Brock, *The Luminous Eye*, 23.

53. Segal, *Edessa*, 89.

to surpass the clarity of well-defined terminology and logical demonstration with the clarity of a more comprehensive and superior form of intelligence.[54]

There are several recurrent themes in the poetic theology of Ephrem. In contrast to the prevalent Platonic and dualistic tendency to denigrate the body, Ephrem places a constant emphasis on the value of the corporeal world:

> If our Lord had despised the body
> as something unclean or hateful and foul,
> then the Bread and the cup of salvation
> should also be something hateful and unclean to these heretics
> for how could Christ have despised the body
> yet clothed himself in the Bread,
> seeing that bread is related to that feeble body.
> And if he was pleased with dumb bread,
> how much more so with the body endowed with speech and reason?[55]

The primacy of faith over reason, logic, or human capacity to understand the divine is a frequent theme for Ephrem, most evident in his composition of an entire cycle called *Madrashe on Faith*: "through faith God reveals Himself to you."[56] Ephrem constantly identified the desire to dominate intellectually an object of understanding as the root of heresy.[57] Ephrem's intimate acquaintance with the Bible demonstrates that for him Scripture is the primary source of any kind of knowledge of God. Fire is often employed as an imagery depicting the divine: "Fire entered Mary's womb, put on a body and came forth."[58] The most common imagery employed by Ephrem is that of putting on and taking off clothing.[59]

The posing of opposite concepts at either end of a paradoxical spectrum is one of Ephrem's favorite ways to describe divine mysteries. One such example is the dynamic relationship between word and silence, which, for Ephrem, must be in a constant state of balance when approaching the mysteries of God. For on the one hand, the use of the word in the presence of an Almighty God would be audacious, while on the other, awe for God's majesty should not lead to absolute silence, thus ignoring God's love and truth.[60] Another polarity whose poetic complexity Ephrem

---

54. den Biesen, *Simple and Bold*, xix.
55. *Madrashe against Heresies* 47:2. See Brock, *The Luminous Eye*, 37.
56. *Madrashe on Faith* 72:2. Brock, *The Luminous Eye*, 29.
57. Brock, *The Luminous Eye*, 43.
58. *Madrashe on Faith* 4:2. Brock, *The Luminous Eye*, 38.
59. Brock, *The Luminous Eye*, 39.
60. den Biesen, *Simple and Bold*, 152.

enjoys is that between word and intellect. While Ephrem demands the subordination of the human intellect to the revelation of God, it would be a mistake to perceive him as anti-intellectual. Rather, both the linguistic and cognitive faculties function as an extension of God's creation process through a creative interchange of interpretation and reproduction.[61]

The core feature of Ephrem's theological method is his understanding of God's self-revelation through symbols. God has endowed the entire creation with "hidden meaning" (*hayla kasya*), which requires the eye of faith to discern his salvific purpose. Ephrem's connection of the spiritual and physical worlds through divine symbols evident in the natural world further exemplifies the value placed on the physical world, against the dualistic tendencies popular in his day. It is through symbolic theology that Ephrem discusses the mystery of the Trinity.[62] The two principle witnesses through which divine symbols are perceived for Ephrem are the creation and Scripture:

> In his book Moses described
> The creation of the natural world,
> So that both Nature and Scripture
> Might bear witness to the Creator:
> Nature, through man's use of it,
> Scripture, through his reading it;
> They are the witnesses
> Which reach everywhere,
> They are to be found at all times,
> Present at every hour,
> Confuting the unbeliever
> Who defames the Creator.[63]

That which is constantly spoken of as "symbols" in Ephrem's theology is in Syriac a *raza* ("mystery," "symbol," "secret"). Of Persian origin, this word is used in the book of Daniel as well as texts from Qumran and is most likely the Semitic concept lying behind Paul's use of the Greek word *mysterion*.[64] The *raze* (plural) typologically connect two different modes of reality, and it is quite a different concept than our modern usage of the word "symbol." Though "symbol" is the word that will be employed with reference to the *raze*, it is important to remember that for Ephrem

61. Ibid., 324.

62. Edmund Beck, *Die Theologie Des Hl. Ephraem in Seinen Hymnen über den Glauben* (Rome: Pontificum Institutum S. Anselmi, 1949) 45.

63. *Madrashe on Paradise* 5:2. Brock, *St. Ephrem the Syrian*, 102–3.

64. Ibid., 42.

(as well as early Christians in general), *raze*, or *mysteria*, are deeply connected to the spiritual reality they symbolize and are not essentially of a different nature from that which is symbolized, in contrast to the way the modern world tends to think of a symbol. The process of instruction by means of symbols and meaning is, for Ephrem, the sum of theology.[65]

The symbol of the eye (of the heart, or soul) refers to one's ability to see God clearly, depending on where that individual stands with regard to sin and right belief. Ephrem likens Eve and Mary to two eyes, one darkened by sin and the other illumined with perfect vision:

> Through the eye that was darkened
> the whole world has darkened,
> and people groped
> and thought that every stone
> they stumbled upon was a god,
> calling falsehood truth.
> But when it was illumined by the other eye,
> and the heavenly Light
> that resided in its midst,
> humanity became reconciled once again,
> realizing that what they had stumbled on
> was destroying their very life.[66]

Ephrem employs several symbols with which to describe Christ, the church, and the relationship between the two. Fueled by his anti-Jewish hostility, Ephrem frequently describes the church as the "nation" which has replaced the original "nation of God":

> Nobler was Melchizedek
> Than the high priests of the Nation
> Among the Nations he officiated and taught
> That the High Priest who was to come to the Nations
> Would be immolated by the Nation.[67]

Motivated by his anti-gnostic/dualistic views, Ephrem showed his attitude toward the corporeal world most clearly in his constant veneration of the physical body of Christ. The body of Christ is at the center of God's relationship with the church in that Christ's body becomes the source of salvation for the church, which

---

65. Griffith, *"Faith Adoring the Mystery,"* 29.
66. *Madrashe on the Church* 37:6–7. Brock, *The Luminous Eye*, 72–73.
67. *Madrashe on Virginity* 8:20. See Murray, *Symbols of Church and Kingdom*, 45.

is made the corporate body of Christ by receiving Christ's body in the Eucharist.[68] Ephrem also employs the biblical symbols of the Vine and Vineyard[69] as well as the Rock and the House on the Rock[70] to speak of Christ and his church.

A concept that did not originate with Ephrem but is nonetheless extremely popular with Ephrem and Syriac Christian writers in general is the robe of glory. Again utilizing his favorite imagery of clothing, Ephrem contrasts Adam and Christ, describing the salvation process in terms of an exchange of clothing:

> All these changes did the Merciful One make,
> Stripping off glory and putting on a body;
> For He had devised a way to reclothe Adam
> In that glory which Adam had stripped off.
> Christ was wrapped in swaddling clothes,
> Corresponding to Adam's leaves,
> Christ put on clothes, instead of Adam's skins;
> He was baptized for Adam's sin,
> His body was embalmed for Adam's death,
> He rose and raised up Adam in his glory.
> Blessed is He who descended, put Adam on and ascended![71]

The robe of glory operates in four stages in the history of salvation: the fall, the incarnation, baptism, and the resurrection of the dead. Adam and Eve were first stripped of the robe through their sin, leading to a desire for Christ to put on the body in order to reclothe Adam and Eve. Through baptism the Christian puts on the robe by putting on Christ and then awaits the resurrection in which one can fully participate in paradise clothed in robes of glory.[72]

Perhaps Ephrem's most famous symbolic imagery is that of the pearl. At the end of the *Madrashe on Faith*, Ephrem added five poems on the pearl, the symbolic device through which he is able to glimpse the mysteries of God.

> One day, my brothers, I held a pearl;
> I saw in it symbols (*raze*), witnesses to the Kingdom,
> Images and signs of His majesty.
> It became a fountain from which I drank the mysteries of the Son.

---

68. Murray, *Symbols of Church and Kingdom.*, 77.
69. Ibid., 95.
70. Ibid., 205.
71. *Madrashe on the Nativity* 23:13. Brock *The Luminous Eye*, 85.
72. Brock, *St. Ephrem the Syrian*, 67.

> Response: Blessed is He who symbolized the Kingdom of the Most High by means of a pearl.
>
> I placed it, my brothers, in the palm of my hand, observing it;
> I continued looking at it on one side and its face was on all sides,
> I found out that the Son is incomprehensible,
> For He is completely light.
> In its luminosity I saw the Luminous One, He who cannot be shaken;
> In its purity is a great symbol (*raza*),
> The Body of Our Lord, untarnished.
> In its undividedness, I saw the undivided truth.[73]

Conclusion

Ephrem and his poetic theological method have been described as representing non-Westernized, Asian/Semitic theology:

> Here is a genuinely Asian Christianity which is free from the specifically European cultural, historical and intellectual trappings that have become attached to the main streams of Christianity . . . Saint Ephrem is thus a writer who can preeminently serve as a link and meeting point between European Christianity on the one hand, and Asian and African Christianity on the other. For those whose Christian tradition is of European background, Ephrem provides a refreshing counterbalance to an excessively cerebral tradition of conducting theological enquiry, while for Asian and African Christians Ephrem is the one great Church Father and theologian whose poetic writings will be readily accessible, without requiring any prior knowledge of Greek philosophical terminology and tradition.[74]

The cultural accessibility afforded non-Western Christians comes not only from the poetry of Ephrem but from the various early Christian traditions that developed across the continents of Africa and Asia. Throughout late antiquity African Christianity expanded rapidly along the Nile River while Asian Christianity traveled the Silk Road. If not for the Western isolation of these communities followed by the Islamic Conquest, there might be more Christians of color today with a church tradition free of slavery and colonialism. Yet the legacy of Near Eastern Christianity empowers the rest of the non-Western, Christian world by offering proof of two fun-

---

73. *Madrashe on Faith* 81:1–3. This passage is translated from the text given by Edmund Beck, ed., *Des heiligen Ephraem des Syrers: Hymnen de Fide*, Corpus Scriptorum Christianorum Orientalium 154 (Louvain: Imprimerie Orientaliste, 1955) 248–49.

74. Brock, *The Luminous Eye*, 15.

damental realities: (1) Christianity has always been multiethnic and (2) Christians are free to develop contextualized modes of expression.

The Western captivity of the Church has rendered non-Western expressions of Christianity not merely an option but a necessity. Christianity's association with European culture is the most influential factor in non-Westerners' reluctance to accept the message of the gospel. As in the case of African American Muslims, it is not the message of the gospel itself but the completely unnecessary and destructive Western packaging that turns millions away from knowing Jesus. If the world is to encounter the transforming power of the gospel, it must be presented in an easily accessible manner. The goal here is for the world to know Jesus as Lord and Savior. Affirmation of non-Western cultural expressions is not the end in itself. This point is crucial for the myriad of Christians who tend to dismiss conversations regarding justice, race, or culture as a secular, liberal agenda irrelevant to the ministry of the church. It is God who has declared all people groups acceptable to him,[75] and to claim that a certain group has any inherent superiority in its understanding of God and his Word is idolatry.

The idolatry of Western culture in the history of the Christian tradition has a twofold effect on the non-Western world: vigorous rejection of the gospel by non-Western non-Christians and self-hatred on the part of non-Western Christians. The latter can be easily detected by the millions of non-Western Christians who make more use of white American worship music and literature in translation than that of their own community. There is perhaps no better example of non-Western Christian self-hatred than a congregation of black or brown Christians worshipping toward the front of the sanctuary, above which hangs a depiction of a blond-haired, blue-eyed Jesus. It is not surprising so many non-Western Christians want nothing to do with Christianity.

The task is clear: seventeen hundred years of Western cultural captivity has made it necessary to place special emphasis on non-Western expressions of Christianity guided by autochthonous leaders. In the same way that Ephrem understood the power of the *madrashe* for the citizens of Urhoy and employed this cultural medium for the proclamation of the gospel, non-Western Christians today must discerningly reappropriate modes of expression accessible to specific milieu. The importance of this task becomes more evident in the increasingly multiethnic context of the city,

---

75. Acts 10:34–5. Unless otherwise noted, all biblical references are taken from the New International Version (NIV) (Colorado Springs: International Bible Society, 1973).

and there are several wonderful examples of encouraging non-Western Christian expression in contemporary ministry.[76]

I have found invaluable use in embracing not only external expressions of ethnicity but also deeply rooted cultural systems of belief and behavior in the urban, black ministerial context. For example, in ministering among urban black youth I have found it much more helpful not only to encourage Christian hip hop, spoken word, and clothing styles but also culturally specific systems of communication and relationships. As ministers of the gospel, it is of paramount importance actively to seek cultural expressions that can be embraced and employed in the ministry of the church. As the people of God continue to embrace the multiethnic expressions for which it has been destined,[77] the door will be opened to a church that truly reflects all nations for those who have been culturally alienated.

---

76. See Richard L. Twiss, *Rescuing Theology from the Cowboys: An Emerging Indigenous Expression of the Jesus Way in North America* (Vancouver, WA: Wiconi International, 2011); Luis Pantoja Jr., Sadiri Joy Tira, and Enoch Wan, *Scattered: The Filipino Global Presence* (Manila: Lifechange, 2004); Orlando Crespo, *Being Latino in Christ: Finding Wholeness in Your Ethnic Identity* (Downers Grove, IL: InterVarsity, 2003); Chan Kei Thong, *Faith of Our Fathers: God in Ancient China* (Shanghai: China Publishing Group, 2006); Kwame Bediako, *Jesus and the Gospel in Africa: History and Experience* (Maryknoll, NY: Orbis, 2004); Efrem Smith, and Phil Jackson, *The Hip-Hop Church: Connecting with the Movement Shaping Our Culture* (Downers Grove, IL: InterVarsity, 2005); James H. Cone, *Black Theology & Black Power*, 7th ed. (Maryknoll, NY: Orbis, 2005).

77. Rev 7:9.

RESPONSE TO BANTU

Armida Belmonte Stephens

Thank you for this opportunity to enter the ancient Near Eastern world to remember the almost forgotten realities of one of the early communities of Christian faith within the Syriac tradition. We are enriched by the scholarship and the wider vista of the history of the church.

The main concern of this paper is that "for the gospel to take firm root among all peoples, the idea of the superiority of Christianity laden with Western cultural values must be rejected. Conversely, non-Western expressions of Christianity should be cultivated and promoted in order to reflect a church that is truly for all peoples." I could not agree more with this statement. Acquainting us with Syriac Christianity as an example of a Christian tradition that has developed independently from the Western church not only contributes to a broader historical understanding regarding the formation and development of the church and orthodoxy but it also awakens our sensibilities to what the Christian church actually *is* today. To learn that this long-enduring faith community still has expression in the world is not only encouraging but also instructive. I am reminded of philosopher-theologian Rubem Alves's insight that the work of the historian is significant not only for the purpose of better coming to know our pasts but also because in the telling of the story of the work of God there is also a birthing of a vision and hope for today and the future.[1] As we hear the call to remember the Syriac story and embrace its present reality, those of us from non-Western traditions are also invited into the remembrance and recapture of our own histories, with hope that the same God who acted and worked within the Syriac tradition also works in our communities of faith today and tomorrow. For this we can be thankful.

While this expanded picture and hopeful reminder serve to build up the church in these ways, they also render a counter-example to the dominant narrative of what the church *is* and how it theologizes for those who would otherwise close their ears to the Christian story and message. As the paper states, "the Western captivity of the church has thoroughly permeated the Christian tradition and is the single great-

---

1. Rubem Alves, *Theology of Human Hope* (New York: Corpus, 1969).

est reason non-Western people have no desire to participate in a religion that is perceived as American, Western, white, or all of the above." This is a sad truth—one that resonates in the Latin American and Latino contexts of which I have been a part—and a difficult reality with which the Western church must grapple.[2] I heartily agree that more work needs to be done to bring particular histories to the forefront, to acknowledge the realities of marginalized faith communities, as well as the need for contextualization, both theologically and ministerially.[3] It seems to me that we are on the same page with respect to the problem of Western imperialism and cultural paternalism. However, some questions come up in my reading of the paper, both with respect to how we frame or envision the problem, as well as with respect to how we move forward in faith and practice beyond a Western paradigm for what is in actuality a diverse, catholic church.

The first issue has to do with framing the situation by the use of such phrases as "the Western church" or "Western captivity of the church." In the spirit of Saint Ephrem's poetic theology, my aim is not to play with semantics or to quibble with language and labels. However, I want to raise the issue insofar as these phrases represent, or fail to represent, present realities accurately. With respect to the phrase "the Western church," who or what exactly is represented in the use of this phrase? It seems that in limiting or narrowing what we call "Western" to people of European background and descent, we inadvertently marginalize communities who may also find their roots or histories in the same times and places but whose stories are not the dominant narrative. I wonder—and this is an honest question—do not African American faith communities consider themselves by and large Western? What of the bicultural, hyphenated faith communities who may inhabit the lived tension of Western and non-Western immigrant identities? Understanding that there are good scholarly, historical, sociological, economic, and political reasons for the specific or particular referents in the use this phrase, I bring up the point only to suggest that

---

2. Philip Jenkins (*The Next Christendom: The Coming of Global Christianity* [Oxford: Oxford University Press, 2002]) describes the many tensions (ethnic, religious, political, etc.) that have resulted from the major shifts in global Christianity.

3. Cf. Justo González, "The Significance of a Minority Perspective," in *Mañana: Christian Theology from a Hispanic Perspective* (Nashville: Abingdon, 1990) 21–30; and Benjamín Valentín's introductory essay in *In Our Own Voices: Latino/a Renditions of Theology* (Maryknoll, NY: Orbis, 2010). See also Craig Ott and Harold Netland, eds., *Globalizing Theology* (Grand Rapids: Baker, 2006); Timothy Tennent, *Theology in the Context of World Christianity: How the Global Church Is Influencing the Way We Think about and Discuss Theology* (Grand Rapids: Zondervan, 2007); Soong-Chan Rah, *Many Colors: Cultural Intelligence for a Changing Church* (Chicago: Moody, 2010); Brian Bantum, *Redeeming Mulatto* (Waco: Baylor University Press, 2010); and Craig Keener and M. Daniel Carrol R., eds., *Global Voices: Reading the Bible in the Majority World* (Peabody, MA: Hendrickson, 2013).

this language perhaps undermines the purposes of the paper and even perhaps further reifies incomplete concepts of what it means to be culturally Western at a point in time in which the very notions of what it means to be Western and the dominance of its narrative are being challenged.[4] So, we should dispense with labels. We are likely in agreement about *who* we mean, but I wonder *what* we mean when we talk about the "Western captivity of the church." Are we talking about the Eurocentric nature of the Western church and its culture and theology? Are we also talking about the accompanying posture that has historically expressed dominance and unshared power with respect to the rest of the church?

The question is an important one because as non-Western Christian traditions and marginalized communities in the West talk about contextualization, we must recognize that the Western traditions, in all their various and distinct faith communities, are also contextualized expressions of the gospel life. To invalidate "Westernness" itself—its culture, traditions, and theology—is wrong-headed, not only because it problematizes the legitimacy of contextualization itself, but it also diminishes the value of our Western siblings' histories, as problematic as non-Westerners or marginalized faith communities might find or have experienced them. Therefore, when describing the Western captivity of the church, it is important to distinguish between a European culture and history on the one hand, and those spiritually misguided postures of superiority and the theological methods of the European-American church on the other hand, that have resulted—broadly speaking, for there are certainly exceptions—in a church witness that has been historically myopic and at odds with many other people.

With respect to and as an example of the latter, one of the significant problems of the Western, Enlightenment tradition has been the famous theory/praxis divide.[5] This divide between faith and practice has manifested itself in American evangelical contexts in the separation of ethics as a distinct discipline from theological studies. Although we have witness from those in pietist traditions and admonishments from theologians as prominent as Karl Barth,[6] we see that spiritual formation continues to play a secondary role in much, but not all, of theological education.[7] The delay

---

4. Michael Foley and Dean Hoge, *Religion and the New Immigrants: How Faith Communities Form Our Newest Citizens* (Oxford: Oxford University Press, 2007). Cf. also Juan F. Martínez, *Los Protestantes: An Introduction to Latino Protestantism in the United States* (Santa Barbara: Praeger, 2011).

5. Cf. Alasdair MacIntyre, *After Virtue* (Notre Dame: Notre Dame University Press, 2007).

6. Cf. Karl Barth, *Church Dogmatics*, I/2, §22.3.

7. Cf. David I. Smith and James K.A. Smith, eds., *Teaching and Christian Practices: Reshaping Faith & Learning* (Grand Rapids: Eerdmans, 2011); and Craig Dykstra, *Growing in the Life of Faith: Education and Christian Practices* (Louisville: Westminster John Knox, 2005).

in the Western theological responses to racialization and the marginalization of the "other" come as no surprise then, and this becomes particularly significant in light of the roots of the white American church itself, having once been marginalized on the European continent as well. For this reason, while the presence of the Syriac church is helpful in reframing the reality of who makes up the Christian church, the example of Saint Ephrem reminds us that the church also needs to hear multiple voices in its theologizing to work toward a more holistic faith seeking understanding and a posture of hope.

This relates to one other aspect I would like to mention. While Ephrem and the Syriac tradition serve to provide us with an alternative narrative or with a more nuanced narrative of the catholic church, it is interesting to note that they were born out of a context where there was much melding of traditions, cultures, and histories. The Syriac Christian tradition developed in a shared space where various peoples, cultures, and powers came together over a period of time—the Persians, the Greeks, and the Romans—to form something new at Urhoy. As a Mexican-American, I can appreciate this backdrop as there are parallels in the *mestizaje* of the Latin American church and in the development of a bicultural Latino church in the U.S.[8] Moreover, in an increasingly diverse world where city neighborhoods are becoming more diverse and complex, we find in urban realities increasing polycentrism in identity formation. In these contexts we can no longer frame conversations using black-white binaries, and similarly the "Western/non-Western" categories are decreasingly helpful when we speak of theological traditions; the presence of Latin American, Asian, and African communities in the U.S. and Europe reminds us that these categories are not so clear-cut.

This raises the question: How does a faith community do theology and theological history when your neighborhood is made up of Blacks, Whites, Latinos, and Asians—all living together? What history—or better yet histories—does a faith community adopt in such contexts in which there is the constant negotiating, not just of personal identities, but of shared histories as a local church and also as a part of the body of Christ? I am also increasingly convinced that as marginalized faith communities and Christians with polycentric identities attempt to escape the so-called "captivity of the Western church," we must also shy away from the temptation of nativist appeals in the expression of our identities (Christian or otherwise) at all levels: socially, geographically, and theologically. I am reminded of the parable of the workers in Matt 20. While the church as the people of God is a flesh and blood real-

---

8. Cf. Virgilio Elizondo, *The Future Is Mestizo* (Boulder: University Press of Colorado, 2000); and Roberto Goizueta, *Caminemos con Jesús* (Maryknoll, NY: Orbis, 1995) 96ff.

ity, it also finds its roots, host, and home in the hospitality of Christ. His flesh and blood body reminds us that our encultured and embodied expressions of the church are at their best good, true, and beautiful expressions of his own body. These must be remembered and celebrated. Yet, we must also find ways of expressing the shared nature of our Christian reality, not only in its spiritual dimensions but in its historical, theological, and practical dimensions in shared spaces of doing life together. That, too, is the challenge of the urban church and what I believe is a compelling and beautiful witness to an unbelieving world.

I would like to close with a couple of questions. How does Ephrem's theological method—free from the constraints of Western dualism—give a way forward for how the Western church lives into the "both/and" reality that is the church where diversity and particularity are celebrated in the wider context of unity and solidarity? Could his theology of the body of Christ give us a way forward to think through the "Western/non-Western" dynamics where issues of history and power surface in order to find an authentic expression of Christian unity? As our world continues to change, are there ways that a symbolic theology can help the church navigate the murky waters of divisions and hostilities present not only in the global but also American church?

"NO SHORTCUT TO THE PROMISED LAND": THE FOSDICK BROTHERS AND MUSCULAR CHRISTIANITY

Amy Laura Hall

There is no royal road to the millennium, no short cut to the Promised Land.

What we need supremely at this time, therefore, is something of the synthetic vision of an Aristotle, an ability to break over the boundaries of parochialism and think in world terms, a willingness to plan constructively on the basis of larger loyalties. This is the only road to salvation. This is where the judgment and common sense of the race would lead us.[1]

I am currently digging into old archives and visiting with living people for a book on masculinity in American mainline evangelicalism, called (for the time-being) *Erecting the Pulpit: Muscular Christianity from Victoria to Viagra*. I focus on ways that North American Protestants have tried to make Christianity seem more virile and generally congenial to white, male authority. I am considering denominational and parachurch efforts that fit under the umbrella of "Muscular Christianity." Since accepting the gracious invitation to speak at North Park Theological Seminary on the topic of "Urban Ministry," I have tried to connect this research to the conference theme. There are what I call "shooting fish in a barrel" examples of "Muscular Christianity," examples that are obviously about reinforcing what might be termed "traditional" versions of Western masculinity. Although he did not like it, the term "Muscular Christianity" was coined for Charles Kingsley (1819–1875), a Victorian clergyman who wrote popular, mass-produced novels for boys and young men with titles like *The Roman and the Teuton* and *Westward Ho!*[2] Kingsley drew from various social Darwinisms and a sense of Anglican superiority to narrate and argue for the potency of English Christianity. His writings strike a different tone than that of Mark Driscoll (b. 1970), the former head of today's Acts 29 matrix of neo-Calvinist

---

1. Raymond Fosdick, *The Old Savage in the New Civilization* (Garden City, NY: Doubleday, 1928) 185, 197.

2. *The Roman and the Teuton* (Cambridge: Macmillan, 1864); *Westward Ho!* (Cambridge: Macmillan, 1855).

church plants, but Kingsley and Driscoll share a similar rhetorical argument. It goes like this: young men are weak, enervated by gender confusion, and they need a form of Christianity that affirms unequivocally male strength and authority. A third "fish in a barrel" figure who falls between Kingsley and Driscoll in time and in tone is Abraham Vereide (1886–1969), an industrialist, anti-labor enthusiast and founder of a network of "Christian Leadership" schemes in the U.S. Vereide's 1961 biographer christened him no less than a "Modern Viking."[3]

I am also interested in less obviously "muscular" characters within evangelicalism, like Harry and Raymond Fosdick, and, apropos to this conference, their collaboration focused in part on cities and serving or sorting people in "urban" areas. Harry Emerson Fosdick (1878–1969) and his brother Raymond (1883–1972) were two progressive evangelicals keen to be leaders for a new era. Harry was the inaugural preacher of the Riverside Church in New York City, a church conceived by John D. Rockefeller Jr., and Raymond Fosdick was a chief advisor to Rockefeller and the President of the Rockefeller Foundation from 1936 to 1948. Their partnership as very well-funded social entrepreneurs is helpful for thinking at the intersection of masculinity, money, and social planning. Each encouraged a particular segment of the relatively educated, mainstream Protestant population to perceive themselves as living through a crisis, in fact, an *unprecedented* crisis that called for new thinking and bold direction. In the overlapping realms of theology and social science, each brother offered himself as a suitable guide. I sketch these details here as a caution— as a caution to be aware of ways that money, social scientific research, ministerial authority, and even architecture itself can reinforce hierarchical, nondemocratic notions of discipleship in postindustrial cities. Frankly, at this point in my research, I have more leads than clear answers, but my questions are useful for left-leaning as well as conservative-leaning evangelicals, for churches keen on concerted efforts toward systemic social justice as well as for those more inclined toward Christian Community Development Association types of organizations.

Phallic Follies

Any good Methodist brought up in the last forty years can tell you, "The church is not a building, the church is not a steeple, the church is not a resting place, the

---

3. Norman Percy Grubb, *Modern Viking: The Story of Abraham Vereide, Pioneer in Christian Leadership* (Grand Rapids: Zondervan, 1961) front cover. Among the dignitaries to praise the book at the time were Senator Frank Carlson, Senator Alexander Wiley, Judge Boyd Leedom, and Congressman Charles E. Bennett. Judge Leedom was with the National Labor Relations Board in 1960, when the book was published.

church is a people"—from a beloved hymn by Richard Avery and Donald March, "We are the Church" (1972). Writing as I do in the shadow of Duke Chapel, I also have some sense that erecting the pulpit is not merely a metaphor for ensuring the potency of Christianity. Sometimes muscular Christianity means quite literally *erecting a pulpit*, inside a large building with an impressive, phallic-gothic steeple. The dazzling mirror of cinema is helpful here. The importance of such an edifice is the theme of a hit movie from 1947 called "The Bishop's Wife," based on a novel from 1928. The bishop in question is the ambitious, anxious David Niven, and he is nearly cuckolded by an angel played by Cary Grant. As this particular Hollywood story goes, the bishop eventually realizes (with help from Cary Grant) that the good Christians of the big metropolis do not need a new cathedral after all. On first viewing what struck me most was how much the gilded portrait of the proposed cathedral, lit through a mystical haze above the bishop's hearth, looks like Duke Chapel or Riverside Church.

Duke Chapel and Riverside Church were both financed by money made through baron-robbery, and each building is meant to serve as a testimony to both the largesse of the benefactor and the importance of the man speaking from the pulpit. Riverside Church is the tallest church in the U.S., still impressively visible even in the city that is the platonic-American form of "Metropolis." Duke Chapel remains one of the most noticeable structures in the city of Durham, visible from all the major highway arteries. The term that I think best suits both structures is the British word "folly." The meaning of the word is contested, but basically a folly is a structure built as a formal whimsy, a mixture of earnest intent and profligate fantasy. Some kind person contributed this on the Wikipedia site for one folly, Castell Coch, in Wales:

> [The 3rd Marquess of] Bute's desires and money, allied with [architect William] Burges' fantastical imagination and skill, led to the creation of two of the finest creations of the late Victorian era Gothic Revival, Cardiff Castle and Castell Coch. The two buildings represent both the potential of colossal industrial wealth and the desire to escape the scene of that wealth's creation.[4]

I am interested in the stories behind the creation of Riverside Church and Duke Chapel, each representing a partnership between industrial wealth and Protestantism. Stories of men of faith building visible testimonies to their prowess and piety make the imagery of muscular Christianity helpfully concrete. Construction of each structure began within a few years of one another (Riverside, 1927; Duke Chapel, 1930).

---

4. See http://en.wikipedia.org/wiki/John_Crichton-Stuart,_3rd_Marquess_of_Bute.

Each building was inaugurated definitely to impress during the Great Depression, Riverside in 1931 and Duke Chapel in 1932. I am curious about how Harry Emerson Fosdick, the senior minister for whom John D. Rockefeller Jr., built Riverside Church, and Franklin S. Hickman, the first Preacher to the University and the first Dean of Duke Chapel, each perceived his own role as an agent of divine providence in their respective cities. In my book I am thinking through how the architecture of each structure promoted ministerial legitimacy during a time of economic distress and during a shift from religion to science as the source for what counted as expertise. I suspect that the gothic grandeur of Riverside leant an air of authority and tradition to Fosdick's antifundamentalist, antitraditional form of evangelicalism. From Duke Chapel's tower to its towering pulpit the whole Duke endeavor helped a regional, newly rich campus, and her chapel dean, to appear older and wiser than if it had been built in the style of a Friends Meeting House. This may be a pretty basic observation, but such historic structures and their storied past continue to shape the definitions of efficacy within Christian communities and efforts in a city.

To worship inside of or in the shadow of such a structure is to worship in a particular way, a way that I think works more through receptivity and awe than through activity and self-confidence. I am not quite prepared to say that it was impossible for Spirit-filled Christian populism to break out inside of a massive structure like Riverside Church or Duke Chapel, but I do suspect that the architecture was intended to make congregants and neighbors sense their place within an orderly structure, rather than to activate participants prophetically to challenge the holiness of the order of things around them.

The Supreme Question

> Humanity stands today in a position of unique peril. An unanswered question is written across the future: Is man to be the master of the civilization he has created, or is he to be its victim? Can he control the forces which he has himself let loose? . . . This is the supreme question before us.[5]

I am curious about ways that these tangible and abiding landmarks to purportedly faithful industry are connected to definitions of Christian ministry in times of perceived crises in cities. In her meticulously detailed account of "the rise of the new biology," scientist and historian Lily Kay writes about the collaboration among researchers and corporate funders through Caltech and the Rockefeller Foundation

---

5. Fosdick, *The Old Savage*, 21.

across several decades of the twentieth century and the ways that this collaboration shaped perceptions of efficacy and purpose:

> The motivation behind the enormous investment in the new agenda was to develop the human sciences as a comprehensive explanatory and applied framework of social control grounded in the natural, medical, and social sciences. Conceived during the late 1920s, the new agenda was articulated in terms of the contemporary technocratic discourse of human engineering, aiming toward an endpoint of restructuring human relations in congruence with the social framework of industrial capitalism . . . the new biology (originally named "psychobiology") was erected on the bedrock of the physical sciences in order to rigorously explain and eventually control the fundamental mechanisms governing human behavior.[6]

I became interested in the period she covers in part due to the formal resemblance of the Rockefeller funded "Science of Man" project, directed by Raymond Fosdick, and the hegemonic Templeton Foundation today. As the Rockefeller Foundation sought to create a thoroughly new and carefully orchestrated science of human behavior, the Templeton Foundation has created and shaped a new field, the ahistorical and seemingly apolitical field known as "religion and science."[7] As Kay explains, the development of a sizeable network of scholarly projects with related goals was the result neither of cosmic kismet nor of spontaneous, collective effervescence: "[T]he rise of the new biology was an expression of the systemic cooperative efforts of America's scientific establishment—scientists and their patrons—to direct the study of animate phenomena along selected paths toward a shared vision of science and society." Kay continues, the new science "would borrow methods not only from physics, mathematics, and chemistry but also from other fields of life science—genetics, embryology, physiology, immunology, microbiology. The new biology aimed to transcend disciplinary boundaries and employ whatever tools the

---

6. Lily E. Kay, *The Molecular Vision of Life: Caltech, The Rockefeller Foundation, and the Rise of the New Biology* (Oxford: Oxford University Press, 1996) 8.

7. For more on the Templeton Foundation, see: http://www.motherjones.com/mojo/2011/09/koch-brothers-million-dollar-donor-club, and http://www.insidehighered.com/news/2013/05/21/some-philosophy-scholars-raise-concerns-about-templeton-funding, and, from the foundation's website: http://www.templeton.org/what-we-fund/funding-priorities/from-beliefs-to-virtuous-behaviors. From Kay regarding an earlier era, "The corporate structure of the philanthropic enterprise mirrored the structure of the business corporation; and the visions of the Foundation's trustees, leaders of business and industry, reflected their ideologies and social world. True, legal distinctions such as tax laws and nonprofit status did differentiate these quasi-public institutions from their parent corporations, but they are proximate mechanistic causes" (Kay, *The Molecular Vision*, 10).

problem at hand demanded."[8] Cooperation and the sharing of methods across fields in the life sciences had previously worked due to professional societies and faculties and such, this being part of the aim of university life itself, but "the design of a large-scale program based on interdisciplinary research encompassing several disciplines was unprecedented."[9]

Kay also describes the way that a progressive, evangelical Protestant zeal for shaping human existence toward order served as a kind of motor for the movement:

> Animated by a potent conjunction of Protestant values and technocratic visions, the Foundation's civic missions were formulated within the dominant cultural categories of race, class, and gender, as well as within a socioeconomic framework that defined norm and deviance for individuals and groups. The Rockefeller philanthropies cultivated scientific and managerial elites in order to address the root causes of social dysfunction: culturally specific and historically contingent forms of maladjustment. Their projects aimed to restructure human relations and to develop social technologies commensurate with the material and ideological imperatives of industrial capitalism.[10]

Further, she adds:

> To extract the full significance of the Rockefeller philanthropies' commitment to social reform, their projects must be viewed on two interconnected levels of commensurability: the economic and the ideological. On the materialistic and utilitarian level, the projects in the social and biological sciences were intended to foster favorable conditions for raising economic productivity and managing social stability—making the world safe for private enterprise. On the level of consciousness and ideology, the reform programs were intended to combat vice, raise moral standards and improve human conduct. The life of labor, the practice of self-control, and the drive for prosperity formed the essential elements along the spiritual-material continuum of a social intervention project based on Protestantism, republican principles, and industrial capitalism.[11]

One way to discern Raymond Fosdick's contribution to this endeavor is through his collection of essays *The Old Savage in the New Civilization*, published in 1928, a collection made up of college addresses, including four commencement speeches given at Wellesley, Colgate, Vanderbilt, and University of Iowa; a Founder's

---

8. Kay, *The Molecular Vision*, 3.
9. Ibid., 5.
10. Ibid., 10.
11. Ibid., 26.

Day address at Mount Holyoke; and lectures he delivered at Columbia, University of Virginia, Colorado College, University of of Georgia, University of Nebraska, and the University of Kansas. (Think of his 1928 book as a historical equivalent of a viral TED talk today on *Problem X* in the *City of Y*, with an *Answer Z* that "we" reading, composting, non-gun-toting people must all endorse.) While Raymond's brother, Harry Emerson, was gaining renown through his preaching and writing, Raymond was speaking on the university lecture circuit, delivering addresses with a focused refrain. The "supreme question" facing inter-war America, indeed the world, is whether "humanity" may find the resolve to overcome both inertia and fear to forge an organized scheme for progress: "Here lies the hope of the future. With such high-visioned and creative leadership we can conquer the most powerful creatures with which man has ever had to contend—creatures which he himself fashioned and set free: his own machines."[12]

This quote is characteristic of Fosdick's rhetorical method of argumentation. Industrialization is a man-made force now let loose on the world, something like Godzilla plus Frankenstein. As he describes this turn, Fosdick uses language that makes the shift seem inescapable, as if the rise of industrialization, while a result of human engineering, was inevitable, ineluctable—a naturally occurring, social-evolutionary shift upward in complexity and size. The question now is whether there is anyone sufficiently evolved, sufficiently "high-visioned" to take in the scope of the monster and steer it. His scrap of an epigraph to the collection sets a particular tone to the question and the implied answer: "a naked Polynesian parading in a top hat and spats." "People" in general are of little use. In his myriad descriptions of "the" human predicament, he casts the average set of workers like faceless extras in a Godzilla movie, making their way without individual distinction through lives without meaning or dignity. What is needed, Raymond Fosdick insists, is "a new Aristotle" to give answers to the leaders so that they may provide direction for the masses (his sixth essay is "Wanted: An Aristotle").[13]

Here, a series of quotes will be helpful for reproducing the effect of his seven essays. First, Raymond Fosdick asserts that he is addressing college graduates or students and their professors during a *singular* moment in time:

> Since the days of Assyria and Babylon—indeed since the days of our Neolithic forefathers—nothing has occurred which has so completely and in so short a time changed the method and manner of living of the human race, as the

---

12. Fosdick, *The Old Savage*, 32.
13. Ibid., 167.

mechanical revolution of the Nineteenth Century. Our great-grandparents would find themselves far more at home in the world of the Venerable Bede or of Alfred the Great than they would in the world we occupy today.

Our fate may overtake us while we are still admiring the slow processes of history... To drift without question of goal, or to steer our course by old reckonings which have not recently been checked, is to court a disaster perhaps without parallel.

Our long analysis leads to one conclusion. We are living in a world that is utterly different from any world that has existed before. Modern science has suddenly compressed the planet we occupy—jamming together into a single community widely diverse peoples and civilizations. On top of this confusion, with prodigal gesture, science has scattered weapons of destruction far more deadly than bewildered man ever before possessed; so that, suddenly armed to the teeth, he is asked to live in peace, crowded together with neighbours whom he never knew before and for whom he has no particular liking.[14]

Second, for "people" life is mostly chaotic and/or meaningless. They (we) require suitably enlightened leadership:

> Civilization has, in fact, become a great machine, the wheels of which must be kept turning or the people starve. For millions of human beings it is a vast treadmill, worked by weary feet to grind the corn that makes the bread that gives them strength to walk the treadmill.

> We know now that we are not completely the masters of the machines we have created. Their pulsations we can control, but their consequences control us. They have risen like living things to dominate our entire civilization. They have called into being hundreds of millions of people who otherwise would not have been born. For these hundreds of millions they are the sole means of existence. Stop the machines and half the people in the world would perish in a month.

> There is real truth in Herbert Spencer's observation that majorities are generally wrong. History is one long record of the scornful overturn of standards which the majority in the preceding generation had fought and died for ... It was the majority that stood behind the Spanish Inquisition. It was the majority that supported the burning of witches. It was the majority in America that upheld in election after election the institution of slavery and passed laws to suppress those who criticized it. It was the majority that rallied behind our

14. Ibid., 7, 31, 49.

unjust war in Mexico in 1845. It was the majority that prohibited the teaching of evolution in Tennessee.[15]

Third, the supreme question facing the time is whether listeners (and readers) will be able to make the leap to entrust the future to those qualified to wield revolutionary science:

> At this point we often make an erroneous assumption. We assume that man's capacity keeps up with his inventions. We assume that, as civilization becomes great, the human stock which is building it also becomes great; that by some alchemy or other there is a rise in individual capacity from generation to generation to match the increasing complexity of our physical environment . . . We cannot be dogmatically sure that there has been substantial improvement in the human stock since the old days of the Egyptians or the Greeks.
>
> But social science today is still lacking in the fundamental groundwork of knowledge. It is still too largely based upon inspiration rather than upon facts. Consequently, social reform gropes in the dark where it should walk with assurance.[16]
>
> That answer calls for boldness, for a spirit of daring, for a certain scorn of the past, for a fearless facing of present facts. It involves the analysis and reconsideration of the worth and utility of human institutions and practices. It means a fundamental reappraisal of things that have hitherto been regarded as more or less sacrosanct . . . In brief, it requires a public opinion, conscious of the growing disproportion of civilization, eager to encourage creative work in the sphere of human relationships. Surely if our colleges and universities are to play an effective part in the great drama of this generation, it will be by instilling into their students, as the coming leaders of public opinion, a spirit of adventurous liberalism, an eagerness for truth wherever it may be found, a willingness to follow facts wherever they may lead.
>
> With all our new knowledge, is it our doom to sit supinely and helplessly in this temporary lull before the approaching crash of civilizations—of populations, rather—driven by hunger, competing for the mere occupancy of the earth? Can the conscious effort of men in any way steer this biological evolution? . . . Can the science of eugenics reshape a process that is tumbling with such gigantic forces? Can the power of man's intellect make this world a worthy and beautiful home to live in instead of a place to fight and freeze and starve in?[17]

15. Fosdick, *The Old Savage*, 11, 64, 85.
16. Ibid., 18, 42.
17. Ibid., 51, 184–85.

Raymond Fosdick casts Christianity chiefly as a cause of inertia, as an ideology whose pull is against the trajectory of time, so that humans who believe in God's revelation in Jesus Christ are stalled in their progress. If human beings are going to answer the supreme question, they must forge a new form of Christian faith.

> The Church and the legal profession, backed by the business interests, are peculiarly intemperate in their condemnation. Particularly here in the United States, in the midst of this present era of conservatism, the whole pressure of social opinion is exerted to make everybody conform to a given standard of ideas, to suppress innovations, to force the heretic to kneel before the scarlet-clad cardinals of the social order in penance for his sins.
>
> As a matter of fact, the derangement of human affairs is so extensive and our whole civilization is relatively so undeveloped that bewildering opportunities await on every hand. Every human idea and institution must be prepared to meet the challenge of facts, to face the measurement of truth and worth. Our views of property, our conceptions of government, our systems of education, our churches, our laws, our philosophies, or notions of right and wrong, our conventional relationships with each other—these are legitimate subjects of analysis, the laboratory materials of the new inquiry. There is no refuge where a human institution can escape questioning. No longer can the world build sanctuaries for the protection of ideas.[18]

The sweep of the case Raymond Fosdick builds is toward the sort of scheme he eventually directs under the Rockefeller Foundation:

> [I]t would seem as if first of all we needed a vision, a synthesis, a programme conceived in terms of the common good, behind which we might marshal the driving force of an awakened world. The curse of man has been his aimlessness, his paucity of ideas in regard to his own career, his disbelief in his own powers to shape his future. Let us have a plan, a chart, an objective. Let us determine where we want to go and the best methods of advance. Let the surveyors and engineers stake out the boundaries of the new homestead and map the roads. And then, with the promise of the new land beckoning ahead, humanity can strike its tents and once more take up the march.[19]

This summary of the scheme is from the Foundation's 1936 Annual Report, written by Raymond Fosdick:

---

18. Ibid., 49, 59.
19. Ibid., 198.

There is, therefore, an essential unity in the program of the Foundation, although it covers wide and diverse fields. The underlying interest is in the general problem of individual and social living, with the aim of progress through understanding. While, necessarily, the old classifications are employed, such as medical science, natural science, and social science, an endeavor is being made to think of the objective in coordinated and synthetic terms and to shape the program toward what has been called the science of man.[20]

New Knowledge

Raymond's brother Harry Emerson said, "Man's architecture has developed from the crude huts of primitive men until our cathedrals and business buildings reveal alike an incalculable advance and an unimaginable future."[21] Harry Emerson preached his best known sermon before John D. Rockefeller, Jr., built the Riverside Church in New York City. As the canonically approved story goes, "Shall the Fundamentalists Win?" cost Harry Emerson his position at First Presbyterian but gained him the equivalent of a progressive, Protestant cathedral. The history is more morally complicated than the usual, liberal "Fosdick equals brave and good; Fundamentalists equal stupid and evil" story. Ivy Lee is considered to be second only to Edward Bernays for creating the field of public relations—or corporate spin. The industrial strategist who orchestrated the wide distribution of "Shall the Fundamentalists Win?" to Protestant clergy across the U.S. was hired initially by the Rockefellers to manage public perception of the Rockefeller empire after what came to be known as the 1914 "Ludlow Massacre," in which strikers and their families were killed during a conflict between laborers and hired guards (mercenaries and the National Guard itself). Three of the mining companies involved were owned by the Rockefeller Family.

My future work will focus on this particular period that encompasses (1) Rockefeller, Jr.'s announcement of plans to build a new church in New York City in 1917 (three years after the massacre); (2) Fosdick's sermon and its subsequent wide circulation in 1922; and (3) the opening of Riverside Church in 1930. I hope to dig into the correspondence (as it remains) between Ivy Lee, Harry Emerson, Raymond, and Rockefeller, Jr., about the architecture of the building and the role of the senior

20. Raymond Fosdick, "The Rockefeller Foundation Annual Report 1936," *The Rockefeller Foundation*, 8, accessed at http://www.rockefellerfoundation.org/uploads/files/d52b902d-7909-4d7e-b04f-5a25cda250cf-1936.pdf.

21. Harry Emerson Fosdick, "Shall the Fundamentalists Win?" sermon preached at First Presbyterian Church, New York, 1922, subsequently published and distributed widely by Ivy Lee, chief publicist for John D. Rockefeller, Jr.

pastor who would come to define not only the church but also the role of progressive evangelicalism in the U.S. It is helpful to read Raymond Fosdick's *The Old Savage in the New Creation* alongside Harry Emerson's "Shall the Fundamentalists Win."

Harry Emerson's use of the passive voice in describing "a great mass of new knowledge that has come into man's possession" seems important in that he does not name that the "great mass" is being amassed under particular auspices and in collaboration with the very industrialists who are erecting the Riverside pulpit:

> A great mass of new knowledge has come into man's possession: new knowledge about the physical universe, its origins, its forces, its laws; new knowledge about human history and in particular about the ways in which the ancient peoples used to think in matters of religion and the methods by which they phrased and explained their spiritual experiences; and new knowledge, also, about other religions and the strangely similar ways in which men's faiths and religious practices have developed everywhere.[22]

The thing he and his brother variously call "knowledge" or "science" is to be the method for understanding "spiritual experiences" and bringing people of different "faiths and religious practices" together. Knowledge is the gauge for determining which beliefs and practices are developed and which are, well, not developed. To be on the side of not-developed is to be in some way akin to Christian Fundamentalism, which Harry Emerson had helped to designate as retrograde and therefore unpatriotic.

As Harry Emerson describes the question of their time, what is needed is a new alchemist who can concoct a faith capable of addressing the new age. In this description Harry Emerson makes two interrelated claims. First, the new faith must be applicable across leisure, work, and worship. Second, the preachers of the new faith must realize that they are not the masters of their discourse. They must learn and incorporate a "new knowledge" from other specialists:

> The new knowledge and the old faith cannot be left antagonistic or even disparate, as though a man on Saturday could use one set of regulative ideas for his life and on Sunday could change gear to another altogether. We must be able to think our modern life clear through in Christian terms and to do that we must be able to think our Christian life clear through in modern terms ... There is nothing new about the situation. It has happened again and again in history, as, for example, when the stationary earth suddenly began to move and the universe that had been centered in this planet was centered in the sun around which the planets whirled. Whenever such a situation has arisen,

---

22. Fosdick, "Shall the Fundamentalists Win?" 2.

there has been only one way out: the new knowledge and the old faith had to be blended in a new combination.[23]

This form of liberalism seems not incidentally to have allowed for a probusiness rearranging of Christianity, to eliminate that which seems impractical to the sorts of men who ran corporations like Rockefeller's Standard Oil or General Electric. Owen D. Young, head of General Electric and member of the board of the Rockefeller Foundation preached from Riverside's pulpit on the importance of a nimble faith capable of serving and not alienating the chief industrialists who were forging the new future of the United States. Young's "What Is Right In Business" appears in a collection of his speeches published in 1930 by the General Electric Company, and the editor specifically notes the speech was "delivered from the pulpit of Dr. Fosdick's church in New York on January 20, 1929."[24] Comparing the spread and growth of intercontinental corporations with the bumpy but ultimately fortuitous spread of automobiles, Young announced:

> So our big business has not justified the fears of our people. Exploiters no longer own the big concerns. Bankers no longer own them. Their shares, like motor cars, are spread from one end of the country to the other in every city and village. And broadly speaking, the vast organizations are in skilled hands and the road is reasonably safe.[25]

How did the Riverside pulpit serve to christen a form of "business" that described "The Golden Rule," as does Owen D. Young, as only rightly "applied by men of great understanding and knowledge, as well as conscience." He continues, such men must be "technicians in the sense of making the connecting link between the golden rule on the one side and the most complicated business transaction on the other."[26] While it would not have initially occurred to me to consider Harry Emerson Fosdick as having a kindred spirit with Bruce Fairchild Barton, author of the apparently infinitely popular (unfortunately, still today) handbook for aspiring and arrived Christian capitalists, *The Man Nobody Knows*,[27] I am now interested in simi-

---

23. Ibid., 3.

24. Owen D. Young and Gerald Swope, *Selected Addresses of Owen D. Young, Chairman of Board of Directors, and Gerald Swope, President, General Electric Company* (New York: General Electric, 1930) 251. I am indebted to Rolf Lunden for pointing toward this particular address of Owen D. Young. See also Rolf Lunden, *Business and Religion in the American 1920's* (New York: Greenwood, 1988).

25. Ibid.

26. Ibid., 256.

27. *The Man Nobody Knows: A Discovery of the Real Jesus* (Indianapolis: Bobbs-Merrill, 1925).

larities between the individualized, spiritualized piety of Barton and the progressive evangelicalism of Fosdick.

The Fosdick brothers recreated Protestant notions of "the promised land" to layer over a narrative of capitalist progress and the expansion of American democracy. Raymond Fosdick oversaw an interdisciplinary program in the biological and social sciences to explain the rationality of hierarchy and social design. The world of their time demanded grand strategists to sort and direct toward an end, or else (the case goes) the machinery of industrialism would crush the people working within it. Those "leaders" who were destined to serve as ecclesial alchemists, market cartographers, or well-funded socializing scientists were to take as their guide a form of ethics that was more about micro-instances of candor or individualized integrity than about questioning the larger system they saw themselves destined by God and evolutionary science to direct. By one reading, Harry Emerson Fosdick's *The Power to See It Through* or *The Secret of Victorious Living*[28] is more consonant with the individualistic, capitalism-friendly piety of *The Man Nobody Knows* than discordant, even though Fosdick and Barton were pitched to differently educated audiences. Many of Harry Emerson Fosdick's readers would have found Barton's candor gauche. Fosdick's references to Shakespeare and Keats was a sign of his vast distance from the striving-upper-middle-managerial style of an advertising executive like Barton (or Barton's Jesus).

Many in Harry Emerson's class-aspiring audience were striving not only to be well established financially but also to be in the know with the well-bred classes of New England. In "Shall the Fundamentalists Win" his description of the coming of the kingdom of God pulls together signs of "high" Western aesthetics and progress as harbingers of God's glory:

> Man's music has developed from the rhythmic noise of beaten sticks until we have in melody and harmony possibilities once undreamed. Man's painting has developed from the crude outlines of the cavemen until in line and color we have achieved unforeseen results and possess latent beauties yet unfolded. Man's architecture has developed from the crude huts of primitive men until our cathedrals and business buildings reveal alike an incalculable advance and an unimaginable future.[29]

Part of what distinguished "Fundamentalists" then was their lack of gracious acceptance of these forms of hierarchical ordering, both aesthetic and moral. Harry

28. *The Power to See It Through: Sermons on Christianity Today* (New York: Harper & Bros., 1935); *The Secret of Victorious Living: Sermons on Christianity Today* (New York: Harper & Bros., 1934).
29. Fosdick, "Shall the Fundamentalists Win?" 6.

Emerson defines "love" largely as a kind of magnanimity or dignity, such that discipleship involves a lack of visible rancor:

> [J]ust now the Fundamentalists are giving us one of the worst exhibitions of bitter intolerance that the churches of this country have ever seen. As one watches them and listens to them, he remembers the remark of General Armstrong of Hampton Institute: "Cantakerousness is worse than heterodoxy." There are many opinions in the field of modern controversy concerning which I am not sure whether they are right or wrong, but there is one thing I am sure of: courtesy and kindliness and tolerance and humanity and fairness are right. Opinions may be mistaken; love never is.[30]

I have much more digging to do into Harry Emerson Fosdick's explicit collaboration with Raymond Fosdick's plans for the Rockefeller Foundation and into how Riverside functioned at the intersection of what counted as progressive leadership and Christian discipleship during struggles over civil rights and labor rights in New York City. In my initial survey it seems Harry Emerson may have often functioned in a way similar to the present-day Jim Wallis, founder of *Sojourners Magazine* and the Sojourners Community. In Wallis's current instantiation at least, he seems not to swerve too far off the mainstream middle of the Democratic Party, making a case for the importance of civility over cantankerousness. In current parlance Harry Emerson seems to have been more liberal than radical, limited in his solidarity with working class and unemployed people in part due to the original structure of his pulpit and the foundation on which and purpose with which the church was built. I am hoping to be surprised with Spirit-filled examples of discipleship *otherwise*.

Firecrackers

> In 1813 eighteen workmen died on the gallows at York, England, on the charge of destroying machinery. They had resented the coming of the new civilization, they had feared the extension of its power and they had struck out blindly to destroy it. It was a pathetic, foolish act. It was like trying to stop a glacier with a firecracker. Remorselessly and irresistibly the machine age has ploughed its way across the life of man.[31]

Through extensive archival research Lily Kay has shown that what is commonly thought of or described as "pure" science, as if "science" is a *thing* that occurs naturally or coincidentally, was during decades of the twentieth century a well-coordinated

---

30. Ibid., 7.
31. Fosdick, *The Old Savage*, 93.

effort to shape research toward a particular end defined by funders.³² The way that Raymond Fosdick and others during his time described "machinery" is formally similar. Industrialization itself functions as a sort of *thing* that has happened. By their reckoning the radical changes that make their moment unique become part of a social-evolutionary version of holy providence. Raymond Fosdick describes their era as the vast result of collective, human ingenuity that now must be mastered by those with the creativity and gravitas to face the task. The "machine age" is part of an ineluctable force, and the original Luddites, as the machine-breakers came to be called, were acting blindly. This description of human history elides details as much as any description of "science" as a thing that just occurs. The revolt of skilled workmen (and women) against the machinery that would result in their unemployment and change the very nature of their craft did not simply take its declining, downward course as a movement and wane. Nor were their efforts swept aside by an inanimate force larger than themselves, like a naturally occurring tsunami of progress. Their revolt was systematically dismantled by the concerted effort of other, actual, acting human beings, real people acting as the arm of the newly industrializing state.

In his article "Machine-Breaking in England and France during the Age of Revolution," Jeff Horn gives these details of the concerted breaking of the breakers:

> Against a grand total of two fatal victims of the Luddites and the Captain Swing movement combined, British courts hanged more than thirty Luddites in 1812–13, and nine of the nineteen executed in 1830, "Swung" for the crime of machine-breaking. These figures do not include the casualties involved in the attacks themselves. In repulsing the Luddite attack on Daniel Burton's steam-loom factory at Middleton in Lancashire on 18 April 1812, five were killed and eighteen wounded before a crowd of colliers returned to finish the job. In addition to the dead and maimed, dozens more Luddites and 200-plus machine-breakers involved in Swing were sent to Australia. Nearly 650 were imprisoned. More generally, [George] Rude found that in the course of more than 20 major riots and demonstrations between 1736 and 1848, the English "crowd" killed no more than a dozen while the courts hanged 118, and 630 were killed by the military. These figures include the "Wilkes and Liberty" movement, the Gordon Riots of 1780, and Peterloo in 1819.³³

To bring this essay full-circle, the design of the Rockefeller funded language and the architecture of the Rockefeller pulpit seem set up in such a way as to encour-

---

32. Here I am summarizing one of Kay's central arguments in her book *The Molecular Vision*. I am grateful to Kara Slade for coming up with the expression "Science as a thing" and for help in editing my prose and securing proper citations. Any mistakes remaining are certainly my own.

33. *Labour/Le Travail* 55 (2005) 143–66, 148.

age a kind of gratefully pensive piety among some hearers ("the people," inasmuch as they were in view as actual listeners) and to rouse activated duty among hearers of a learned class, hearers aspiring to be of use in leading the humanity on to the next era. In his continual erasure of workers as actual agents rather than as merely descriptors, and in his pointed dismissal of resistance as futile, Raymond Fosdick offered a narrative that functioned well for the industrialists he himself served. By ignoring altogether the agency of individuals who decided for the state repression of workers in the machine-breaking era, he served his own industrialist friends badly—at least inasmuch as Raymond was trying to be a true brother in Christ to the men he was advising. I am interested to learn more about how prophetically, or not, Raymond's brother functioned in the Riverside pulpit. I am interested in this history as much for the sake of the wild west laborers and their families, whom schemer Ivy Lee sought rhetorically to bury, as for the leaders determined to describe themselves as men of good faith and as good citizens of the city.

RESPONSE TO HALL

Reggie Williams

After reading Dr. Hall's paper, I doubt that I will ever look at a church bell tower the same way again. The evidence that Hall presents about Rockefeller and the Fosdick brothers suggests an insidious history of collaboration between the pulpit and wealthy power-brokers of industry. Church in this arrangement is not a community that represents the loving presence of Christ in the world, nor is it a place where the faithful share concern for the poor and the outcast. Instead, the church characterized in the work of Rockefeller and the Fosdick brothers is a massive phallic symbol representing corporate interests in urban communities that are having their way with the least powerful in society. Consequently, Hall cautions us to take heed to "the ways that big money, social scientific research, ministerial authority, and even architecture itself can reinforce hierarchical, nondemocratic notions of proper discipleship in an industrial (or postindustrial) city." This caution is fascinating. As a fellow Christian ethicist I understand Professor Hall's paper as a caution to be aware of the loyalties that shape our language of Christ and faithful Christian discipleship. Christianity that is faithful to the witness of the gospel must be aware that personal and communal loyalties have a natural and inevitable effect upon our morality as Christians and upon the type of Christian discipleship that we advocate.

The language of natural and inevitable progress from Raymond Fosdick describes congruence between science, industry, capitalism, and God's providence. Fosdick's Christian argument for congruence between capitalism and the will of God is disturbing and flies in the face of the language of justice that is woven throughout the Bible.

In Hall's paper Raymond Fosdick's interpretation of human progress betrays deviant loyalties. Hall's research here is constructively troubling. At various points I see parallels with my own research on the harmful intersection of race and religion in modernity. The connections between our work reminds me of something that James Baldwin said about black consciousness and the absurdity of the African American experience. Baldwin said, "To be a Negro in this country and to be relatively conscious is to be in a rage almost all the time."[1] I heard Baldwin in the questions that Hall's research provoked. The first question that I have really involves several interrelated ones: What is the connection between the Fosdick/Rockefeller partnership and Harlem? Why put the church in Harlem, and why then?

Taylor Branch tells us that Harry Fosdick initially turned down Rockefeller's request to take the helm of his new church in Manhattan because its new building was situated on Park Avenue. Fosdick was not interested in being known as "the minister of another elite church in the swankiest part of New York," nor was he interested in being known as "the pastor of the richest man in the United States."[2] But Rockefeller would not take no for an answer in his pursuit of Fosdick. In order to acquire Fosdick as pastor of his church in New York, Rockefeller's congregation abandoned their new building, and at Fosdick's request, they built a new one nearer to New York's poorer neighborhoods in addition to discarding the Baptist label from the church name.

The location and the time in which the church opened its doors—Morningside Heights in 1930—corresponds with a watershed moment in African American history. The early 1930s saw the last moments of the Harlem Renaissance, and given what Hall's research tells us, the role of Riverside Church in that space at that moment should catch our attention.

Consider Hall's observation about the effect of the architecture of the church on its worshippers: "[T]he architecture was intended to make congregants and neighbors sense their place within an orderly structure, rather than activate participants to challenge the order of things around them." I hear Hall's comments in the context of a description of class and gender disparities. Given the fact that the church opened its doors in Harlem—Morningside is on the lower west side of Harlem, that it opened in Harlem on the tail end of the Harlem Renaissance, and that a year before the stock-market crash had plunged the world into the Great Depression, I'm wondering how race factored into Fosdick's Riverside ministry in Harlem? My first question then is really a series of interrelated questions around the presence of Riverside in Harlem during the Harlem Renaissance and within the Harlem Renaissance urbanization of black life, from the farm fields of the south to the factories in the North. What was the gospel message that Riverside Church was proclaiming in that space? What was the role of faith in Harlem's emerging urban center, and

---

1. Mathew H. Ahmann and Stephen J. Wright, *The New Negro* (New York: Biblo and Tannen, 1969) 109.

2. Taylor Branch, *Parting the Waters: America in the King Years, 1954-63* (New York: Simon and Schuster, 1988) 39.

how did Riverside participate in it? What were the threats to the people and the city that Riverside saw and was compelled to address? What were the loyalties driving the vision of Christian discipleship as it was communicated from Riverside?

The migrants to Harlem left the southern United States and colonized places along the Atlantic coast looking for something other than the forced compliance to capitalism and white supremacist terrorism to which they were subject. What did the Fosdick/Rockefeller connection have to offer them? Did it offer anything to them at all?

Like Professor Hall, I do not have answers to these questions. I am only asking questions that her essay provoked. Peter Paris tells us that Riverside has maintained a rich and vibrant outreach to the community surrounding it.[3] In that regard it would be interesting to compare the ministries of Harry Fosdick and Riverside Church with that of Adam Clayton Powell Sr. and Abyssinian Baptist Church. Powell was intentional about placing Abyssinian in Harlem for the sake of the migrants who were gathering there. Abyssinian is little more than a thirty-minute walk from Riverside Church, into the heart of the community that was languishing in the grips of poverty when Riverside was established. The plight of the black migrant in the urban north after World War I was the dawn of the poor, inner city, black neighborhood, birthed in the context of a what Langston Hughes described as a "dream deferred." Grinding inner city poverty in the wake of the Great Depression followed the hope-filled move to Harlem for most southern migrants. Both churches were situated to be active participants in this critical urban moment.

Abyssinian was the largest African American church in the country when it opened its doors at 138th and Lennox Avenue in 1923, seven years before Riverside Church did. The two pastors in Harlem were also situated within the middle of an intellectual and spiritual stew. Gary Dorrien claims that Fosdick was a giant of liberal modern Christianity, who sought to articulate a middle way between fundamentalism and atheism, reconceptualizing what might be considered fundamentalist Christianity in light of the influence of modernity. White Christian liberals like Fosdick accommodated American society, making little distinction between human achievement in modernity and industry and the "civilizing virtues of Western Christian gentility."[4] It might not be too much of a stretch to say that for white

---

3. See Peter J. Paris, *The History of the Riverside Church in the City of New York*, Religion, Race, and Ethnicity (New York: New York University Press, 2004).

4. Gary J. Dorrien, *The Making of American Liberal Theology: Imagining Progressive Religion, 1805–1900* (Louisville: Westminster John Knox, 2001) xix.

Christian liberals in early twentieth-century America, Christianity and civilization were virtually synonymous.

That was not the case with Powell's black church. Accommodation to American civilization in 1930 was death-dealing for African Americans. To cooperate with the hypnotic effect of the architecture as Hall describes it and to accommodate oneself as an African American to the racial hierarchy of society meant accepting one's place within an orderly racialized, white-supremacist structure, where the historically vicious depictions of people of color served to illustrate their natural and inevitable inferiority to whites. How did the Rockefeller/Fosdick collaboration engage this social problem when they intentionally sought out Harlem for ministry?

The questions that Hall's paper provoked has had me focus on a sliver of time in the life and ministry of Harry Fosdick. That is not a fair treatment of him or of the multitude of ministries offered by Riverside Church. Professor Hall has also not engaged the larger intellectual stew of New York's theological environment within which Fosdick was situated. Riverside Church has continued to engage its community as the demographics have changed over the years, which has inevitably caused the church and its leadership to participate in dialogue with different constituencies on different topics. I am grateful for Hall's encouragement to pay attention to the loyalties that are active within our claims to proper Christian discipleship.

THE LORD OF THE RINGS

Isaias Mercado

Muy buenas tardes! I greet you in the name of our Lord and Savior Jesus Christ. I am the senior pastor of the Carpenter's House (La Casa del Carpintero), a church located in the Humboldt Park community area of the northwest side of Chicago. I am an urban pastor.

Power, Purpose, and Plan

The text that I would like to deal with today is Acts 1:8: "But you will receive power when the Holy Spirit comes on you; and you will be my witnesses in Jerusalem, and in all Judea and Samaria, and to the ends of the earth."

The Scripture selected speaks about three important realities that we need as urban pastors: *power, purpose, and plan*. This passage is written in the context of an emerging church developing in a very dynamic and complex city, and Jesus' first instruction is empowerment! Without a doubt, if we are going to work in the city, we will need *power*, power to sustain our faith as we witness oppression and poverty daily. We will need power to give hope to the hopeless and strength to the weary, and we will need power to speak on behalf of the voiceless and transform the unjust structures that continue to perpetuate this situation.

We are to obtain that power through the Holy Spirit. The Holy Spirit is "*the mysterious power or presence of God in nature or with individuals and communities, inspiring or empowering them with qualities they would not otherwise possess.*"[1] The Spirit of God will equip and empower us in the areas of weakness. It is important to remember that power is found in knowing that God is with us. As we face these difficulties and minister in the city, we can be empowered with the knowledge that, although what we see with the eyes of our flesh seems grim and sad, we are inspired by God to seek change and transformation. Eldin Villafañe in his classic work *The Liberating Spirit*[2] shares an insightful comment on Karl Barth where Barth envisioned from afar a new generation of thinkers that would develop a theology of

---

1. Paul Achtemeier, *HBD*, 401.
2. (Grand Rapids: Eerdmans, 1993) 163.

the Spirit, not written from the dominant perspective of Christology, but from that of Pneumatology. We need to continue to develop a theology of the Spirit that addresses the urban challenge.

As an urban pastor, I have been overwhelmed by the needs, hurts, and lament of the people. Sadly, we have to prioritize tragedies. In the vernacular of my people in Humboldt Park, "We have some jacked up folks." Therefore we must seek to be continuously empowered, baptized, and inspired in our ministry through the Holy Spirit. This is the only source that will sustain us as we minister. I pray that the Spirit of the Lord can replenish and recreate strength in you and your ministry as you continue to work in rebuilding the city.

The second reality to which the text points is purpose. Our purpose is to become witnesses. A witness is someone who has evidence or has seen or experienced an event. We are witnesses of Jesus' life, death, and resurrection. This is the center of our message. We are witnesses to the complete gospel for the complete human experience. We must be witnesses to the lament but also to the glory, pain and healing, suffering and joy, despair and peace, brokenness and restoration, chaos and order that are part of the urban journey. We can celebrate through repentance personally, socially, and systemically. We can experience God's love, forgiveness, security, care, joy, prosperity, mobility, and shalom.

However, there must be a balance. According to Eric Law's book *The Wolf Shall Dwell with the Lamb*, in the cycle of gospel living most affluent, white Christians focus on the resurrection, while people of color usually focus on the cross.[3] The point has been made several times in this conference: we must provide spaces to lament those situations that are in need of God's redemption. As pastors, we must create opportunities for people to cry out to God and ask for God to bring justice to his people, but we must also create spaces to celebrate God's goodness, faithfulness, and mercy. Even in the most despairing situations, we must find ways to see God working on behalf of his children. Lament and celebration must go hand in hand. Such is the rhythm of life.

The third reality is the need for a plan. In our passage we read about several rings: in Jerusalem, Judea, and Samaria, and to the ends of the earth. Even as Jesus spoke to his disciples, he set a plan on how to expand the gospel throughout the region. We must begin with the place we call home and then go to our neighbors and eventually our community. We must constantly be aware that although the message

---

3. (St. Louis: Chalice, 1993) 73–74.

is the same, the needs and strategies of and for the people we are ministering to might change.

When I was a student at McCormick Theological Seminary, Professor Mark Wendorf introduced me to a concept or theory for defining urban growth. It is based on the model developed by Ernest Burgess from the University of Chicago many years ago. His theory is based on a series of concentric circles or rings that divide a city into five zones.

This theory is obviously not a perfect instrument or description for every city. It is clearly focused on the industrial cities of the United States. We know that there are new patterns and theories about urban city that are necessary and possibly even more helpful. However, Burgess's overall description has helped me to understand the religious implications for ministry in the city. Below is a description of each ring with accompanying questions Professor Wendorf raises that pertain to ministry in each circle.

Ring one is the main business district in the downtown area. Residential options are limited and usually only for the very rich or single homeless people. Churches heavily depend on their members coming from other circles or rings. This is a circle of privilege and power. Among the questions that arise, how willing and able are the members to travel to the church? Will the church initiate some type of transportation ministry for its members who live at some distance? As the homeless become more prevalent in this circle, how do we help members not be frightened by their surroundings, and how do we meet the needs of the members and the homeless?

The second ring is known as the warehouse district. The factories here are usually owned by the people in circle one. In the last twenty years we have seen factories converted into lofts and jobs have been moved either to the suburbs or overseas. Given these realities, as the value of the land increases in this circle, how long can the church hold out before it needs to move locations as well? Will the new upper class moving into this circle be willing to accept the more needy members of this church and community? As the change creates problems between the needy and the developers, whose side will the church take?

The third ring is where the poor working class live. This is the hood, the place of my own church in Humboldt Park. The needs are great, and high congestion and crime are realities. Service agencies are frequently found here. How will the church fund the services needed in this community? Will the church partner with an agency or another denomination to help support the services provided to this community? Who will be the members of this congregation?

Rings four and five are the suburban areas; in Chicago this would be areas like Oak Park and Forest Park. These are middle-class neighborhoods with nice lawns and nice stores, and for residents in my community something we only saw in movies. Change comes here as well though. As the racial and class population changes in this circle, will the churches create spaces to welcome these new members? Will churches partner with new congregations by renting property until these churches can find their own location? Will churches simply close or abandon the area to service more appropriate "racial or class related" congregations?

Conclusion

These rings give us a quick glance at the various needs in each area. We understand that we cannot preach the gospel to the homeless the same way we would preach to someone who owns a home and has his retirement set. This theory obviously raises many questions for churches in these circles/rings. Although it is not a perfect theory, it provides a framework by which we can view our approaches and ministries in these circles. It shows us that before we insert ourselves into ministry we must seek to understand the plight, the needs, the values, and the story of those we are going to serve. It reminds us that everything is constantly changing. Therefore, our plan must also change. My prayer is that, wherever you may live and serve, our God may be the Lord of the rings.

ANNOTATED BIBLIOGRAPHY ON URBAN MINISTRY

Altman, Neil. *The Analyst in the Inner City: Race, Class and Culture Through a Psychoanalytical Lens*. 2nd ed. New York: Routledge, 2010. In bringing psychoanalysis to the marginalized world Altman addresses the gap in the relationship of class, culture, race, and the psychological world and identifies how this can negatively affect self-image. This edition includes updated case studies and clinical studies to explain his theories.

Augustine. *City of God*. Translated by Henry Bettenson. New York: Penguin, 1972. This classic work was written in relation to the decline of Rome. Augustine attacks paganism while offering theological insights, the views of Greek philosophers, and a defense for Christianity. His work underscores the difference between earthly and eternal cities and shows that the city of God transcends time and civilization.

Bakke, Raymond. *A Theology as Big as the City*. Downers Grove, IL: InterVarsity, 1997. Bakke provides a hopeful theological picture of urban ministry. To assist in addressing the growing needs of urban people he explores God's view of the city and what Scripture says to instruct the church's engagement with the city.

Batey, Richard A. *Jesus and the Forgotten City: New Light on Sepphoris and the Urban World of Jesus*. Grand Rapids: Baker, 1992. Batey contests the claim that Jesus knew only a rural setting and shows how he was influenced by the culture, architecture, and society of Sepphoris. The excavations of Sepphoris are shown through illustrations and photos.

Block, Peter. *Community: The Structure of Belonging*. San Francisco: Berrett-Koehler, 2009. Block offers strategies for building community in our fragmented society. His perspective is not particularly religious, but he lays out a framework for transformation that involves creating opportunities for strategic conversations that can lead to mutuality and interdependence.

Boesak, Allan A., and Curtiss P. DeYoung. *Radical Reconciliation: Beyond Political Pietism and Christian Quietism*. Maryknoll, NY: Orbis, 2012. The authors examine biblical reconciliation and emphasize the need to address the roots of injustice. Political pietism is seen when shallow attempts— often by the white, rich, and privileged—are made to fight for an equal society. True biblical reconciliation is deeper and requires the privileged to lay down their rights in order to lift the oppressed.

Branson, Mark Lau, and Juan Martinez. *Churches, Cultures and Leadership*. Downers Grove, IL: InterVarsity, 2011. The authors combine biblical, sociological, anthropological, theological, and communication studies to equip leaders working in urban settings. Case studies, exercises, and Bible studies bridge the gap between abstract ideas and application and give practical guidelines for intercultural competency within the church.

Bretherton, Luke. *Christianity and Contemporary Politics: The Conditions and Possibilities of Faithful Witness*. Hoboken, NJ: Wiley-Blackwell, 2010. This book explores the interaction between political theory and theology through case studies and theological reflection. Modern challenges such as immigration and consumerism are addressed.

Brueggemann, Walter. *Peace*. St. Louis: Chalice, 2001. The church's responsibility to bring God's peace into the world must be rooted in a vision of God's compassion and justice. Brueggemann engages the biblical text to offer the hope of God's desired future of a fully expressed peace. Of particular interest is his explanation of the difference between a theology of the "haves" and a theology of the "have nots." He challenges the church to engage not only in the theology of celebration but also to embrace the reality of brokenness.

———. *The Prophetic Imagination*. 2nd ed. Minneapolis: Fortress, 2001. This is an important book that distinguishes between the prophetic critique of reigning ideologies, the pathos of the prophetic message, and the energizing words of prophetic hope that envision an alternative reality. Brueggemann links the prophets with the life and ministry of Jesus.

Cannon, Mae Elise. *Just Spirituality: How Faith Practices Fuel Social Action*. Downers Grove, IL: InterVarsity, 2013. Cannon explores how spiritual practices have shaped the public activism of seven remarkable leaders in Christian mission and social change: Mother Teresa, Dietrich Bonhoeffer, Watchman Nee, Martin Luther King Jr., Fairuz, Desmond Tutu, and Oscar Romero. The book reminds urban ministry practitioners that it is the practice of spiritual disciplines that fuels lives of ministry and service.

Carroll R., M. Daniel. "A Biblical Theology of the City and the Environment: Human Community in the Created Order." In *Keeping God's Earth: The Global Environment in Biblical Perspective*, edited by Noah J. Toly and Daniel I. Block, 69-89. Downers Grove, IL: InterVarsity, 2010. In examining the biblical evidence regarding the city Carroll shows that the Bible presents the multidimensional impact of sin on the city and its surrounding environment and also gives a wonderful picture of the future hope of a glorious city in a renewed creation.

Christiano, Kevin J. *Religious Diversity and Social Change: American Cities, 1890-1906*. Cambridge: Cambridge University Press, 1987. This study assesses the effect of mass migration and urbanization at the time of the transition from the nineteenth to the twentieth century. A connection is made between cultural shifts and the development of the denominational system.

"City." In *Dictionary of Biblical Literature*, edited by L. Ryken, J. C. Wilhoit, and T. Longman III, 150-54. Downers Grove, IL: InterVarsity, 1998. This article provides a helpful survey of the biblical material regarding the city and also gives theological reflections for the life of faith today.

Cone, James H. *Black Theology & Black Power*. 7th ed. Maryknoll, NY: Orbis, 2005. This study, originally published in 1969, is the first systematic approach to black theology. The focus is on liberation and the salvific elements of the gospel. Cone's approach to the Christian faith seeks to show what is necessary for African Americans to survive in modern society.

Conn, Harvie M. *The American City and the Evangelical Church: A Historical Overview*. Grand Rapids: Baker, 1994. Conn examines the emergence of a "wicked city" stereotype among evangelicals in the twentieth century. By tracing the history of the role of the church in the city, Conn asserts that the story of the evangelical church and the American city is more complicated and more ambiguous than the generalizations typically offered.

Conn, Harvie M., and Manuel Ortiz. *Urban Ministry: The Kingdom, the City, and the People of God.* Downers Grove, IL: InterVarsity, 2001. This is a textbook offering a historical and biblical perspective on cities and suggestions of ways to understand and minister within contemporary cities throughout the world. The authors trace four stages of development of cities throughout history and then seek to provide a biblical foundation for urban mission.

Corbett, Steve, and Brian Fikkert. *When Helping Hurts.* Chicago: Moody, 2009. By expanding the definition of poverty to include more than financial need, Corbett and Fikkert stress the importance of holistic work in poor areas. They provide a critique of past church-based development programs and give examples for healthy church engagement with the poor.

Cox, Harvey. *The Secular City.* New York: MacMillan, 1965. This foundational study reviews the shift from rural American Protestantism to the rise of an urban context. Cox argues for the positive effects secularity has on institutions and the presence of God in both secular and religious settings.

Dawn, Marva J. *The Sense of the Call: A Sabbath Way of Life for Those Who Serve God, the Church, and the World.* Grand Rapids: Eerdmans, 2006. Dawn invites Christian clergy and leaders into a "Sabbath way of life" through which God's grace revitalizes us and shines through us to others. She describes four central components to a Sabbath way of life: (1) resting in prayer; (2) ceasing our busyness; (3) feasting in the delight of ourselves and of Christian community; and (4) embracing the mission and cost of our call. Her rejection of the "balance paradigm" may be especially helpful for urban ministers in that she recognizes that a paradox of Christian ministry is the call to suffering and self-denial that is accompanied by the mandate to love ourselves.

De La Torre, Miguel. *Liberating Jonah: Forming an Ethics of Reconciliation.* Maryknoll, NY: Orbis, 2007. This reading of Jonah integrates contemporary social and political ethics with a theological perspective rooted in Liberation Theology. The focus on reconciliation re-examines more traditional interpretations of power and prophetic witness.

Dreier, Peter, et al. *Place Matters: Metropolitics for the Twenty-First Century.* Lawrence: University Press of Kansas, 2013. Where we live affects the jobs, education, shopping, cultural experiences, and medical services to which we have access. *Place Matters* challenges the reader to see the political influence of poor government policies that caused increased segregation of the poor and the wealthy in metropolitan areas. The urban crisis is both a moral and economic crisis for America. The authors provide commentary and guidance on political and government systems to seek reform.

Ekblad, Bob. *Reading with the Damned.* Louisville: Westminster John Knox, 2005. Ekblad examines the religious, cultural, and economic gaps that tend to exist between the churched and the unchurched as each group approaches Scripture. He challenges the reader to read from the perspective of those on the fringes of society and in doing so to rediscover the simple yet powerful "good news."

Elizondo, Virgilio. *The Future is Mestizo*. Boulder: University Press of Colorado, 2000. The author addresses the growth in the Hispanic population in the twentieth century and highlights the effects of Latin culture on music, culture, and religion.

———. *Galilean Journey: The Mexican-American Promise*. Maryknoll, NY: Orbis, 2007. Elizondo explores the parallels between Galilean Jews and Mexican Americans by presenting background to Mexican-American identity, an in-depth look at the gospel, and principles for bringing the kingdom to earth. He offers a prophetic look not only at Mexican-Americans but all Christians in the United States.

Ellis, Carl F., Jr. *Free at Last? The Gospel in the African American Experience*. Downers Grove, IL: InterVarsity, 1983. Ellis stresses the importance of African Americans knowing their history and identity. He provides a history of African Americans in the United States and an assessment of the amount of freedom offered to them in modern culture.

Ellul, Jacques. *The Meaning of the City*. Grand Rapids: Eerdmans, 1993. Ellul's historical analysis shows cities to be places with a tendency to destroy human beings in favor of human works. Cities are both a place of rebellion against God and places of grace. Ellul recognizes that Christianity's eschatological hope lies in a redeemed city and creates a theology applicable to urban ministry.

———. *The Presence of the Kingdom*. New York: Seabury, 1967. This influential ethicist explores the Christian place and purpose in the world and how Christians should engage a system affected by sin. Specifically, the church is to bring life both to individuals and society at large.

Flemming, Dean E. *Contextualization in the New Testament: Patterns for Theology and Mission*. Downers Grove, IL: InterVarsity, 2005. Flemming provides a treatment of the ways the gospel is expressed and embodied in context-sensitive ways in different NT books. From the context of the first-century church lessons are provided for the church's current missional tasks.

Fuder, John, and Noel Castellanos. *A Heart for the Community: New Models for Urban and Suburban Ministry*. Chicago: Moody, 2009. The authors offer advice for ministering both in urban and suburban settings and deal with the changes occurring with the shifts in population out of cities. They summarize current issues and models for ministry.

Gee, Alex, and John Teter. *Jesus and the Hip Hop Prophets*. Downers Grove, IL: InterVarsity, 2003. This text is divided into "tracks" and explores the lyrics of Tupac Shakur and Lauryn Hill to discover the spiritual truths they hold. The authors connect prophetic writings with urban life to find hope in harsh circumstances.

Gehring, Roger W. *House Church and Mission: The Importance of Household Structures in Early Christianity*. Peabody, MA: Hendrickson, 2004. Gehring explores how meeting in house churches affected mission and outreach in the early church and discusses the implications of house churches for leadership, ethics, and mission.

Gibbs, Eddie. *The Rebirth of the Church: Applying Paul's Vision for Ministry in our Post-Christian World*. Grand Rapids: Baker, 2013. This book addresses issues concerning the response of the contemporary Western church, which is broken and marginalized, to a post-Christian, secular, and pluralistic society. The author finds helpful the comparison of contemporary society with Paul's first-century context. The church needs to go back to a missional ecclesiology, especially in the urban context.

Gilbreath, Edward. *Reconciliation Blues*. Downers Grove, IL: InterVarsity, 2006. This is a personal perspective on the need for continuing dialogue about reconciliation in the evangelical church. The author highlights the unique nature of the African American evangelical experience by discussing important historical African American figures and the historical and current state of reconciliation.

Gordon, Wayne. *Real Hope in Chicago*. Grand Rapids: Zondervan, 1995. This book traces the author's story as a white man moving to Chicago's south side and starting Lawndale Community Church. The church employs over 150 people, supports students through college, runs a medical clinic, and was key in offering the neighborhood hope. The book highlights how very different people can unite to bring transformation to poor communities.

Gornick, Mark R. *To Live in Peace: Biblical Faith and the Changing Inner City*. Grand Rapids: Eerdmans, 2002. This is an excellent proposal for inner-city ministry that is both theologically grounded and experientially tested. On the basis of personal examples from his church plant in inner-city Baltimore and insights from biblical passages, Gornick repeatedly challenges the church to be "with" their communities, rather than "for" or "in" them.

Green, Clifford J., ed. *Churches, Cities, and Human Community*. Grand Rapids: Eerdmans, 1996. Green reviews the history of ten denominations working in cities across America and offers guidance for urban ministry in the future.

Hauerwas, Stanley. *Resident Aliens: Life in the Christian Colony*. Nashville: Abingdon, 1989. Hauerwas offers a visionary perspective of the church's role in a secular society. He emphasizes that the church is a holy people that holds to values not recognized by the outside world.

Heschel, Abraham. *The Prophets*. New York: Harper & Row, 1962. This is a classic, pioneering work that probes the emotional investment of God—and his prophets—in the life and destiny of humanity and of Israel. Heschel explores the prophetic call and message of each of the writing prophets and the phenomena connected to each prophecy.

Heuertz, Christopher, and Christine Pohl. *Friendship at the Margins: Discovering Mutuality in Service and Mission*. Downers Grove, IL: InterVarsity, 2010. The emphasis of this work is on the mutual change required for those who engage in service. This is a call for mission framed by friendship. This is a good resource for spirituality in urban ministry.

Holland, Joe, and Peter Henriot. *Social Analysis: Linking Faith and Justice*. Maryknoll, NY: Orbis, 1983. This study is a bit dated, but it introduces the "pastoral circle" tool for Christians to observe, judge, and act to establish social justice. The principles are still applicable in present day society.

Holli, Melvin G., and Peter d'A. Jones. *Ethnic Chicago: A Multicultural Portrait*. Grand Rapids: Eerdmans, 1997. The authors explore the diverse ethnic history in Chicago—African American, Asian, Indian, Chinese, Hispanic, Korean, Polish, Ukrainian, German, Greek, Japanese and Swedish communities. Immigration patterns and the adaptation process show the growth of Chicago is similar to the growth of other large urban centers.

Hooks, Bell. *All About Love: New Visions*. New York: Perennial, 2000. Bell Hooks is a black feminist author, cultural critic, and social activist whose work, although not explicitly Christian, is helpful. This book is the first in a trilogy attempting to construct a new American love ethic. Hooks challenges the popular romanticized view of love and discusses how issues of justice, community, spirituality, honesty, mutuality, and even loss are part of love.

Horrell, David. *After the First Urban Christians: The Social-Scientific Study of Pauline Christianity Twenty-Five Years Later*. Edited by Todd Still. London: T. & T. Clark, 2009. This collection of seven essays revisits and updates the areas covered by Meeks in *The First Urban Christians*. The social and historical context of early Christianity is explored and questions are posed for future Pauline study.

Jacobsen, Dennis A. *Doing Justice: Congregations and Community Organizing*. Minneapolis: Fortress, 2001. Fourteen years of personal experience ground Jacobsen's discussion of church-based community organizing. He gives practical suggestions for working for justice for the poor in the public realm.

Jacobsen, Eric O., and Eugene H. Peterson. *Sidewalks in the Kingdom: New Urbanism and the Christian Faith*. Grand Rapids: Brazos, 2003. The authors highlight the importance of analyzing the physical environment of cities for ministry and mission. They see physical factors as nourishing opportunity for ministry. The combination of theology and urban theory provides practical resources for those doing urban ministry.

Jennings, Willie James. *The Christian Imagination: Theology and the Origins of Race*. New Haven: Yale University Press, 2010. This monumental work excavates some of the deep theological architecture in the construction of race in the modern world. With historically attentive explorations of displacement and intimacy Jennings reimagines theology connected to bodies and land in communities of belonging.

Katongole, Emmanuel. *The Sacrifice of Africa*. Grand Rapids: Eerdmans, 2011. Katongole reflects on the contrast between the thriving of Christianity in Africa with the increasing level of poverty and violence in Africa. He shows the importance of stories and imagination in shaping our worldview and challenges how our perspective has been shaped by the colonial narrative, which allows for the sacrifice of Africa.

Keller, Timothy. *Center Church: Doing Balanced, Gospel-Centered Ministry in Your City*. Grand Rapids: Zondervan, 2012. Keller offers an analysis of the gospel and how gospel ministry can be contextualized for the city. Keller's church, Redeemer Presbyterian Church in New York City, serves as the laboratory for the implementation of his principles.

Kilpin, Juliet, ed. *Urban to the Core: Motives for Incarnational Mission.* Leicester: Troubador 2013. Reprint, Eugene, OR: Wipf and Stock, 2014. *Urban to the Core* is a reflection on personal stories and the work being done through Urban Express, an urban mission and church planting organization which prioritizes the inner cities and those living in the margins in Britain. Kilpin is passionate that any church mission strategy that fails to prioritize the city is incomplete.

LaGrand, James B. *Indian Metropolis.* Champaign: University of Illinois Press, 2002. This work explores the history of the American city and Native American urbanization. Chicago Native American stories are presented through first hand oral and written accounts.

Linthicum, Robert. *Building a People of Power: Equipping Churches to Transform Their Communities.* Federal Way, WA: World Vision, 2005. Linthicum shows that Christians should be a people filled with the power of God to transform cities. He differentiates between the power used to dominate and that used to liberate and presents strategies to organize, build relationships, and create leaders and communities.

———. *City of God, City of Satan: A Biblical Theology of the Urban Church.* Grand Rapids: Zondervan, 1991. Linthicum reflects on the dominant perspective of cities as centers of evil and sinfulness. By examining the etymology and theological meaning of the city of Jerusalem, Linthicum proposes a biblical urban theology that avoids an all good or all bad categorization and which calls Christians to engage the city as a battleground for ministry. Using Jeremiah 29 as a paradigm, he encourages those called to urban ministry to "pray for the *shalom* of the city," which often involves spiritual, economic, and political reform.

———. *Empowering the Poor: Community Organizing among the City's "Rag, Tag, and Bobtail."* Monrovia, CA: MARC, 1991. Linthicum uses his experience in North America to overcome superficial attempts to organize the community and work with the urban poor. He offers strategies and ways to build coalitions for mission in urban centers.

Lipsky, Laura van Dernoot, and Connie Burk. *Trauma Stewardship: An Everyday Guide to Caring for Self While Caring for Others.* San Francisco: Berrett-Koehler, 2009. An occupational hazard of urban ministry is the risk of vicarious, or secondary, trauma that occurs from being in relationship with individuals, families, and communities whose lives are often marked by trauma, violence, and loss. This book helps urban ministry practitioners understand the impact that bearing witness to trauma has upon their lives and helps them manage trauma's impact.

Livermore, David. *Cultural Intelligence.* Grand Rapids: Baker, 2009. Despite using jargon at points, Livermore's perspective on Christian multicultural engagement is thoughtful, thorough, and accessible. With a blend of sociological and organizational perspectives he explores cultural knowledge, identity, awareness, and behavior.

Marsh, Charles. *The Beloved Community.* New York: Basic, 2005. This vivid narrative shows the Civil Rights Movement is inextricably tied to the movement for justice in Christianity. Despite the divisions often drawn between justice and the church, Marsh shows how many of the Civil Rights Leaders were a part of the Beloved Community.

Marsh, Charles, and John Perkins. *Welcoming Justice: God's Movement toward Beloved Community*. Downers Grove, IL: InterVarsity, 2009. Marsh, a historian and theologian, and Perkins, a social activist, provide a history of God working for justice and equality. Martin Luther King Jr. created a vision for a beloved community, but this text shows how God's vision for the beloved community extends beyond King's words. The people of God are all called to participate in this community.

Martinez, Juan F. *Los Protestantes: An Introduction to Latino Protestantism in the United States*. Westport, CT: Praeger, 2011. This book provides an assessment of the current status of American Protestantism. With 20 percent of Latinos identifying as Protestants, this book makes a significant contribution.

McRoberts, Omar M. *Streets of Glory: Church and Community in a Black Urban Neighborhood*. Chicago: University of Chicago Press, 2005. Using the lens of a tough Boston neighborhood McRoberts shows what is really happening with the church in the inner city. He observes that churches are often filled with congregants who do not live in the local neighborhood.

Meeks, Wayne A. *The First Urban Christians: The Social World of the Apostle Paul*. New Haven: Yale University Press, 1983. This book is a classic study of Pauline Christian communities in the Greco-Roman city. Meeks uses the letters of Paul to engage the subjects of urban community, city versus country, women, social stratification, and other pertinent topics related to Greco-Roman cities.

Meyers, Eleanor Scott, ed. *Envisioning the New City: A Reader on Urban Ministry*. Louisville: Westminster John Knox, 1992. This is a compilation of thirty essays relating to urban ministry; the articles are written by seminary professors, lay and community leaders, and pastors with the intent to offer hope to churches and their communities.

Mott, Stephen. *Biblical Ethics and Social Change*. Chicago: Oxford University Press, 1982. In this important work Mott examines social change rooted in biblical principles and shows the necessity of intentional change to take up the cause of the oppressed and to create justice. He also treats ethical issues involved in social change including civil disobedience and revolt.

Myers, Bryant. *Walking with the Poor*. Maryknoll, NY: Orbis, 1999. This is a holistic approach to poverty alleviation and social change. Myers provides a theological framework for the work of Christian NGOs and international development organizations. The reclaiming of human identity and vocation as stewards of God's creation is shown to be necessary for shalom to be restored.

Myers, Joseph R. *Organic Community: Creating a Place Where People Naturally Connect*. Grand Rapids: Baker, 2007. Myers offers tools to help create environments where people can connect naturally and find a sense of community. He outlines nine organizational tools by which church leaders can assess and develop communities.

Newbigin, Lesslie. *The Gospel in a Pluralistic Society*. Grand Rapids: Eerdmans, 1989. This influential work shows how Christian faith can be affirmed in a modern pluralistic society. Newbigin assesses contemporary culture and reviews the work of Walter Wink, Michael Polanyi, Robert Wuthnow, Alasdair MacIntyre, and Hendrikus Berkhof.

O'Connor, Kathleen. *Lamentations and the Tears of the World.* Maryknoll, NY: Orbis, 2002. O'Connor presents an exegetical and theological commentary on the book of Lamentations. Despite the seemingly gloomy content of Lamentations, O'Connor sees a comforting witness. The difficult reading of Lamentations challenges those who live in denial, such as those in the United States capitalist society, to reclaim humanity and move towards compassion and justice.

Orsi, Robert, ed. *Gods of the City: Religion and the American Urban Landscape.* Bloomington: Indiana University Press, 1999. This collection of essays examines the role of urban religion in twentieth-century America. The text emphasizes the critical and formative role that cities have played on the religious life of the nation. Scholars covering diverse fields such as art history, anthropology, and religious studies contribute to this work.

Osiek, Carolyn A., and David L. Balch. *Families in the New Testament World: Households and House Churches.* Louisville: Westminster John Knox, 1997. The authors analyze the material and social environment of the Greco-Roman household, and what we know of early Christian families and house churches. They seek to provide a more accurate foundation to inform our modern family structure discussions.

Owens, Marcia, and Samuel Wells. *Living Without Enemies.* Downers Grove, IL: InterVarsity, 2011. The authors show how the gift of presence is a form of love that combats violence in the face of many unsuccessful programs and litigation. This form of radical acceptance helps overcome the powerlessness and offers pastors a tangible way to engage a violent world.

Paulsell, Stephanie. *Honoring the Body: Meditations on a Christian Practice.* San Francisco: Wiley, 2002. It is easy for urban ministers to be "heart, soul, and mind" people whose gaze is perennially directed upward toward God, outward to the needs of those whom they serve, and inward to the mental chatter that occupies their heads. Paulsell reminds Christians of the necessity of also directing attention and care to our physical bodies.

Perkins, John. *Beyond Charity.* Grand Rapids: Baker, 1993. Perkins challenges complacency and greed in the modern church and offers insights for community development and social justice.

———. *Restoring At-Risk Communities.* Grand Rapids: Baker, 1995. This is a comprehensive guide to community development which offers practical advice about racial reconciliation, education, finances, and real estate.

Peters, Ronald E. *Urban Ministry: An Introduction.* Nashville: Abingdon, 2007. This is a good, basic introduction to urban ministry which notes challenges and offers helpful perspectives for church workers. It tries to bridge the gap between seminary education and the skills actually needed to work in an urban setting with an optimistic yet realistic approach.

Peterson, Eugene. *Under the Unpredictable Plant.* Grand Rapids: Eerdmans, 1992. Peterson's creative reading of Jonah is a thoughtful and pastoral exploration in "vocational holiness" and integrates wise reflections on his own journey. It offers perspectives on spirituality, writing and literature, and the contemporary challenges of pastoral ministry in a changing church.

Putnam, Robert D. *Bowling Alone: the Collapse and Revival of American Community*. New York: Simon & Schuster, 2000. Putnam shows how society has become more fragmented over the last few decades. He discusses the term "social capital" and how it has diminished by looking at various institutions and segments of society.

Putnam, Robert D., and Lewis Feldstein. *Better Together: Restoring the American Community*. New York: Simon & Schuster, 2004. In following up on *Bowling Alone* the authors treat segments of society that have seen social capital increase—including churches. By providing specific examples from an urban setting, social interactions are shown to improve lives. They offer the suggestion that small groups are a key to building greater connection in society.

Rah, Soong-Chan. *Many Colors: Cultural Intelligence for a Changing Church*. Chicago: Moody, 2010. The changing demographics in the United States require the church to become more capable of dwelling in a multicultural context. Historical and case studies provide practical guidelines for the church to engage different cultural settings.

———. *The Next Evangelicalism: Freeing the Church from Western CulturalCaptivity*. Downers Grove, IL: InterVarsity, 2009. As Philip Jenkins recorded how Christendom shifted from the West to the Global South and East, Rah highlights how Evangelism too must make this global shift. Evangelism cannot remain captivated by the white, individualistic, and materialistic church. Rather, it must be awakened to the change and adapt to the real shift in the modern church.

Rocke, Kris, and Joel Van Dyke. *Geography of Grace: Doing Theology from Below*. N.p.: Street Psalms, 2012. In the authors' words this book is a "dialogue between Scripture and the street." It is a recontextualization of the biblical message of grace told through the experience of those on the fringes of society. The authors write from their experience in impoverished urban areas of the majority world.

Rogerson, John W., and John Vincent. *The City in Biblical Perspective*. Biblical Challenges to the Modern World. London: Equinox, 2009. This brief academic work has two parts that explore the biblical perspective on cities through social and archeological lenses. The first (three chapters) focuses on the city in the OT; the second part (four chapters) deals with the NT. The concern is for application to present realities in the United Kingdom.

Sandnes, K. O. *A New Family: Conversion and Ecclesiology in the Early Church with Cross-Cultural Comparisons*. Studies in the Intercultural History of Christianity 91. Bern: Lang, 1994. This study of early Christian converts explores the way Christian fellowship could take the role of establishing a new family, especially for those who encountered resistance from their nuclear family.

Sennett, Richard. *Flesh and Stone*. New York: Norton, 1994. Sennett provides a history of the city from ancient Athens to present New York City with a focus on what people experienced bodily—how they encountered space, what they smelled, tasted, wore, how they bathed, etc. He deals with the impact of Christianity on the city and also with the results in modern urban life.

Sherman, Amy. *Restorers of Hope: Reaching the Poor in Your Community with Church Based Programs That Work*. Eugene, OR: Wipf and Stock, 2004. This is a collection of stories about churches that have successfully engaged some of the poorest neighborhoods in the United States. Sherman offers strategies for the church to embody the gospel in such communities.

Sherwood, Yvonne. *A Biblical Text and Its Afterlives: The Survival of Jonah in Western Culture*. Cambridge: Cambridge University Press, 2000. This detailed book examines an expansive body of scholarship on the story of Jonah and its interpretive history from Jewish, Christian, and secular perspectives in literature, popular culture, and biblical studies.

Sider, Ronald J. *Linking Arms, Linking Lives: How Urban-Suburban Partnerships Can Transform Communities*. Grand Rapids: Baker, 2008. Sider challenges the stereotypes of suburban and urban dwellers and seeks to foster collaboration for stronger ministry. He offers practical and theologically grounded guidelines based on the experience of pastors, practitioners, and theologians to aid those ministering to the poor.

———. *Rich Christians in an Age of Hunger: Moving from Affluence to Generosity*. Nashville: Word, 1997. Sider provides a thorough examination of the causes of poverty and hunger from political, economic, sociological, and religious perspectives. He also explores practical solutions that can be carried out by all followers of Christ.

Skinner, Tom. *Black and Free*. Grand Rapids: Zondervan, 1968. Skinner, a former African American gang leader in Harlem, became a popular and influential evangelist. This early work provides a history of African Americans in the United States and offers solutions that offer hope in the midst of inequality and oppression.

———. *How Black is the Gospel?* Philadelphia: Lippincott, 1970. This book provides a contextualization of the gospel for the African American community. Skinner shows how the gospel illuminates the fight for justice and liberation. Reconciliation comes when both African Americans and whites surrender themselves to Christ.

Smith, Efrem. *The Post-Black and Post-White Church*. San Francisco: Josey-Bass, 2012. Smith explores what it means to be the church in a multi-ethnic urban context and pays attention to urban subculture as well. Guidelines for leadership in this setting are offered through ministry models, case studies, and the example of Christ.

Smith, Efrem, and Phil Jackson. *The Hip-Hop Church: Connecting with the Movement Shaping Our Culture*. Downers Grove, IL: InterVarsity, 2005. The authors show the necessity for the church to connect with the Hip Hop culture to reach the current young urban culture. They suggest ways to engage this culture through breakdancing, poetry, deejays, rap, and the like.

Smock, Kristina. *Democracy in Action: Community Organizing and Urban Change*. New York: Columbia University Press, 2004. Smock analyzes the techniques used by ten organizations of varying racial and economic demographics working for community organization. She shows the strength and weaknesses of five community organization models: power-based, civic, transformative, community building, and women-centered ones.

Spina, Frank Anthony. *The Faith of the Outsider: Exclusion and Inclusion in the Biblical Story.* Grand Rapids: Eerdmans, 2005. With a biblical interest attentive to the insider-outsider dynamics of Israel's story, Spina highlights the exclusivity of Israel's election and the inclusivity of God's mission through Israel. Through readings of Esau, Rahab, Jonah, Ruth, and others, Spina draws attention to the importance of "outsiders" in God's redemptive plan of salvation.

Taylor, Barbara Brown. *An Altar in the World: A Geography of Faith.* New York: HarperCollins, 2009. After leaving congregational ministry Taylor turned her attention to "doing church" beyond the walls of the local parish. In this book she describes how simple daily activities—such as paying attention to the world around you, praying, and saying no—free us to experience the sacred in daily life. The book is helpful in practicing spiritual disciplines.

Twiss, Richard. *One Church, Many Tribes: Following Jesus the Way God Made You.* Ventura, CA: Regal, 1979. Twiss offers hope for sharing the gospel from the perspective of a Native American Evangelical from the Rosebud Lakota/Sioux tribe. While acknowledging the pain caused by white Christians in the past, it explores reconciliation and how white and Native American churches can form reciprocal relationships.

Usry, Glen, and Craig S. Keener. *Black Man's Religion: Can Christianity Be Afrocentric?* Downers Grove, IL: InterVarsity, 1996. By including both a historical-cultural perspective and a view of the current black church, Usry and Keener find what the past lends to modern Black Christian identity.

Villafañe, Eldin. *The Liberating Spirit: Toward an Hispanic American Pentecostal Social Ethic.* Grand Rapids: Eerdmans, 1993. Villafañe focuses on Hispanic American sociocultural experience and on Hispanic Pentecostalism to offer a Spirit-driven ethic which is directly applicable to Hispanic urban contexts and relevant for others.

———. *Seek the Peace of the City: Reflections on Urban Ministry.* Grand Rapids: Eerdmans, 1995. Villafañe with humor tells of his experience in urban ministry. He explores what it means to walk with the poor and engage in urban theological education and ministry.

Villafañe, Eldin, et al. *Transforming the City: Reframing Education for Urban Ministry.* Grand Rapids: Eerdmans, 2002. Six case studies offer helpful advice for ministering effectively in urban contexts. Educators and church leaders highlight potential dangers and opportunities for working in various inner city settings.

Volf, Miroslav. *A Public Faith: How Followers of Christ Should Serve the Common Good.* Grand Rapids: Brazos, 2011. Volf gives a comprehensive view of how the church can engage a pluralistic society for its good. He is aware that no single path exists to engage modern culture, but he asks timely questions about faith and the modern world.

Wallis, Jim. *God's Politics: Why the Right Gets it Wrong and the Left Doesn't Get It.* New York: HarperCollins, 2005. Wallis's approach to political secularism and faith recognizes that the separation of church and state does not prevent the translation of spiritual values for the public. He separates faith from political ideologies and shows faith to be interested in morality at large instead of being focused on particular political issues.

———. *The Soul of Politics: Beyond "Religious Right" and "Secular Left."* New York: New, 1995. From his experience of living in urban ghettos and traveling to third world countries Wallis shows the need to move past the liberal and conservative divide. A new view of politics with a theological base broadens human rights from the individual to the community. The text is more visionary that practical.

Ward, Graham. *Cities of God.* London: Routledge, 2000. This unusual book analyses western cities in the 1970s, but it does so by analyzing contemporary film, literature, and architecture on the one hand and theologians such as Augustine and Gregory of Nyssa on the other. The goal is to provide a systematic theology that paves the way for building good cities.

Warner, Stephen, and Judith Wittner, eds. *Gatherings in Diaspora: Religious Communities and the New Immigration.* Philadelphia: Temple University Press, 1998. This collection brings together chronicles of immigrants to America and their religious experience in the period after 1965. It includes the experiences of people from various countries and religions, explores how people adapt religiously to the new context, and notes how much more important religion often is for immigrants than it was for them in their home country.

Wells, Sam. *God's Companions: Reimagining Christian Ethics.* Oxford: Blackwell, 2006. Wells defines ethics as a reflection of God's abundance and argues that God offers all that is necessary to dwell with him. The text combines his own experience in poor neighborhoods with scholarly sources to explore the idea of Christian ethics.

Westermann, Claus. *Praise and Lament in the Psalms.* Translated by Keith R. Crim and Richard N. Soulen. Atlanta: John Knox, 1981. Westermann divides the OT poetic material into psalms of praise and lament and determines that the two modes determine all manner of speaking to God. He questions whether lament must always lead to praise and promotes a dialogical theology and the importance of lament in that dialogue. Lament, therefore, moves beyond the role of simply being a stepping stone in the move towards praise.

Wilkerson, Isabel. *The Warmth of Other Suns: The Epic Story of America's Great Migration.* New York: Random House, 2010. This well-documented work chronicles the exodus of African-Americans from the Southern states to the Northern cities. The great migration serves as a benchmark that altered the course of U.S. history, and Wilkerson reveals the stories behind the event.

Wilson, William Julius. *When Work Disappears: The World of the New Urban.* New York: Vintage, 1996. This book shows the effects of joblessness in urban ghettos, such as crime and drugs. It offers a thorough and balanced view of the problems and also suggests potential solutions.

Winter, Gibson. *The Suburban Captivity of the Churches: An Analysis of Christian Responsibility in the Expanding Metropolis*. New York: MacMillan, 1962. This older work treats the church's suburban flight and the implications for those left in the inner city. It is still an important book for the Protestant church and offers ways to integrate the fragmentation resulting from this church movement.

Yong, Amos. *Hospitality and the Other: Pentecost, Christian Practices, and the Neighbor (Faith Meets Faith)*. Maryknoll, NY: Orbis, 2008. Yong contests that non-Christians can be confined to a group needing conversion and argues that hospitality must be extended to invite all people into a loving community. With the Trinity as a model the church must be loving and welcoming to all people, regardless of race, ethnicity, and religion.

NORTH PARK THEOLOGICAL SEMINARY SYMPOSIUM ON THE THEOLOGICAL INTERPRETATION OF SCRIPTURE

SEPTEMBER 26–SEPTEMBER 28, 2013

Urban Ministry

PRESENTERS

VINCE BANTU
PhD Candidate, Catholic University

M. DANIEL CARROLL R.
Distinguished Professor of Old Testament, Denver Seminary

DENNIS EDWARDS
Senior Pastor, The Sanctuary Covenant Church

AMY LAURA HALL
Associate Professor of Theological Ethics, Duke Divinity School

DAVID LEONG
Assistant Professor of Missiology, Seattle Pacific University

ISAIAS MERCADO
Senior Pastor, The Carpenter's House

SOONG-CHAN RAH
Milton B. Engebretson Associate Professor of Church Growth and Evangelism, North Park Theological Seminary

PAUL TREBILCO
Professor of New Testament Studies, University of Otago, Dunedin, New Zealand

CHANEQUA WALKER-BARNES
Assistant Professor of Pastoral Care and Counseling, McAfee School of Theology

RESPONDENTS

NATHAN BILLS
   ThD Candidate, Duke Divinity School

STEPHEN CHESTER
   Professor of New Testament, North Park Theological Seminary

KURT FREDRICKSON
   Associate Dean for Doctor of Ministry and Continuing Education, Fuller Theological Seminary

DANIEL WHITE HODGE
   Director of the Center for Youth Ministry Studies, North Park University

ELIZABETH PIERRE
   Adjunct Professor of Pastoral Care, North Park Theological Seminary

JESSICA RIVERA
   Education Director, The Carpenter's House

ARMIDA BELMONTE STEPHENS
   PhD Candidate, Trinity Evangelical Divinity School

REGGIE WILLIAMS
   Assistant Professor of Christina Ethics, McCormick Theological Seminary

www.ingramcontent.com/pod-product-compliance
Lightning Source LLC
Chambersburg PA
CBHW081352230426
43667CB00017B/2804